AMERICAN KERNEL LESSONS

AKL: ADVANCED

ROBERT O'NEILL
EDWIN T. CORNELIUS, JR.
GAY N. WASHBURN

Diana Aguilar. Bartz

"is the owner"

Longman

American Kernel Lessons: Advanced

Library of Congress Cataloging in Publication Data

O'Neill, Robert.
  American kernel lessons: advanced student's book.

  (Longman American English)
  1. English language—Textbooks for foreigners.
I. Cornelius, Edwin T.   II. Washburn, Gay N.,
1948-   .   III. Title.   IV. Series.
PE1128.048   428.6′4   81-23637
ISBN 0-582-79741-1   AACR2

First printing 1981

5   4

Cover Design: Frederick Charles Ltd.
Interior Design: James M. Wall

Special thanks to Robert Walbridge for collaborating on the listening activities, to
Penny Laporte for her work on the Teacher's Manual and to Linda Markstein for her
contributions to the Student's Test Book

Longman Inc.
95 Church Street
White Plains, N.Y. 10601

Distributed in the United Kingdom by Longman Group Ltd., Longman House, Burnt
Mill, Harlow, Essex CM20 2JE, England, and by associated companies, branches and
representatives throughout the world.

Printed in the U.S.A.

We wish to thank the following for providing us with photographs:
Page 1, left: Barbara Swenson. Page 10: NYC Dept. of Transportation. Page 11, top: Tony Spina/
Detroit Free Press; bottom: U.S. Dept. of Transportation. Page 16: NYC Dept. of Transportation.
Page 18, top and bottom: NASA. Page 19, top and bottom: NASA. Page 24: Metro-Goldwyn-Mayer
Inc. Page 26, left: Barbara Swenson; right: Villette Harris. Page 27, top: Anne Darling/Bank Street
Information Office; bottom: Educational Facilities Laboratory/Rondall Partridge. Page 32: Allen
Butte/Literacy Volunteers of America, Inc. Page 34, top: Villette Harris; middle: WHO Photos; bot-
tom: UN/Bill Graham. Page 35: EPA-Documerica. Page 42, top: Cosmos Tours; bottom: National Park
Service/U.S. Dept. of the Interior. Page 43: Ray Scott; Page 48: Hawaii Visitors Bureau. Page 50: UPI.
Page 51, top: PICTUREPOINT—LONDON; bottom: National Archives. Page 56: U.S. Geological
Survey/Dept. of the Interior. Page 66, top: Fox Photos Ltd.; bottom: HUD Photo. Page 74, left: New
York Public Library Picture Collection; right: Paramount Pictures Corporation. Page 75: National
Safety Council. Page 80: The School of Visual Arts Public Advertising System. Page 88, left: Jaguar
Rover Triumph Inc.; right: Volkswagen of America/Doyle Dane Bernbach Inc. Page 90, top: USTA/
Russ Adams; bottom: Villette Harris. Page 91, top: Bill Hayward; bottom: Barbara Swenson. Page 96:
The Bettmann Archive. Page 98, bottom: New York University. Page 99: Angel Cuevas. Page 104:
Susan Clee/Positive Images. Page 106, top: Marilyn K. Yee/The New York Times; bottom: Joe
di Dio/National Education Association. Page 112: Jack Schneider/Dept. of Energy. Page 114, top:
Museum of the City of New York; bottom: British Airways. Page 115, top: U.S. Dept. of Transporta-
tion; bottom: Portland General Electric Company.

Cover Photos:
Top right: U.S. Geological Survey; center, left to right: Russ Adams/USTA, National Education Association, United Nations; bottom left: NASA.

We also wish to thank the following illustrators:
Pages 12, 52 and 83: Anna Veltfort. Pages 38, 39, 82 and 84: Janet Lampart. Page 40: Milo Hess. Page 43: Karen
Hitt. Pages 65 and 72: Nilda Scherer. Page 67: Presse-Illustrations-Bureau. Page 121: Marty Norman.

CONTENTS

WNYN-TV

1 | What kind of building is this?
Is it in the city or the country?

This is the headquarters of station WNYN-TV, a small television station in New York City. Most of the programs it presents are syndicated; that is, they are produced and distributed by other companies. But WNYN produces its own news programs. These shows are popular because they concentrate on local news and special events. The news department staff is also originating a series of special programs about problems and issues of particular interest to New Yorkers. These "specials" often include interviews with experts on these topics. Right now, WNYN is expanding its news department so that it can produce more specials.

Questions
1. Does WNYN produce most of the programs it shows?
2. What does it produce?
3. Why are WNYN's news programs so popular?
4. What kind of specials is the news department originating?
5. Why is WNYN expanding its news department?

2 | Where is this woman?
How old is she?
What do you think she does?

Hello. My name is Marsha Nelson. I'm a TV news reporter. I was born in Arizona, but I grew up in California. I lived there for twenty years. Then I moved to Ohio and worked for a small newspaper in Cleveland for five years. After that, I came to New York and got a job at WNYN. I'm still working for WNYN and I enjoy the kind of work I'm doing. I do shows about important problems and issues. My work usually involves doing interviews and I particularly enjoy that part of my job. Our program coordinator has just suggested the idea of doing a special on traffic problems in the city. I'm thinking about the idea now and I'm considering the possibility of making it a one-hour show.

Ask and answer questions about this woman, like this:
Ask what this woman's name is.
A: What's this woman's name?
B: Marsha Nelson.

Now you do it. Ask:
1. where Marsha was born
2. where she grew up
3. how long she lived there
4. where she worked for a newspaper
5. how long she was there
6. where she works now
7. who has just suggested an idea to her
8. what she is doing about it

**Where is this man?
How old is he?
What do you think he does?** | **3**

My name is David Denton. I've lived in New York City all my life. I even went to college here. I studied radio and television. After I graduated from college, I spent three months in Europe. That was two years ago. Since then, I've been trying to get a job in television. I have an interview today at WNYN-TV for a job as a cameraman. But I don't think I'll get the job because I haven't had any work experience. I don't understand it. How can I ever get work experience if I can't get a job?

Ask and Answer
Ask:

1. where David was born
2. if he grew up there
3. where he went to college
4. what he studied
5. when he graduated
6. what he's been doing since he graduated
7. where he has an interview today
8. why he doesn't expect to get the job

4 | **Where are these people?
Whose office is this?
How do you know?**

The man behind the desk is Robert Russo. Bob is the director of the morning and evening news programs at WNYN-TV. He directs the shows, but other people report the news. He wants to expand his department. He hired Marsha Nelson a few years ago and she has built up a special features section. She needs a full-time cameraman now. So today Bob is interviewing David Denton for the job. David hasn't had any real work experience, so he probably won't ask for a very high salary. Bob may decide to offer David a job.

Answer the questions with short answers, like this:

A: Who is the director of WNYN's morning and evening news shows?
B: Bob Russo is.

1. Who directs the shows?
2. Who reports the news?
3. Who hired Marsha Nelson?
4. Who's sitting in Bob's office now?
5. Who's interviewing David Denton?
6. Who might offer David a job?

UNIT 1 Grammar

1 Present continuous vs. simple present: verbs that rarely take the continuous

A. Comment

1. Verbs expressing a state (*be, seem, know,* etc.) do not take the continuous: I *believe* her. He *looks* tired. I *know* that man. I *doubt* it. He *needs* a shave.
2. Neither do verbs expressing sense perception (*see, hear, taste,* etc.): She *feels* happy. That ice cream *tastes* good.
3. You *see* whenever your eyes are open. You *hear* whenever there's sound. But you *look at* and *listen to* something selectively or on purpose: He *heard* the radio in the living room, so he went in and *listened to* the news. The verbs *see* and *hear* do not usually occur in the continuous, but *look at* and *listen to* occur in both the simple and continuous tenses: A reporter is *looking at* a house on fire. He *sees* a fireman fall off a ladder.

B. Situation

The president is going to hold an important press conference on the economy this evening. You are a radio announcer. Use the clues given to describe the events as they happen.

Example: the press room/fill up/with people
The press room is filling up with people.
I/not see/the president/yet
I don't see the president yet.

1. many reporters/wait for/the president
2. they/seem/anxious
3. I/hear/the president/now
4. he/enter/the room
5. he/smile/and/wave
6. he/know/many reporters/personally
7. they/look at/the president
8. he/look/nervous
9. he/walk to/the podium
10. he/need/another microphone
11. an aide/adjust/the new microphone
12. the press conference/begins
13. the president/see/a reporter raise her hand
14. the reporters/listen to/him

2 Present continuous vs. simple present: verbs with different meanings

A. Comment

Some verbs have two different meanings. In one meaning they can take the continuous. In the other meaning they cannot.

1. *Think* and *consider* can be state verbs of opinion. In this sense they occur in the simple present tense.

   What *do* you *think* of my idea?
   I *consider* it a very good one.

   Think and *consider* can also mean *to give attention to* or *to go over in one's mind*. In this sense they can take the continuous.

   I'*m thinking* of going to Florida for my vacation.
   We'*re considering* her job application.

2. *Have* can describe an action and in this sense it can take the continuous.

   They'*re having* lunch.
   Are you *having* a good time?

   But when *have* is used to indicate possession, it is used in the simple form.

   She *has* a new car.
   He *has* no experience.
   Do you *have* time to talk to me now?

B. Situation

Margaret Klein and Peggy Hill work at WNYN. They are talking about David Denton. Fill in the blanks with the simple present or present continuous form of the verb.

Example:
PEGGY: Where's Grace Lee?
MARGARET: She's   (have)   lunch with David Denton.
           She's *having* lunch with David Denton.

PEGGY: Is he a good candidate?
MARGARET: I 1. think he is. But he 2. have no previous work experience.
PEGGY: Has Bob Russo offered him a job yet?
MARGARET: Not yet. He's 3. think about it.
PEGGY: What do you think of him?
MARGARET: I 4. think he 5. have a pleasant personality. He certainly 6. have a lot of enthusiasm. But I think he 7. have a tough time finding a job.
PEGGY: What did Grace Lee say about his qualifications?
MARGARET: She 8. consider them very carefully.
PEGGY: Well, who's this Mike Horton?
MARGARET: He's the one who 9. have 15 years of experience in promotion and advertising.
PEGGY: Where is he now?
MARGARET: He's 10. have an interview with the head of the advertising department.
PEGGY: Is Bob thinking of hiring him?
MARGARET: I'm not sure. He 11. think Horton 12. have a lot of potential, so I guess he's 13. consider it.
PEGGY: Is David Denton the only candidate Bob has for the cameraman job?
MARGARET: Yes. Bob 14. not consider anyone else right now.

4

3 | Present perfect and present perfect continuous

A. Comment

One common use of the present perfect and present perfect continuous tenses is to express actions occurring within periods of time that began in the past and continue up to the present. Notice the division of time in the chart.

PAST ONLY	PAST-TO-PRESENT		PRESENT
Past Tense Carol worked for a small company for five years.	*Present Perfect* She's worked at this TV station for three years.	*Present Perfect Continuous* She's been working at this TV station for three years.	*Present Continuous* She's working at this TV station now.

1. The simple past is used for lengths of time completely in the past. They do not continue up to the present.
2. The present perfect continuous usually means that the action started in the past and continues up to the present. It always has this meaning when used with *for* or *since*.

   I've *been watching* TV for an hour.
   She's *been living* in Chicago since 1980.
3. The present perfect usually has this past-to-present meaning when used with verbs of continuous duration (*live, work, study,* etc.): They've *lived* here all their lives. With these verbs, either the present perfect or the present perfect continuous can be used to show that the action continues up to the present.

   They've *worked* for this company for a long time. *or*
   They've *been working* for this company for a long time.
4. State and perception verbs that do not usually occur in the present continuous do not occur in the present perfect continuous either. (See Comment 1A.)

   How long *have* you *had* your present job?
   I've *known* her all my life.
   He's *been* here for a long time.

B. Practice

You are talking to a new friend. Notice the question forms:

A: I lived in California years ago.
B: *Oh? How long did you live there?*
A: Twenty years.

A: I'm living in Indiana.
B: *How long have you been living there?/How long have you lived there?*
A: Three years.

A: I'm working on my homework now.
B: *How long have you been working on it?*
A: Since seven o'clock.

Now you do it. Working with a partner, ask and answer questions with *how long*.

1. I studied at the University of California.
2. I worked in a factory once.
3. I was in London once.
4. I work in television now.
5. I studied Spanish in school.
6. I'm studying Chinese now.
7. I'm looking for another job.

8. I worked for a newspaper once.
9. I live in a large apartment building.
10. I'm waiting for an interview.
11. I know your boss.
12. I play tennis.
13. I have two dogs.

C. Situation

Make a list of things you have, own, do or are doing, similar to exercise B above. Read your list to somebody else. Stop after each item and let the other person ask you a question starting with *how long*.

D. Discussion

Think about the present. Describe things you started doing some time ago and still do now. The following ideas may be helpful:

1. Describe where you're attending classes, for how long and what you've learned.
2. Do you have a job? Describe it and tell what you've done on the job.
3. Do you play any sports? Describe what you do and how long you've been doing it.

5

UNIT 1 Dialog/Communication Practice

DIALOG 🎞️

Listen to the dialog and complete David's part.

(Bob Russo's assistant, Margaret Klein, is introducing David.)

MARGARET: Mr. Russo, this is David Denton.

MR. RUSSO: How do you do?

DAVID: Glad (1) ~~to meet~~ *to meet you* ✓

RUSSO: Come in. Please . . . sit down.

DAVID: Sorry (2) *I'm late.* I—*usually*

RUSSO: That's all right.

DAVID: I (3) *usually try to* be pretty (4) *punctual* ✓, but (5) *this morning —*

RUSSO: I understand. Don't worry about it. Go ahead . . . please sit down. Now, let's see. . . . I have your resumé here. I would like to ask you a few questions.

DAVID: (6) *OK* ✓

RUSSO: You haven't had a job in television before, have you?

DAVID: Well, no, . . . actually, I (7) *haven't.* But I've (8) *I had a lot of* camera (9) *experience* In college (10) *we had a t.v. station* on campus I (11) *was* the camera crew (12) *for nearly* 2 years.

RUSSO: I noticed that in your resume. Was your work confined to studio productions?

DAVID: Oh, no. We (13) *did* a lot of field production (14) *too* . . . I . . . went out on assignments (15) *all the time.* We (16) *did a* WFK News *program* that was (17) *pretty popular.* I'd (18) *like to* tell (19) *you* a little bit (20) *about it* if (21) *I could.* It (22) *was called* Odyssey. Maybe (23) *you've heard about* the (24) *program?*

RUSSO: No, I'm afraid I haven't.

DAVID: There (25) *was* quite a nice write-up *about it* (26) *in the paper* last year.

RUSSO: Well, . . . I . . . uh . . . see here that you graduated from college two years ago. You haven't been working since you graduated—is that right?

DAVID: Well, uh . . . I (27) *haven't.* But (28) *I've been working* for (29) *the college*

RUSSO: Well, let me tell you a little bit about the job.

(Thirty minutes later. The interview is almost over.)

RUSSO: Well, I think that with the camera experience you've had, you should be able to do the work all right. But it's going to be a lot different than the kind of thing you've been used to.

DAVID: (30) *different?*

RUSSO: Well, I'm thinking particularly about the question of handling responsibility.

DAVID: Oh, I (31) *don't mind* having (32) *a lot of responsibility* ! In (33) *college,* I (34) *had to* produce shows (35) *all of myself* by I had (36) *to prepare for every thing.*

RUSSO: That's just the point I'm trying to make. Here at WNYN, a cameraman works as an assistant to a reporter.

DAVID: (37) *an assistant*

RUSSO: Yes. And the reporter's the "boss," so to speak.

And the reporter tells you what to do on each assignment.

DAVID: Oh . . . Well, uh . . . wouldn't be (38) *any problem for me.* I . . . I don't mind (39) *working with other people.*

RUSSO: Hmm. I'd like to set up an interview for you with Grace Lee, our chief program coordinator.

DAVID: You mean (40) *I'm going to get the job?*

RUSSO: I'd say there's a good chance. We need a cameraman right away. But I want you to talk with Ms. Lee before we make a final decision.

COMMUNICATION PRACTICE

Apologizing

David was late for his appointment. He said:
Sorry I'm late.
Bob Russo responded:
That's all right.

Comment

Here are some expressions of apology:

Sorry.	I'm terribly sorry.
I'm sorry.	I feel terrible about it.
I'm awfully sorry.	Oh, I'm so sorry.

Situation

You are at a party and the following things happen. Choose one of the expressions above to complete each apology. You may use some of the expressions more than once.

1. You arrive an hour early:
   _____ . I got the time mixed up.
2. You spill coffee on the rug:
   _____ . Let me help you clean it up.
3. You break a glass:
   _____ .
4. You go into the wrong room and wake up the baby:
   _____ . Will she be able to go back to sleep?
5. Your party is so loud that it disturbs the neighbors:
   _____ . We'll turn down the music.
6. You knock a lamp off the table and break it:
   It was such a beautiful lamp. _____ .
7. You forget someone's name:
   _____ . I've forgotten your name.

Note that apologies are often followed by an excuse or a comment of some kind.

Apologize for other embarrassing things you might do at somebody's house or office.

6

LISTENING

A student has been attending classes given at the college to help prepare people who are going to be applying for jobs.

Getting Ready to Listen

1. How do you feel when you are in an interview situation with either a prospective employer while looking for a job or with a teacher while talking about academic problems?
2. If you were being interviewed by a prospective employer, how would you try to conduct yourself? What kinds of things would you tell the interviewer about yourself?
3. Suppose you were an employer. What qualities would you look for in someone applying for a job with you?

Vocabulary

sell yourself: convince others of your abilities
on the line: in a situation where you have to prove yourself
a mock interview: a pretended interview, for practice
freeze up: get tongue-tied; be unable to speak due to fear
do it cold: [informal] do it without a rehearsal; without previous preparation
(right) off the top: [informal] without thinking about it; spontaneously
primed: prepared

Now listen to the interview.

Comprehension Checkup

Choose the phrase that correctly completes each statement, based on the interview.

1. The adviser suggests that if you're nervous, you should
   a. use your nervous energy to present a positive image of yourself.
   b. try to make the interviewer think you are calm and confident.
2. After practicing with friends in a mock interview, the student says
   a. the real interview comes out just perfect.
   b. he still tends to freeze up in the real interview.

3. The adviser thinks
   a. it is important to stick to the central issue of the interview.
   b. some casualness and reference to outside interests can be good.
4. If you do talk about outside things, such as hobbies, you should
   a. brief yourself first on what your strongest points are.
   b. relate them to the job you are applying for.
5. Employers are often eager to find employees that
   a. have several years of experience.
   b. are positive about themselves.

Listening for Emotion

The adviser tells the student that a strong, positive attitude about his own success will work in his favor. Yet, during this interview the student expresses uncertainty, doubt and nervousness.

Listen to the interview again. How does the student show his nervousness?

Transfer

Do a job-counseling session similar to the one you listened to on tape. Prepare notes with questions, problems, advice, etc. in advance.

Job-counseling session:
SPEAKER 1: person getting ready to go out and apply for a job (has specific problems and questions to discuss with the adviser)
SPEAKER 2: adviser (has specific suggestions to make)

UNIT 1 Reading

Graph 1. **Distribution of Workers in Occupations in the United States, 1977.**

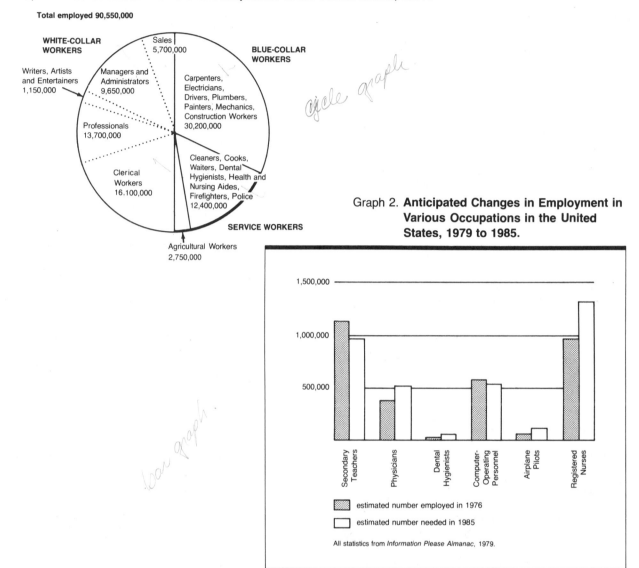

Total employed 90,550,000

WHITE-COLLAR WORKERS

Sales 5,700,000

Writers, Artists and Entertainers 1,150,000

Managers and Administrators 9,650,000

BLUE-COLLAR WORKERS

Carpenters, Electricians, Drivers, Plumbers, Painters, Mechanics, Construction Workers 30,200,000

Professionals 13,700,000

Cleaners, Cooks, Waiters, Dental Hygienists, Health and Nursing Aides, Firefighters, Police 12,400,000

Clerical Workers 16,100,000

SERVICE WORKERS

Agricultural Workers 2,750,000

Graph 2. **Anticipated Changes in Employment in Various Occupations in the United States, 1979 to 1985.**

1,500,000

1,000,000

500,000

Secondary Teachers

Physicians

Dental Hygienists

Computer-Operating Personnel

Airplane Pilots

Registered Nurses

[gray box] estimated number employed in 1976

[white box] estimated number needed in 1985

All statistics from *Information Please Almanac*, 1979.

Words and Expressions

clerical worker: a person who works as a clerk or office worker (typist, secretary, etc.)

professional: a person who works in a job that requires lots of knowledge and training, such as law, medicine, dentistry, etc.

physician: a medical doctor

Comprehension Checkup

Read each sentence below and write *1* if it applies to Graph 1, *2* if it applies to Graph 2, and *1–2* if it applies to both of them.

   2   **1.** This graph gives information about the future.

   1   **2.** This graph gives information about only one year.

  1–2   **3.** This graph shows numbers of people in various jobs.

  1–2   **4.** This graph gives figures on all workers in the United States.

Finding Facts

Use the graphs to answer the following questions:

1. What are the four major types of workers? *managers & adm. agricultural workers, blue collar workers & service workers*
2. How many people were employed in agricultural work in the United States in 1977? *2,750,000*
3. Which category of white-collar workers had the largest number of workers? *clerical workers*
4. Which category of white-collar workers had the smallest number of workers? *writers, artists & entertainers.*
5. What are two examples of blue-collar jobs? *Carpenters & painters*
6. Which two occupations will require fewer workers in 1985 than in 1976? *dental Hygienists & airplane pilots.*
7. In 1985 will there be more computer-operating personnel or more airplane pilots? *more computer operating*
8. In 1985, which occupation will require the greatest number of workers? *registered nurses.*
9. Which occupation will have the greatest percentage increase from 1976 to 1985? *registered nurses*
10. Which occupation will require the fewest workers compared to the other occupations? *dental Hygienists*
11. Which graph would be most useful to you in planning a career? *graph #2*
12. Which graph would give a better idea of what people do for a living in the United States? *Distribution of workers.*

Vocabulary Building

WNYN interviewed an economist about the future of the labor force. Use the list of words below to choose the correct word form for each blank in the interview.

VERBS	NOUNS	ADJECTIVES
distribute	distribution	distributed
estimate	estimate (= calculation)	estimated
	estimation (= opinion)	
anticipate	anticipation	anticipated
employ	employment	employed

WNYN: What kinds of changes in the work force do you 1. anticipate in the next five years?

ECONOMIST: For decades, heavy, labor-intensive industry has been a major source of 2. employ *ment* in the country. Recently, we've seen the work force become increasingly 3. distribute *d* among the service industries and I think that this trend will continue. In addition, certain relatively new industries are going to grow very rapidly and 4. employ many more people than they do now. The information processing field is one of those. I 5. estimate that this field will double its number of employees over the next decade.

WNYN: Is that 6. estimate *estimation* based on firm data?

ECONOMIST: Not really. But I feel that this industry is *anticipation* making important technological strides and the 7. anticipate *anticipation* in the computer industry is that more and more people will be using computers for all sorts of purposes. Why, I saw one 8. estimate that said that 50% of all families in the United States would have a home computer by the year 1990. That's going to 9. employ a lot of people!

WNYN: Predictions about future employment opportunities are important to many people—especially those young men and women who 10. anticipate entering the work force soon. Just how much faith can they put in the predictions of economists such as yourself?

ECONOMIST: Well, it's easy to make accurate 11. estimate *estimations* about the future 12. distribute *distribution* of workers in some fields— we will need fewer people in education throughout the '80s, for example. But in my 13. estimate *estimation*, it's difficult for us to 14. anticipate very many major trends in 15. employ *ment* with much accuracy at this time.

Discussion Topics

1. Do you have a job now? What do you do? How did you get into this field?
2. What do you like about your job? (If you are a full-time student, consider that your job.)
3. Do you think that the kind of job you have will eventually become obsolete? Is there anything about your job that could not be taken over by computers?
4. What jobs do you think will become obsolete in 100 years?
5. What new kinds of jobs will there be in the 21st century?
6. What jobs do we have now that didn't exist 100 years ago?

Writing Topics

Choose one of the topics and write a composition of 250–300 words.

1. Do people now have the same attitudes towards work and their jobs as people did 100 or 200 or 300 years ago? Discuss the changes or the similarities in attitude and possible causes for the changes.
2. Describe the most important achievement of your life. What did you do? Why was it important to you? How has it changed your life?
3. Describe what you consider would be the ideal job or career. Include details about hours, pay, working conditions and duties.

unit 2
transportation PUBLIC OR PRIVATE?

WNYN-TV looks at some of the basic issues.

**Is this a business or a residential street?
Would it be easy to cross this street on foot?**

1 Center Avenue is like a thousand other roads in any big city. Crowded with the heavy trucks and other vehicles that use it every day, it is very busy and noisy. Mrs. Norma Clay, who lives near it, describes it as "a death trap and a scandal."

A lot of children cross it every day on their way to school. Her eight-year-old son, Donald, is one of them. A few days ago a huge truck almost hit him, and he was almost killed. Mrs. Clay says:

> The road is far too dangerous for children to cross, and the authorities know it. But they refuse to do anything about it. We want them to build a bridge or a tunnel. But they say it costs too much. How many children have to get hurt or killed before they do something?

Only last month a truck hit another child.

Doctors tried to save him, but he died. Every year thousands of children die or are badly injured on our streets and highways.

Ask and Answer

Imagine you are a reporter for WNYN. Interview first Mrs. Clay then a city official.

Ask Mrs. Clay:
1. How near _Do you live_?
2. How often does your son _visit you_?
3. How many other children _do you have_?
4. Why do you think _____?
5. What do you think _____?

Ask the city official:
1. Why can't you _____?
2. How much does a bridge _____?
3. Do you know how many children _____?
4. What happened last month when _____?

10

How does the air look?
Do you think it's healthy? | 2

Cities can die too. Some cities are already dead. Why does this happen? Who or what is responsible? One cause is traffic jams. Traffic jams like this happen every day. People get headaches and lose their tempers because they can't move. These traffic jams also cause noise and air pollution. The air becomes harmful to breathe. Trees and plants are killed by the chemicals in the air. People are being killed by this pollution too. Our cities are being destroyed by automobiles, and the problem is getting worse all the time.

Ask and answer questions beginning with:
1. How often _____?
2. Why _____?
3. What _____?
4. What _____?
5. Are only plants and trees _____?
6. By what _____?
7. Is the problem _____?

3 | Is this a new or an old subway station?
Would you enjoy taking trains like this to work?

Perhaps public transportation is the answer. The problem is that public transportation is often slow and very crowded. Schedules are not always reliable. In some cities, public transportation is uncomfortable or even dangerous. But more and more cities are building clean, safe and convenient systems of mass transportation. As the systems improve and driving becomes less convenient, more and more people are taking some form of mass transportation to get to work.

Ask the people in your class:
1. how they get to school/work
2. how they prefer to travel
3. what the advantages/disadvantages are of their present means of transportation

UNIT 2 Grammar

1 Questions with *who/what*

Who hit Donald?
What does Mrs. Clay want?

A. Comment

1. If *what* or *who* is the subject (the "doer" of the action), do not use the question auxiliary words *do, does* or *did*.
2. If *what* or *who* is the object, use the auxiliary words *do, does* or *did*.

B. Situation

You are interviewing a person who takes the train to work every day. Notice the two kinds of questions you could ask.

Something gives her headaches.
What gives you headaches?

She does something every day.
What do you do every day?

Now ask questions with *who* or *what* and listen carefully to your partner's answers.

1. Someone drives him/her to the train station every day.
2. Something happens when it rains.
3. Something often comes late.
4. He/She always sees someone on the train.
5. The conductor always collects something.
6. Something is always very crowded.
7. Something breaks down almost every week.
8. He/She always complains about something.

C. Practice

Look at the picture and make a question with *who* or *what* for each verb given.

Example: sit
Who is sitting next to the fat man? *or*
What is the fat man sitting on?

1. smile
2. hold
3. fall
4. talk
5. play

2 Questions with *how much/how many*

A. Comment

1. Use *how much* before noncount nouns and *how many* before plural count nouns.
2. The same rules for *what* and *who* apply for *how much* and *how many*. When they go with the subject, you do *not* use the question auxiliary words *do, does* or *did*. (See Comment 1A.)

B. Situation

You are interviewing a bus driver. Ask questions with *how much* or *how many*.

Examples:
Many people take the bus to work.
How many people take the bus to work?

He takes in a lot of money every day.
How much money do you take in every day?

1. He/She gets a lot of crazy questions every day.
2. Accidents happen on this street every day.
3. The bus driver sees accidents every week.
4. He/She knows other bus drivers.
5. His/Her bus uses a lot of gas.
6. He/She spends some money on his/her lunch each day.
7. He/She works many hours every day.
8. Many people ride his/her bus every day.
9. He/She has met some celebrities.
10. A lot of time is wasted in traffic jams.

3 Passive

A. Comment

In English, the subject of a sentence usually has more emphasis than the object. Compare these sentences:

Buses are repaired in this garage. (passive)
Mechanics repair buses in this garage. (active)

If you want to focus attention on the buses, use the passive sentence. But if you want to focus attention on the mechanics, use the active sentence.

To indicate the "doer" of the action in a passive sentence, use *by:*

Buses are repaired *by mechanics* in this garage.

B. Situation

A reporter is interviewing Dr. Campbell, a specialist in environmental protection. Respond as Dr. Campbell does.

Examples:
REPORTER: Do cars cause *any damage?*
CAMPBELL: *Yes, a lot of damage is caused by cars.*

REPORTER: Are cars destroying *our cities?*
CAMPBELL: *Absolutely. Our cities are being destroyed by cars.*

1. Do any trucks use this road?
2. Are trucks using it now?
3. Do trucks make much noise?
4. Do trucks cause any damage?
5. Is anyone organizing a protest march?
6. Are several people organizing it?
7. Does traffic cause any problems?
8. Are the authorities doing anything about traffic problems?

4 Present continuous: extended meaning

A. Comment

The present continuous form can also be used to indicate actions or attitudes that are continuing to develop. Some common verbs used with this meaning are:

start (to + verb)	get (+ adjective)	change
begin (to + verb)	grow (+ adjective)	rise
become (+ adjective)	prepare	fall

It*'s starting to rain.*
My small town *is changing* into a city.
My work *is getting* more difficult.
You'd better put on a sweater. The temperature *is falling.*
The students *are preparing* for their next exam.

B. Discussion

Think of things you have read in the newspaper or heard on the news. Use verbs from the list in 4A to complete the sentences.

Example:
The cost of living is *rising.* As a result, people are *becoming angry.*

1. There's a war on in _____. People there are _____ing _____.
2. There's an economic crisis in _____. People are _____ing _____.
3. The next Olympic games will be in _____. Already people there are _____ing _____. Athletes are _____ing _____.
4. There'll be an election soon in _____. Candidates for office are _____ing _____.
5. It's *(season)* in _____. The trees and flowers are _____ing _____. People are _____ing _____.
6. Labor conditions are poor in _____. Workers across the nation are _____.

5 Adjective + infinitive

The air becomes impossible to breathe.

A. Pattern

The air	is impossible to breathe.
It	is impossible to breathe the air.

B. Practice

Make more sentences like this:

It's difficult to find parking places.
Parking places are difficult to find.

It's easy to get a taxi in this city.
A taxi is easy to get in this city.

1. It's expensive to build a good public transportation system.
2. But in the long run they are more economical to build.
3. Of course it's not as comfortable to ride in them.
4. It's more comfortable to ride in a big Cadillac.
5. But it's getting more and more expensive to buy gas.
6. Pollution is also difficult to live with.
7. Perhaps in ten or twenty years our cities will be more pleasant to live in.

C. Discussion

Make some more sentences of your own, using this construction. For example, talk about the place you live in and compare it with another place you know, like this:

I think London is pleasant to live in, but I feel that Paris is far more exciting to visit.

UNIT 2 Dialog/Communication Practice

DIALOG

Listen to the dialog and complete Marsha's part.

GRACE: What did they say about the viewer survey report?

MARGARET: The information's being prepared now. They promised we'd have the complete report in a couple of weeks.

GRACE: Oh, what takes them so long with these things? They're not much good to us if we don't get them promptly. Well, . . . let's get started. This is going to be a very short meeting. Uh . . . Where's David?

MARGARET: I don't think he's come in yet. He does know about the meeting.

GRACE: Hmm . . . Well, we'll go ahead without him. I've got another appointment at eleven thirty. Now, . . . I want to go over plans for our special features this month. What have you got, Marsha?

MARSHA: First of all, there's (1) ~~there's~~ *the special on space exploration*

GRACE: Right. How much have you done on that so far? *got in touch with prof. Daniels*

MARSHA: (2) ~~Well~~ *Oh! I finally (3) managed . He said ~~together~~ with prof. Daniels* *he'd* (4) ~~be the program~~ *be the program . And I'm (5) ~~just~~ delighted*

GRACE: Oh, good! We've scheduled that for the twenty-third. Are you going to be ready by that time?

MARSHA: Oh, (6) *no problem .*

MARGARET: Is that going to conflict with the dates for the Denver project?

GRACE: No, . . . No, the trip will be the week after that.

MARGARET: Bob's really excited about that one.

MARSHA: (7) ~~~~ *talking about?* (8) *what* trip? (9) *What's the* "Denver Project"?

GRACE: Well, . . . Bob wants to talk to you about that himself. All I can say is that it's going to be the biggest and most important assignment you've ever had at WNYN.

MARGARET: He just got the final O.K. this morning to go ahead with the project.

GRACE: Well, let's see . . . Any problems? Uh . . . How many other deadlines do we have? Uh . . . Are we all set for Friday's program on the airline strike?

MARSHA: Yes. And (10) *the other 2 programs.* the housing industry (11) ~~&~~ . noise pollution . . . They're (12) *they're both being* edited (13) *right now .*

MARGARET: Oh, it's eleven thirty, Grace. Time for your appointment.

GRACE: Oh, O.K. I'd better go. Uh . . . we'll get together again on Thursday.

(Marsha goes back to her office . . . She finds David there.)

MARSHA: David! You (14) *missed the meeting*

DAVID: I just walked in. Got tied up this morning. You know the program you want to do on the new hospital?

MARSHA: Yes, of course. We're (15) *supposed go over there* (16) *on tuesday to do the story*

DAVID: Yeah, I know. Well, I spent three hours with the people at the hospital this morning, and planned the whole thing. I think they understand what they're supposed to do when we do the recording on Tuesday.

MARSHA: (17) *You were* over there (18) *this morning*

DAVID: Yeah . . . Well, I was passing by and I thought I might as well stop in and set things up for Tuesday. I thought you'd be happy about *you . Voila*

MARSHA: David! (19) *Why did* (20) ~~~~ thing? You *did* (21) *not even know* what kind of (22) *I wanted*

DAVID: Oh, I think you'll like the story angle I came up with.

MARSHA: That's (23) *not the point* ! (24) *We're supposed to be* a team. I'm (25) *I'm responsible* story, and (26) ~~~~ the video . . . (27) *remember . you're responsible for*

DAVID: Sorry. It won't happen again . . .

COMMUNICATION PRACTICE

Introducing a New Subject

Marsha was talking to David about the meeting. David ignored her comment and brought up a new subject. He said:

You know the program you want to do on the new hospital?

Comment

Very often speakers will introduce a new subject of conversation by using a question or statement that arouses the interest of the listener. When the listener already knows something about the new subject, expressions like these are used:

A: (Do) You know the program you want to do on the new hospital?
B: Yes. What about it?

A: (Do) You remember the man we met on the train?
B: Yes, of course. What about him?

A: (Do) You remember my telling you about the new guy at the office?
B: Yeah. What about him? Isn't he working out?

When the listener doesn't know anything about the new subject, expressions like these are used:

A: You'll never guess who I saw today.
B: Really? Who?

A: You wouldn't believe what happened at the office today!
B: What? Tell me.

A: Something awful happened to me today. My wallet was stolen on the bus.
B: How terrible! Did you have much money in it?

A: I had an interesting/funny/strange/unusual/etc. experience at work today.

B: Yeah? What happened?

Practice

Introduce the following topics of conversation to your partner. Use expressions like those above to fill in the blanks. After your partner responds, continue the conversation by giving more information.

1. _____ that strange man we met on the flight from Paris to New York?

2. _____ that new TV set I bought last week?

3. _____ the apartment on 12th Avenue I looked at a couple of weeks ago?

4. _____ who I met on line at the movie last night.

5. _____. My boss gave me a big raise!

6. _____ the letter I wrote to the electricity company asking for a refund?

7. _____ that my dog was lost?

LISTENING

Colin Campbell is being interviewed about traffic in our cities.

Getting Ready to Listen

1. What are some of the advantages and disadvantages of the automobile in modern society?
2. How have cars affected life in cities?
3. Do you think life in the cities would be improved if cars were eliminated?

Vocabulary

well-founded: based on fact
irreversible: not capable of being changed back to a previous state
it's revealing: it tells us (something)
thrive on: prosper
get off on: [informal] derive special pleasure from
crumble: fall apart

Now listen to the interview.

Comprehension Checkup

Choose the phrase that correctly completes each statement, based on the interview.

1. Part of the problem of traffic is that planners and architects
   a. are convinced that it is irreversible.
   b. believe that it can be solved.
2. There have been proponents of the idea that
   a. traffic problems are irreversible.
   b. cars should be eliminated.
3. Parking the car close to home or in the garage shows
   a. that people feel a personal relationship with their cars.
   b. that people are more secure with their cars nearby.
4. We need to consider what the problems we have with cars
   a. imply psychologically about society.
   b. indicate about the technological aspects of city planning.
5. An important environmental aspect of this problem is that
   a. exhaust fumes from cars cause damage to buildings.
   b. some plants actually seem to thrive on exhaust fumes.

Listening for Tone

Listen to the interview again. Is Mr. Campbell generally optimistic or pessimistic about the problem of traffic in the cities?

Transfer

Imagine that you are conducting an interview for a local radio or TV station on the problem of traffic in the city where you live. Discuss the problems as well as the possible solutions.

SPEAKER 1: interviewer
SPEAKER 2: city-planning expert worried about the rapid increase in number of cars, pollution, etc.

Gerry's Big Decision

(1) When Gerry sold his car and swore that he'd given up the expensive automobile habit forever, his friends laughed and told him he'd change his mind when he got tired of walking. Gerry considered that and decided to buy a ten-speed bicycle. That would serve his needs for everyday transportation and, besides, would add nothing to the pollution that had become a problem in the city where he worked as a computer programmer. In addition, he would get more exercise. He selected a fine English bike and found the short trip home from the bicycle shop pleasant and exhilarating. But he wondered how it would be to ride to work through heavy city traffic.

(2) It was about eight miles to the office where Gerry worked. The first two miles from his suburban apartment had a wide road with a special lane for bicycles clearly marked. That would be no problem, but he had to leave the bicycle lane to take the freeway to the other side of the city. As he entered the freeway, he passed a sign that read "Non-Motorized Vehicles Prohibited." Gerry stopped his bicycle and pondered the sign. That meant him, sure enough. But if he didn't take the freeway, he'd have to take the winding, stop-and-go roads through the suburbs. He decided not to turn back.

(3) The air on the freeway was thick with exhaust fumes, and breathing them as deeply as he did nearly made him sick. Not only that, but the speeding cars threw dust and bits of rock into the air.

Gerry discovered very quickly that few motorists had any patience with bicyclists.

(4) He found himself being blinded by dust in his eyes with nearly every passing car. But he stuck it out until he had to cross the

first exit from the freeway. Then he discovered he could not cross fast enough to please the hurrying motorists. After he came dangerously close to being hit by a garbage truck, Gerry took the next exit from the freeway. "So much for the freeway," he said to himself. "Now let's see how I do in the city traffic."

(5) By this time in the morning, traffic was at its peak, and Gerry learned that there were few motorists that had any patience with a bicyclist. If he rode on the shoulder of the road, cars treated him as a pedestrian and tried to zip past him to make turns into cross streets.

Just for a moment, he considered riding on the sidewalk instead . . .

(6) If he rode in the lane of traffic as a vehicle, cars hovered impatiently near his back wheel—not at all happy with his slower pace. He found himself being intimidated by the bigger, more powerful vehicles, and he realized that if he ever had a showdown with one, he'd be the loser. For a moment, he considered riding on the sidewalk, away from the cars and their impatient drivers. But he knew that pedestrians were even more unpredictable than drivers, weaving aimlessly down the sidewalks. Without a horn, he'd run into dozens before he reached his job. So he stayed in the heart of traffic and dealt with the cars as best he could.

(7) By the time he reached the office, he was in a nervous sweat, agitated by his experience with city traffic. He'd have to calm down and relax if he was going to be able to handle the pressures of his job adequately.

He took one look at the crowded elevators . . .

(8) But first, he had a problem to solve. If he left his bicycle parked on the sidewalk, chained to a parking meter or a sign post, it would get stolen, whether it was locked or not. So he hauled the bicycle into the lobby of the building and paused for a minute, considering the elevators. They were crowded with workers and customers. No chance of taking it up to his eleventh-floor office. So he left the bicycle chained to a banister near the front doors and went up to his office. No more than ten minutes later, the security guard called him and told him he could not leave his vehicle parked in the lobby. Well, he could leave it there for today, anyway. But he'd have to find another place to park. The guard suggested the university a few blocks away. There were lots of bicycle racks there.

(9) Gerry hung up the phone completely disillusioned. It seemed as if the city was completely against bicycles as a solution to the traffic and pollution problems it had. Yet he knew that of all the solutions proposed, the bicycle was the most economical and beneficial to the city and its inhabitants.

(10) Gerry straightened his clothing and ran a comb through his hair. He pulled himself together as best he could. Perhaps tomorrow the ride to work would be more pleasant.

Words and Expressions

came to a stop: stopped
figured on: thought about, expected
stuck it out: continued without giving up (in spite of difficulty)

Comprehension Checkup

Choose the correct statement.

1. The main reason Gerry sold his car was
   a. to cut down on expenses.
   b. to solve his transportation problems.
   c. to do his part in cutting down on pollution.
2. Gerry wanted to take the freeway because
   a. it had a specially marked bicycle lane.
   b. it was the most direct route to his job.
   c. he thought traffic conditions would be better there.
   d. a sign said that bicycles were allowed there.
3. One thing Gerry didn't like about riding on the freeway was that
   a. it was a winding, stop-and-go road.
   b. there were too many bicyclists in his lane.
   c. trucks slowed down for him.
   d. he was blinded with dust thrown by speeding cars.
4. When Gerry reached his office,
   a. he was very happy with his experiment of riding his bike to work.
   b. he was ready to handle the pressures of his job.
   c. he was very upset.
   d. he decided never to ride his bicycle in the city again.

Paraphrasing

Some of the sentences below are accurate paraphrases based on the story. Others are not accurate. Write *true* in the blank if the paraphrase is accurate. Write *false* if it is not. The numbers in parentheses refer to the paragraphs that the paraphrases are about.

_____ 1. Bicycles were allowed on the freeway. (1)
_____ 2. The air was difficult to breathe. (2)
_____ 3. Some drivers threw rocks at Gerry. (3)
_____ 4. It was difficult to see. (4)
_____ 5. Crossing the freeway exits was dangerous. (4)
_____ 6. A truck almost hit him. (4)
_____ 7. There were lots of cars on the streets. (5)
_____ 8. Many motorists had respect for the needs of the bicyclist. (5)
_____ 9. Gerry didn't try riding near the shoulder of the road. (6)
_____ 10. He tried riding where most of the traffic was. (6)
_____ 11. He tried riding on the sidewalk. (6)
_____ 12. He left his bicycle on the sidewalk. (8)
_____ 13. The elevators were too crowded for him to put his bicycle in. (8)
_____ 14. He left his bicycle just outside the building. (8)
_____ 15. The guard made him move his bicycle immediately. (8)
_____ 16. Gerry decided to give up on riding his bicycle to work. (10)

Vocabulary Building

Choose the best meaning for the underlined words in the sentences below. If you are not sure of the meaning, read the paragraph the word comes from again and try to guess the meaning from context. Paragraph numbers are in parentheses.

1. Gerry's ride was <u>exhilarating</u>. (1)
   a. cheerful and exciting   **b.** exhausting   **c.** peaceful
2. He tried riding on <u>the shoulder of the road</u>. (5)
   a. the center of the road where there are a lot of cars
   b. just off the road where there are pedestrians
   c. the side of the road where cars don't usually go.
3. Gerry didn't want to have <u>a showdown</u> with a car. (6)
   a. a confrontation   **b.** a discussion   **c.** an argument
4. Gerry could imagine pedestrians <u>weaving aimlessly</u> down the sidewalks. (6)
   a. talking busily to their companions   **b.** filling up the sidewalks completely   **c.** walking along, changing directions frequently
5. The guard said that there were lots of <u>bicycle racks</u> at the university. (8)
   a. places where he could ride his bicycle safely
   b. places where he could get his bicycle repaired
   c. places where he could leave his bicycle

Writing Topics

Choose one of the topics and write a composition of 250–300 words.

1. You are an automobile owner who does not like bicyclists on public streets and roads, and you have been asked by the local newspaper to write an article about your views.
2. You have been using roller skates as a means of transportation, and the local newspaper has asked you to write an article. In your article, describe the advantages of using roller skates, and try to persuade people to use roller skates instead of automobiles.
3. In many countries, hitchhiking is a popular way for people to travel. In some parts of the world, including the United States, it is often considered dangerous. Discuss the advantages and disadvantages of this mode of transportation.
4. You have invented an entirely new form of transportation. Discuss your invention, and describe its advantages.

unit 3
SPACE EXPLORATION

This is part of a special program that WNYN-TV produced for its evening news show.

What do you see in this picture?
Where was this picture taken?

This is a photograph of the planet Earth, taken from the moon. The Earth has just risen above the moon's horizon. Of course, few people have actually seen it from the moon, but most of us have seen photographs like this one. These photographs show us the Earth as we've never seen it before. And they make us think of it in a different way, not as a vast planet under our feet, but as a green and blue ball racing through space—just a large spaceship that we call home.

Ask and answer:
1. what this is a picture of
2. where it was taken from
3. how many people have seen the Earth from the moon
4. how many of us have seen photographs like this one
5. what the photographs show us
6. how we think of the Earth when we look at the photographs from the moon

What is this a picture of?
Why is this rocket special?

People used to only dream about space travel, but now we have orbited the Earth and walked on the moon. Today we are used to the idea that space can be explored. The success of the first space shuttle, the Columbia, was an important development in the space age. First launched in 1981, the Columbia can travel into space and then return to earth for the next trip into space. All earlier space-going vehicles have either been left in space or have burned up falling back into the earth's atmosphere. Three more shuttles are planned, and this fleet of reusable shuttles will greatly reduce the cost of space travel and research. Eventually, the shuttles may carry material for space stations and factories into space to establish industry and, perhaps, even colonies in space.

Ask and answer questions, like this:
Ask what we have done in space.
A: What have we done in space?
B: We have orbited the Earth and walked on the moon.

Ask:
1. what an important development in the space age was
2. what the Columbia can do
3. what always happened to earlier space-going vehicles
4. how many more shuttles are planned
5. how the shuttles will affect space travel and research
6. what may eventually happen

3 | What is this a picture of?
Are there any people living there?

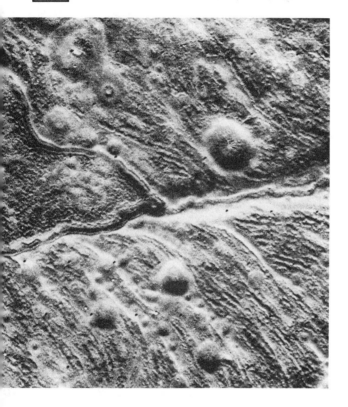

This is a picture of the surface of Mars taken by Viking Orbiter 1 from a distance of 1,360 miles. Shortly after this picture was taken, Viking Lander 1 landed on the surface of Mars and sent back the first close-up photographs ever taken of the Martian surface. The planet Mars has fascinated people for many years. About 100 years ago, an Italian astronomer looked through his telescope and reported that he could see canals on Mars. Ever since he did that, people have been asking the same question, "Is there life on Mars?" We now know that Mars is cold, dry and almost certainly lifeless. Eventually, scientists hope to send robots to explore the surface and collect samples of the soil. Although Mars is a wonderful place to visit scientifically, it is not very likely that it will have any human visitors anytime in the foreseeable future.

Ask and answer:
1. what this is a picture of
2. what happened shortly after this picture was taken
3. what an astronomer did 100 years ago
4. what people have been wondering since he did that
5. what scientists hope to do in the future
6. whether many human visitors will go there

How many stars are there in this picture? | 4

People have been interested in the stars ever since they first looked up into the sky. Some of these stars may have their own planets. If that is so, we can suppose that intelligent life may exist on some of them. The problem is that the nearest star is four light years away. In other words, light from it has been traveling for four years when it finally reaches us. Probably nobody from Earth will ever visit that star because it would take a rocket a hundred thousand years to get there.

Questions
1. How long have people been interested in the stars?
2. What may some of these stars have?
3. What can we suppose if some stars have their own planets?
4. What is the problem with the distance to the nearest star?
5. How long has light from the nearest star been traveling when it finally reaches us?
6. Why, in all probability, will no one from Earth ever visit that star?

UNIT 3 Grammar

1 Use of *just* with the present perfect

The earth *has just risen* above the moon's horizon.

A. Comment

In Unit 2 you used the present perfect to indicate an activity that occurred within a period of time that began in the past and continued up to the present. The present perfect also has other uses. In the example above, we use the present perfect with *just* to indicate something that happened very recently.

B. Transfer

These people have just finished something at work. Ask what they have just done.

Examples:
the bank officer

A: What *has* the bank officer *just done?*
B: She'*s just approved* an important business loan.

the teacher

A: What *has* the teacher *just done?*
B: He'*s just corrected* his students' homework.

1. the housewife
2. the salesclerk
3. the mechanic
4. the secretary
5. the student
6. the police officer
7. the government official
8. the musician

2 Use of the present perfect for a past action

A. Comment

Ever is sometimes used with this meaning in questions. In the example above, the present perfect is used to indicate an action done in the past, but with an importance or relevance to the present. In this meaning, the time the action occurred cannot be stated. In these cases, *ever* means "in your lifetime."

B. Practice

Ask and answer questions using the present perfect with *ever*, using the cues below.

Example:
be/to South America

A: *Have* you *ever been* to South America?
B: Yes, *I have*. In 1979. (No, *I haven't*. Have you?)

1. have/new car
2. go/swimming in the ocean
3. eat/raw fish
4. be/to New York
5. try/to run ten kilometers

C. Discussion

Find out about other people's experiences. If you are interested, you can ask additional questions about the experience.

Note: If you ask additional questions, you will probably have to switch to the past tense. Remember that the present perfect indicates a relationship between the past action and present time, so this tense is used in talking about one's experiences *up to now*. But when you ask about a detail of the experience, you are asking about facts related to the past action itself, not the present.

Examples:
A: *Have* you ever *been* in the hospital?
B: Yes, once when I *was* a child.

A: What *was* wrong?
B: Oh, not much. I *had* a minor operation.

1. travel (Have you ever been to Mexico, France, etc.?)
2. movies (Have you ever seen . . . ?)
3. sightseeing (Have you ever been to . . . ?)
4. unusual sports (Have you ever tried parachuting, water skiing, mountain climbing, etc.?)

3 Used to

People *used to dream* about space travel.

A. Comment

The form *used to* is used for things that people regularly did in the past but no longer do. Compare the underlined verbs in these sentences:

Statement: He <u>used</u> to live in Detroit.
Question: <u>Did</u> he <u>use</u> to live in Detroit?
Negative: He <u>didn't use</u> to live in Detroit.

B. Situation

Many changes take place in people's lives as they grow older—some little and some big. Think about the things you used to do and the change that has occurred. Make sentences using *used to* and *didn't use to*. You can use these topics for ideas.

Example: food
I *used to hate* green beans, but *now I love* them.

1. sports
2. jobs
3. clothes
4. entertainment

C. Practice

Ask questions using *did . . . use to*. Have short conversations with your partner, like this:

A: I take the bus to work now.
B: *Did* you *use to do* that?
A: No, I *used to* ride my bicycle.

4 Be used to

Today we *are used to the idea* that space can be explored.

A. Comment

The expression *be used to* + *-ing* verb or noun means *be accustomed to*.

When I moved to Toronto, I hated the cold weather. But now I'm *used to it*. I'm *used to wearing* heavy clothes. (The weather is ordinary to me; wearing heavy clothes is normal for me now and I don't mind it.)

B. Practice

Form sentences like this:

I'*m used to riding* my bicycle to work.
George *is used to working* all night.
My grandparents *were used to getting up* early.

Now you do it. Form at least six sentences.

C. Practice

Compare the underlined verbs: I <u>used to take</u> the train to work, but now I'<u>m used to</u> walking. Jean has recently moved from a small town in Florida to Chicago. Complete these sentences about Jean with *used to* or *is used to*.

1. When Jean first came to Chicago, she didn't like taking the train to work. In Florida, she_____ drive to her office. However, she_____ taking the train now and she doesn't mind it at all.
2. It was always warm in Florida, so she_____ wear light clothes all year long. But she_____ wearing heavy clothes in the winter now.
3. In Florida, she_____ go to the movies only occasionally. In Chicago, she_____ going almost every week.
4. Her new job is very demanding. In Florida, she_____ work only seven or eight hours a day. Now she_____ working longer hours.

Think of more things Jean regularly did in Florida (things she *used to do*) and things that are ordinary for her now (things she's *used to doing*). Make three more sentences.

UNIT 3 Dialog/Communication Practice

DIALOG 🔲

Listen to the dialog and complete Marsha's part.

DANIELS: Hello.

MARSHA: Is (1) *this 889-7654*

DANIELS: Yes, it is.

MARSHA: I'd like to (2) *speak to Prof. Daniels*, please.

DANIELS: Speaking.

MARSHA: (3) *Oh*. Professor Daniels, (4) *this is* Marsha Nelson.

DANIELS: Who?

MARSHA: Marsha Nelson. We're (5) *doing the special program on space exploration*. (6) *spoke to you* about (7) *two weeks* ago. . . .

DANIELS: Are you with the Hartley Foundation?

MARSHA: No, I'm (8) *calling from* WNYN-TV. You *asked me to* (9) *call you* this week (10) *to arrange a time for our interview*. Do (11) *you remember?*

DANIELS: Oh, the television program! Yes. Yes, of course. Forgive me. Since we spoke the last time, I've been involved in two other projects.

MARSHA: Oh, (12) *that's all (13) understand.*

DANIELS: Let me get my appointment book. Hold on for a minute, will you?

MARSHA: (14) *certainly*

DANIELS: Hmm. Now, let's see . . . uh . . . Are you planning to do the interview here at the university, or will I have to go into the studio?

MARSHA: Oh, (15) *here in your lab*, if at all possible. (16) *interesting things* (17) *in the lab*. I think it *would be important* (18) *to record* (19) *the program* *you here*.

DANIELS: Of course. Well, in that case, I could do it on Wednesday of next week, or . . . Hmm . . . How about this Friday?

MARSHA: (20) *Friday would be* perfect.

DANIELS: Friday's fine. There's just one thing—it'd have to be fairly early Friday afternoon. Since I'll be catching a six o'clock flight to Chicago, I'll have to leave here by around . . . four o'clock.

MARSHA: That's fine. How would it be *if we set it up for* (21) *2 o'clock*, then? It (22) *shouldn't take more than an hour.*

DANIELS: Good. Two o'clock, here at my office in Goddard Memorial Center. Will you be able to find it all right?

MARSHA: Oh, no problem. I (23) *used to take courses* (24) *at the U*

DANIELS: Now, . . . Should I prepare a short lecture?

MARSHA: Oh, no. You (25) *don't have to do that.* We'd *like to* (26) *keep it* as (27) *informal* as (28) *possible*. I'll prepare (29) *a couple* (30) *ask you questions*.

DANIELS: Fine. See you on Friday then.

MARSHA: (31) *Friday*, (32) *at two o'clock*. Thank you, Professor Daniels.

DANIELS: Goodbye.

(Marsha hangs up, then buzzes David Denton on the intercom.)

DAVID: Extension 32.

MARSHA: David, I (33) *just talked with Prof. Daniels*. The (34) *interview* is set for (35) *this Friday*

DAVID: At the university?

MARSHA: Uh-huh. At (36) *his office at* Goddard Center. We're (37) *supposed to be there at 2 o'clock* sharp.

DAVID: O.K. Meet you at his office?

MARSHA: Well, . . . uh . . . all right, (38) *that'd be* best. Since (39) *you'll need* I'll (40) *go many* I'll (41) *meet you* there. *Van with the equipment*

COMMUNICATION PRACTICE

Refusing and Accepting Offers Politely

PROFESSOR DANIELS: Should I prepare a short lecture?

MARSHA: Oh, no. You don't have to do that.

Comment

Marsha didn't want Professor Daniels to prepare a lecture for the TV interview. She wanted the interview to be as informal as possible. However, to be polite, she said, "You don't have to do that." It would have been rude if she had responded to his suggestion by saying, "No! Definitely not!"

Should I . . . ?/Would you like me to . . . ?

(polite refusal) Oh, no.	You don't have to do that. Please don't bother doing that. It's perfectly all right. Don't bother.
(polite acceptance) Oh,	please do! that would be fine. that would be wonderful. that would be very thoughtful of you.

Situation

A friend is planning to come visit you for a few days. He/She is making preparations for the trip and suggests doing certain things. Refuse or accept each suggestion politely.

1. Should I bring my stereo with me?
2. Should I bring the color slides I took on my trip to Mexico?
3. Would you like me to bake a cake to bring with me?
4. Should I bring a present for your parents?
5. Would you like me to bring some vegetables from my garden?

Making Polite Suggestions

How would it be if we bought a new car this year?

How would you like to empty the ashtray for me?

What would you think about going to the movies tonight?

Comment

Note that the verb is in the past following the expression "How would it be if . . . ?"

Situation

In the following situations, make polite suggestions to accomplish the things you want done:

1. You are in a meeting that has been going on for more than two hours. You're tired and want to go home. You'd rather continue the meeting tomorrow.
2. Your friend wants to go to a movie tonight, but you'd rather go tomorrow night instead.
3. You and your friend were going to go to a soccer game together, but you've decided you'd rather stay home.
4. You're talking to your wife/husband. You think both of you should buy new bicycles.

LISTENING

In this interview, a space scientist talks about space war movies, current efforts to pick up signals from other parts of the galaxy and about attitudes of the people who work in space research projects.

Getting Ready to Listen

1. Do you think there are other forms of life in the universe?
2. Should we human beings here on Earth try to communicate with extraterrestrial life (if it exists)? How? Why?

Vocabulary

jockeying: moving about with skill so as to get in good position

"mookies"; "chewbakki": names used to designate strange creatures from other planets in certain science fiction films

plaques: engraved tablets, here intended as messages from Earth to intelligent beings in outer space

intelligent signal: signal from some intelligent life form

matter of faith: belief in something not based on proof or facts

get our heads around: [informal] try to understand

Now listen to the interview.

Comprehension Checkup

Read each of the statements below and decide if they accurately restate what the scientist said in the interview. Write *yes* if they do and *no* if they do not.

_____ 1. The scientist says he enjoys the movies about space wars and star wars that film producers are making these days.

_____ 2. The way these movies show spaceships battling in outer space is very accurate scientifically.

_____ 3. Efforts are being made to send signals out into space in an attempt to contact other intelligent beings.

_____ 4. We are listening all the time, trying to pick up signals from other parts of the solar system.

_____ 5. Radio telescopes are far more sensitive than optical telescopes.

_____ 6. Radio telescopes are being used to look in the visible spectrum for possible signals from outer space.

_____ 7. Astronomers who studied the heavens four or five hundred years ago were really philosophers.

_____ 8. There used to be a lot of superstition about what should be done in space, but all of that has changed now.

_____ 9. From a space scientist's point of view, the movies we have today about space are good because they popularize things that will be possible in future years.

Listening for Specialized Language

Scientists, doctors, engineers and other professional people often use a very technical kind of language when they speak to one another that is difficult for non-professionals to understand.

Listen to the interview again. Does the space scientist use a technical style of language or does he try to use language that is easily understood by everyone? List examples of words and/or phrases that you think are "technical."

Discussion

1. Do you think there are intelligent beings on any other planets? If so, are they friendly or hostile?
2. What are your views about UFOs (Unidentified Flying Objects)?
3. Do you think you or anybody you know will ever get a chance to travel in space?
4. If you could, would you like to take a trip to the moon? Why or why not?

1 The surface of the red moon was barren and still. Steve radioed their landing position to Exploration Base Four and then he and Perry strapped on the heavy spacesuits and left the shuttle. "Nice place to visit . . ." Perry breathed into the intercom. "Yeah," Steve answered unenthusiastically. "Let's get those rock samples and get out of here. This place is spooky."

2 The heavy gravity on the large moon made movement difficult and Steve could hear Perry breathing hard through the intercom. He left Perry and headed for a low ridge of rocks jutting through the red dust of the moon. When he reached the ridge, he began to search for the variety of rocks he was required to take back to the Space Lab. Iron ore was the most interesting to the company. If he found an iron ore site worth mining, he'd get a handsome commission. "Then maybe I could quit this lousy job," he told himself. A startled gasp sounded in his ear.

3 "Hey, Steve?"

4 "Yeah?"

5 There was no other sound. Steve turned and looked at Perry. But instead of Perry, he saw two Perrys, one next to the other, at slightly different angles. A strange mist surrounded the two images he saw and then he realized that the mist was expanding in all directions. Suddenly he saw what

---

Words and Expressions

spooky: frightening
a handsome commission: a big fee, a generous payment
all turned around: completely disoriented, all mixed up in
    direction, lost

Comprehension Checkup

The main events of the story are given in scrambled order below. Put them in the correct order from beginning to end.

_____ Perry screamed and then was silent.
_____ Steve and Perry began exploring for certain rocks.
_____ Steve followed his own footsteps back to the shuttle.
_____ The mist appeared.
_____ They landed on the moon.
_____ Perry became lost in the mist.
_____ Steve took off from the moon.
_____ Perry tried to get back to the shuttle.

Making Inferences

Which of the following statements can be inferred from the story? Write *right* or *wrong* for each one. The numbers in parentheses refer to the paragraphs where the inferences are made.

_____ 1. Steve and Perry do not consider space exploration unusual. (1)

_____ 2. They were happy to be exploring this particular moon. (1)

_____ 3. They work for a mining company. (2)

_____ 4. Steve was not very happy with his job. (2)

_____ 5. The mist enveloped Steve before it enveloped Perry. (5-15)

_____ 6. Perry encountered something terrible after he became lost in the mist. (13)

_____ 7. Steve nearly ran into the shuttle because he couldn't see it through the pink mist. (15-16)

seemed like hundreds of images of Perry.

6 Just then Perry dropped his tools. "What's going on, Steve?" he stammered. His fear was plainly audible.

7 "I don't know, Perry. What are you seeing?"

8 "You. I mean, lots of different you's . . ."

9 "Yeah. Me too. Can you still see the shuttlecraft?"

10 "No. This pink stuff is spreading all over the place. Good lord, Steve! I've got images of you all around me, everywhere I turn." Steve could see the images of Perry turning frantically, in total confusion.

11 "Perry, stay calm! Do you remember which way the shuttle was? Can you find your way back to it?"

12 "Yes. I mean, I don't know. I think it was back this way." Steve saw all the images of Perry move in the wrong direction and then disappear into the weblike mist.

13 "Perry, wait! Don't move! That's the wrong way. You're all turned around!" For a moment, there was no answer—just labored breathing. And then Perry screamed. "My God! Oh, my God! Steve! Steve! Oh, God!" Steve grabbed the sides of his helmet, trying to shut out the awful sound of his friend's screaming. But it continued, mercilessly, bringing his own panic to an unendurable level. And then, abruptly, the screaming stopped.

• • •

14 Steve was doubled over with fear. His heart pounded so hard that his chest hurt. He could hear his own rasping breath in the intercom, but no sound came from Perry.

15 Steve forced himself to straighten up. Something was out there. Something had gotten Perry. He had to get away, get back to the shuttle. The pink mist still floated around him,

hazy and yet fibrous. Now he saw reflections of himself. He saw himself turn and stagger and stare at himself again. The mist multiplied his image a hundred times or more. He had to find the shuttle. But how? Everywhere he looked he saw himself again and again and his terror multiplied by the second. Then he looked down. His footprints were real. The mist wasn't reflecting them.

16 Like a man running in a dream, Steve pursued his own footsteps, dragging his legs as fast as he could against the strong gravity. He moved as though something were after him. He never took his eyes off the ground, never let them wander away to confront the images of himself fleeing. He nearly ran into the shuttle head on.

17 He turned the combination to the air lock and threw himself into the chamber when it opened. Then he found the second lock and shut the doors on whatever was out there. He didn't bother to remove the suit but went straight to the cockpit and engaged the engines. The mist engulfed the shuttle, sending back reflections of himself through the windows. Taking a deep breath, he slammed down the ignition key.

18 The force of the liftoff nearly threw him sideways into the narrow aisle. The mist disappeared and with it his images. Steve stared out the windows, gasping, listening to his heart slow down, feeling the paralyzing fear leave him. He sat up and set a heading for Exploration Base Four. Then he looked up, startled. He saw himself reflected in the cockpit windows; staring. The dim green light from the control panel illuminated his face. Just one face, his, and he saw that it was wet with tears.

Vocabulary Building

Match the following words with the definitions. (You won't need to use all of the definitions.) If you don't know the meaning of a word, go back to the story and read the part that the word comes from and try to guess the meaning from the context. The numbers in parentheses refer to the paragraphs where the words can be found.

1. lousy (2) _____
2. audible (6) _____
3. rasping (14) _____
4. cockpit (17) _____
5. liftoff (18) _____

a. the part of an aircraft where the pilot sits
b. very bad; unpleasant
c. visible
d. rough in sound; harsh
e. the start of the flight of a space vehicle
f. very difficult
g. able to be heard

Discussion and Writing Topics

1. Why do people want to explore space? What benefits can there be to space exploration? Do you think the endeavor is worth the money it requires and the risk of losing lives? Give your views.

2. What qualities do you think an astronaut ought to have? Why? Consider physical, mental and emotional qualities. What about ordinary people who might travel in space in the future? Will it be necessary for them to have the same qualities? Discuss your ideas and views.

3. You were invited to travel to the moon to visit a new colony that was established there, and you have just returned from your trip. Describe the way people live in the moon colony and compare it to the way they live on Earth.

UNIT 4
EDUCATION TODAY:
what's wrong and what's right?

WNYN looks at education in a changing society.

Formal education often ends as soon as people reach a certain age. But a lot of men and women are going back to school. Some adults are continuing their education. Others are just beginning it.

The man in this picture is learning to read and write. The young woman talking to him is not a student, so she must be the teacher.

People can go on learning until they are eighty or ninety. There is really no age limit. This woman must be at least fifty. She is learning how to drive.

People are never too old to learn. We can go on learning until the day we die.

Questions
You are interviewing someone about this classroom. These are the answers you are given; make questions for them.

1. As soon as people reach a certain age.
2. A lot are.
3. To read and write.
4. No, she isn't.
5. No, she's the teacher.
6. No, he's older than she is.

Questions
Make questions for these answers.

1. Until they're eighty or ninety.
2. No, there really isn't.
3. At least fifty.
4. How to drive.
5. No, they're never too old.
6. Yes, we can.

26

How old are the people in this picture? Where are they? 3

This is a modern classroom. Education is changing very rapidly today. In the past teachers made children sit still for hours. They made them memorize everything. Today many teachers wonder if it is possible to make children learn at all. They say you should let children learn and discover things for themselves.

Questions
1. What used to happen in the past?
2. What did teachers make children do?
3. What do many teachers believe now?
4. What should you let children do?

 4

Where are these people? How old are they? How do you think they feel? Why do you think they feel that way?

These students don't like school, but their parents make them go. School is a kind of prison for them. They quit school as soon as the law lets them. Many of them want to find jobs, but the law will not let them work until they reach a certain age. So they have to stay in school. Often they do not learn anything at all and hate every minute of it.

Role Play
One person is the interviewer. The other takes the role of one of these students.

Ask the student:
1. how he/she likes school
2. why he/she goes
3. if he/she will stay in school
4. if he/she wants to find a job now
5. why he/she doesn't have a job now
6. if he/she learns a lot in school

UNIT 4 Grammar

1 *Must* used to express assumptions

The young woman is not a student, so she *must be* the teacher.

A. Comment

The modal *must* is often used to express an assumption of truth. *Must,* like all modals, can also be used with a continuous form (*must be learning*).

B. Practice

Make assumptions about the other students in picture 1 based on these facts about the man.

Example:
That man is learning to read and write. Then the women *must be learning* to read and write too.

1. The man lives in Los Angeles.
2. He's learning to do simple math.
3. He's doing the exercises.
4. He has a lot of homework every day.
5. The teacher gives the man books to take home.
6. The teacher likes helping the man learn to read.

C. Situation

David Denton lives in a large apartment building. All of the apartments have balconies. David often sits out on his balcony for hours. Here is what he observed on some other balconies one day last summer. What assumptions do you think he made at the time?

Example:
Apt. 7B—people singing "Happy Birthday."
They *must be having* a birthday party in 7B.

1. Apt. 4R—smoke and the smell of food cooking.
2. Apt. 5C—rugs hanging over the railing of the balcony.
3. Apt. 6S—a man and a woman shouting at each other.
4. Apt. 4B—a small boy crying.
5. Apt. 5N—a dog scratching at the door.
6. Apt. 5L—loud music, laughter, many voices.

D. Transfer

Now think of somebody you know very well but who is not with you now. Think of that person's daily activities and then make sentences with *must be . . . ing* like this:

I have a friend. He works in a factory from eight to four. It's nine o'clock right now. He *must be working* in the factory at this moment.

2 *Until, as soon as*

The law will not let them work *until* they reach a certain age. They quit school *as soon as* the law lets them.

A. Comment

1. *Until* indicates the end point of an action: They waited until six o'clock and then they left. She worked until she was tired.
2. *As soon as* indicates when an action starts: The students began working as soon as the teacher came in.
3. *Until* can be followed by a time (until six o'clock) or by a subject and verb (until she was tired). *As soon as* can only be followed by a subject and a verb (as soon as the teacher came in).
4. The simple present tense is used with *until* or *as soon as* when it refers to future time: She will work until she *is* tired. The students will begin working as soon as the teacher *comes* in.

28

B. Practice

Examples:

A: Wait here. I'll be back in a few minutes.
B: O.K. I'll wait here *until you get back*.

A: The train's going to stop. We have to get out.
B: All right. I'll get out *as soon as it stops*.

Now answer as *B* does. Use either *until* or *as soon as*.

1. The bell's going to ring soon. You have to go to class.
2. Stay under this tree. The rain's going to end soon.
3. Watch this television show with me. It's going to end soon.
4. The lesson's going to end soon. Ask your question then.
5. Stay with me for a few minutes. I think I'll feel better soon.
6. Mary's going to come soon. Wait for her!
7. Study this carefully. Then you will understand it.
8. Finish your dinner. Then come dancing with me.

C. Transfer

Complete these sentences.

1. I'm going to study English until ___5:00 pm___
2. As soon as I speak English well, *I'm going to look for a job*
3. As soon as I have the time, *I'll call you back*.
4. *I'll meet you at the main door* as soon as this lesson is over.
5. As soon as I have enough money, *I'll buy new shoes*.

D. Discussion

Suppose you are going to retire in two years. Talk about how retirement will change your life. What will you do until you retire? What will you do as soon as you retire?

3 | *Make* and *let*

Teachers *made them sit* still for hours.
They say you must *let children learn and discover* things for themselves.

A. Comment

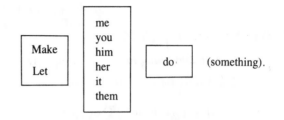

Notice that the verb in box 3 is in the simple form.

B. Situation

Two women are talking about their school days fifty years ago.

A: When I was at school, we had to do a lot of homework.
B: Yes, our teachers certainly *made us do* a lot of homework.
A: And we never took an active part in the lessons.
B: No, our teachers never *let us take* an active part in the lessons either.

Now answer as *B* does, using sentences with *never let us* or *made us*.

1. When I was at school, we worked very hard.
2. We never talked in class.
3. We bought lots of books.
4. We stood up when the teachers came in. *stay sitted*
5. We didn't play games.
6. We had lots of tests.
7. We never came late.

C. Discussion

Think of things your teacher or parents made you do when you went to school: What didn't they let you do? What are some of the things you think we should let children do in modern schools that they couldn't do before? What are some of the things that you think teachers should still make children do?

DIALOG

Listen to the dialog and complete Bob's part.

MARGARET: I see you're working on something right now, Bob. As soon as you finish, I'd like to talk to you for a few minutes.

BOB: (1) _It's ok_? Come on in . . .

MARGARET: Oh, no, I don't want to interrupt you. I can wait until you're finished.

BOB: (2) _You might have_ long wait! I'm (3) _working on budget figures_.

MARGARET: I thought you'd finished the budget. Didn't you turn it in on Friday?

BOB: Uh-huh. But the controller's office (4) _just sent it back to me_. I've _been_ given instruction to cut it (6) _by 20%_.

MARGARET: They must be kidding! How can you do that?

BOB: That's (7) _what I'm trying to_ figure out. I can't (8) _very well_ cut down on (9) _our daily news program_.

MARGARET: No, . . . Well, what about the other departments? _can't cut editorial they_

BOB: We (10) _can't cut editorial_. And (11) _we only got_ 40 specials put in (12) _budget_ for (13) _the whole_ year. I (14) _can't cut out_ any of those—we'd (15) _loose a lot of viewers_.

MARGARET: Well, what else is there?

BOB: (16) _staff travel_ . . . (17) _equipment_ _they're trying to cut everybody's_ (18) _Salaries_. I'd sure (19) _hate_ salary! Well, (20) _take_ your case, for example. You've (21) _been employed here_ for (22) _2 years now_. It'd be (23) _pretty_ salary cut, _I have a 20%_ (24) _wouldn't it?_

MARGARET: A salary cut? _wouldn't do that even if I do that_

BOB: (25) _you know I can't_ (26) _make it come out right now_.

MARGARET: Well, why do they want to cut our budget in the first place?

BOB: That's (27) _what I had to figure out_. Our (28) _ratings_! They've (29) _been going_ down.

MARGARET: Hmm . . . Well, would it help if we could show that we've had a big increase in number of viewers?

BOB: (30) _Of course it would_! But (31) _the last 3 reports have been_ terrible. That's why (32) _they're making us cut back_.

MARGARET: Bob, listen! I got a call from John this morning. He told me he had some very good news for us.

BOB: The (33) _new viewer survey report?_

MARGARET: Well, he wouldn't tell me anything else. But he must be referring to the latest survey. He said he'd get back to me in a few days.

BOB: (34) _Would you mind calling him back right away?_

MARGARET: Now?

BOB: Sure. Find out if (35) _he's really got something good to report_. Tell him (36) _we can't wait_ We've (37) _got to know how_. Gee, if (38) _we could show that_ our audience (39) _for the month_ is up . . . by as much as 30%, . . . even 25%, it (40) _just might_ But (41) _I can't talk to him_ until (42) _I have something definite_.

MARGARET: Well, let me see what I can find out. I'll go call him right now.

BOB: (43) _let me know_ as soon as (44) _you find out any thing._

MARGARET: Oh, I will!

BOB: Thanks. Oh, Margaret? You said (45) _you wanted to talk to me about something_.

MARGARET: Oh, that . . . It can wait.

COMMUNICATION PRACTICE

Making Polite Requests

Bob Russo wants Margaret to make a phone call. He says:
Would you mind calling him back right away?

Agreeing to Polite Requests

You can agree to requests by using these expressions:

Sure.
Not at all.
Of course.
Certainly.
I'll be happy/glad to.

Refusing Requests

You can refuse requests by using expressions like these:

I'm (really) sorry, but	I can't.
	I'd rather not.
	it isn't convenient.
	I'm using it.

I'd like to, but	I can't.
	it isn't convenient.
	I'm using it.

Situation

Read each situation below and make a polite request. Your partner will then agree or refuse to do what you ask.

Example:
A friend is visiting you and you want to move a table from one room to another.

A: Would you mind helping me move this table?
B: Not at all.

1. You're busy cooking and there's someone else in the house (husband/wife/child/friend). The phone rings.
2. You want to paint your ceiling, but you don't have a ladder. Your neighbor does.
3. You've finished school and are looking for a job. Your teacher knows this. You need a letter of recommendation from him/her.

4. Your bicycle is broken, but you want to go on a bike trip on Saturday with some friends. Your brother has a new bicycle.

5. You're on a bus and it's very warm inside. Your neighbor is sitting next to a closed window.

6. You and a friend are going to the beach together. You had agreed to leave at one o'clock, but now you want him/her

to pick you up at two o'clock.

7. You need to make a quick trip to the supermarket, but your baby is asleep. Your neighbor sometimes babysits for you.

8. You want your best friend to lend you his/her car. (You're a terrible driver.)

LISTENING

Three people are interviewed about their views of continuing education. One is a man in the street, the second is a woman who is on her own and the third is a teacher.

Getting Ready to Listen

1. Is it necessary for people to go to school to continue their education after they have completed their formal schooling in high school?

2. If you were going to take continuing education courses, would you prefer practical courses like automobile repair or abstract courses like English literature?

3. Why might some people like to study subjects like automobile repair and plumbing?

Vocabulary

(I wouldn't . . .) if I had to!: [informal—adds strong emphasis to the preceding negative statement]

it didn't do me a bit of good: I didn't get any benefit out of it

get in control of my life: bring some order into my life

takes the place of: substitutes for

shape their lives: give direction or purpose to their lives

zero in on: concentrate on, aim directly at

alleyways: [informal] side tracks, narrow paths

Now listen to the interview.

Comprehension Checkup

Choose the phrase that correctly completes each statement, based on the interview.

1. Continuing education, according to the interviewer, means that
   a. you continue studying for as many years as you can.
   b. you go back to school after you've finished high school or college.

2. The man in the street, who was interviewed first, thought that
   a. his twelve years in school had done him a lot of good.
   b. he hadn't gotten much out of going to school.

3. He felt like a prisoner when he was in school because
   a. he had to stay at school if he wasn't properly dressed.
   b. they tried to regulate his life there.

4. In the second interview, the woman said she was taking night classes in order to
   a. learn some things she needed to know.
   b. qualify for a high school diploma.

5. She feels she needs to learn skills like auto repair and plumbing because
   a. she has no one else to rely on.
   b. she has a family to support.

6. In the last interview, the teacher said she thinks continuing education is a way for people to
   a. focus on things that are important to them.
   b. complete their high school education.

7. Although the teacher feels that no one is ever too old to keep learning, she admits that
   a. it's very difficult for older people to get the G.E.D.
   b. there are certain things people can't do as they get older.

Listening for Emotion

Listen to the first interview with the man in the street again. Did the interviewer expect the answers the man gave or was he surprised by some of them? How do you know?

Discussion

1. If you could go to any university in the world you wanted to, which one would you choose? Why?

2. How did you feel when you were in high school? Did you feel like a prisoner?

3. What are the best and the worst memories you have of your elementary school days?

Is Our Educational System Inadequate?

In the United States, it is required that all children attend school, public or private, for twelve years.

1 There are exceptions to this rule, of course, as in the cases of certain religious or ethnic groups where education is only required until the eighth grade. And there are some groups of people that see no purpose to an education whatsoever and ignore this requirement altogether. But for most, and reasonably so, a twelve-year education is the minimum.

2 In view of the complexity of our society and the changes taking place in communication, technology and the economy, one would think that a person would need at least twelve years of education in order to cope. However, in recent years, a great many people have begun to question the purpose of having compulsory education for twelve years.

"Functional illiterates"—a growing problem . . .

3 One big reason the question is being raised is the fact that an alarming number of young people who graduate from the school systems are unable to handle simple, everyday tasks, such as reading a newspaper, filling out a job application or balancing a checkbook. These people are considered "functionally illiterate" by experts on the subject, who estimate that one out of five adults in the United States falls in this category. Without a mastery of everyday skills, it is extremely difficult for these people to comprehend and deal with the demands of society. And as our language becomes more technical and the laws more complex, life in general can only become more frustrating.

4 Of course, efforts are being made to correct the problem as various agencies and colleges try to reach these people. But they are difficult to reach. Many are embarrassed by the situation and prefer to live with rather than correct the problem. In many cases, those who were unsuccessful in school are easily discouraged when they try to learn again, and the dropout rate is high.

The dilemma . . .

5 It is clear that the public school system has failed to meet the needs of these people. Furthermore, many parents, educators and politicians think that the system still fails to properly educate vast numbers of students. Yet it seems equally clear that the problems the public school system faces are too complex to be handled by increased government control. Each area of the United States has a unique set of requirements for the education

of its young that cannot be satisfied by one general policy.

Upgrading of the system is helping some students.

6 An upgrading of present education systems has been called for by parents and officials. It has long been a complaint that the public school system is geared to the needs of the slowest learners. Bright students, unchallenged by the material and the pace of teaching, become bored and channel their energies into less productive diversions. Often the most difficult children are the brightest. This has sparked the initiation of programs like TAG (Talented and Gifted) to provide more challenging material and an accelerated learning pace for these children. Also, some schools now have programs allowing advanced students to obtain college credits while still in high school. And some students can complete their graduation credits early and then take jobs or enter college immediately.

Alternatives and changes seem to be helping the situation.

7 But there are those who argue that the educational system is still inadequate in meeting the demands of society. Perhaps this is true, but until a more adequate system is developed, we must live with the one we have and deal with its problems individually. Despite the many faults of our system, the fact remains that the opportunity for a basic education is denied to no one. What individuals get out of that education, however, depends a lot on how much they put in.

Words and Expressions

live with (a problem): accept, adjust to (a problem)
dropout rate: proportion (of students) who quit (school)
geared to: designed for
called for: requested, demanded

Comprehension Checkup

Are these statements *true* or *false*, based on the reading?

_____ **1.** In general, a twelve-year education is considered the minimum needed.
_____ **2.** Some people who graduate from the school system are functionally illiterate, even after spending twelve years in school.
_____ **3.** Increased government control of the school system is the answer to our educational problems.
_____ **4.** There are new special programs that pay particular attention to very intelligent children.
_____ **5.** Some people don't have the chance to get an education.

Identifying the Main Idea

Which one of the sentences given best expresses the main idea of the paragraph?

1. Paragraph 3
  a. There are many people in our society who do not have basic reading and writing skills.
  b. Some people say that compulsory education has failed because many people go through twelve years of schooling and still cannot read or write well enough to get along in society.
  c. Life is becoming more and more frustrating as language and laws become more complex.
2. Paragraph 5
  a. The public school system has failed to meet the needs of functional illiterates.
  b. The public school system fails to educate a great number of children properly.
  c. The public school system is failing in many ways, but increased government control cannot solve its problems.
3. `Paragraph 7
  a. The value a person gets from an education is his or her own responsibility.
  b. Our school system has many faults, but at least everyone has the opportunity to get an education.
  c. We have to accept our educational system and try to solve its problems.

Vocabulary Building

The words and phrases below have approximately the same meaning as certain words and phrases used in the reading. Read the paragraph the word comes from and find its synonym.

1. at all (1)
2. obligatory (2)
3. would rather (4)
4. improvement (6)
5. direct (6)
6. shortcomings (7)

Discussion Topics

1. What things couldn't you do if you were illiterate?
2. How could you manage in the situations listed below if you couldn't read or write?
  a. in a restaurant
  b. at a bank
  c. applying for a driver's license
  d. trying to get a telephone number
  e. applying for a job
  f. receiving a letter from a friend
3. The reading expresses the viewpoint that most school systems are geared to the needs of the slowest learners. Do you think this is true in your country?
4. Do you believe in compulsory education? Tell why you do or why you don't. Give examples to support your viewpoint.

Writing Topics

Choose one of the topics and write a composition of 300–350 words.

1. School is a waste of time. (Tell why you think so, what children learn or don't learn in school, etc.)
2. Education in my country. (Tell how long students go to school, whether education is compulsory or not, what subjects are emphasized, etc.)
3. My school experience. (Tell what schools you have gone to, how you felt about school at the time, what kind of teachers you have had, what the good points and bad points were about the system, etc.)
4. Education in the future. (Give your ideas of how people will learn in the future, what the differences will be, whether there will be computers or not, whether there will be teachers or not, etc.)

unit 5
The Rich and The Poor

WNYN did a special on poverty and wealth in the world.

1 **Where are these people?**
Are they rich or poor?
How do you know?

Economically, the world can be divided into two parts. The difference between them is that one part is poor and the other is wealthy. In the poor countries of the world, a lot of people never get enough to eat. In wealthy countries, a lot of people eat too much. The tragedy is that there are more people in the poor countries than there are in the wealthy countries. It is estimated that approximately 80% of the world's population cannot afford to have proper food, housing or medical care.

Ask and Answer
Get someone else to tell you:
   1. the economic difference between the two parts of the world
   2. the difference in eating habits of the people in both parts
   3. which part has a higher population
   4. what it is that 80% of the people in the world don't have

What are these people doing?
Is this good farmland? **2**

The poorer countries are often referred to as the Third World. They have special problems. Often their land is too poor to grow anything on. The land can be improved, but a lot of things have to be done first. New farming methods have to be introduced, people have to be educated and reliable sources of water and energy have to be found.

Many of these problems are too complex for one country to solve alone. Outside help is needed, but it has to be the right kind of help. Money is not enough. Newly developing countries need to be helped to be able to help themselves.

Ask and Answer
Get someone else to tell you:
   1. how the poorer countries are often referred to
   2. how this can be changed
   3. what must be done first
   4. why outside help is needed
   5. why money is not enough to help developing countries

3 Where do you think this picture was taken? Why is the air so dirty?

Rich countries have problems too. They are not always very pleasant places to live in. Often it is those things which make them rich that also make them unpleasant.

In many places, the products that make the country rich also pollute the air and water. Most people put up with this because they feel that a certain amount of pollution is necessary and unavoidable. Other people insist that the factories should get rid of the waste so that it doesn't pollute the environment. They say that they would rather do without some products. They believe that the quality of life is more important than the standard of living. The factory managers say that it would be too expensive to meet more rigid pollution standards. They say that people want and need their products and that it is worth the pollution of the environment.

Ask and Answer
Working with a partner, ask and answer questions with these phrases:
1. rich countries . . . too?
2. pleasant places to live?
3. makes them unpleasant?
4. the air and water?
5. put up with it?
6. the factories should get rid of the waste?
7. do without?
8. the quality of life?
9. the factory managers say?

Discussion
Which do you think is more important, the quality of life or the standard of living?

UNIT 5 Grammar

1 Too + infinitive

Their land is *too* poor *to grow* anything on.

A. Comment

The example sentence above means that it is impossible to grow anything on the land because it is poor. To indicate that something is impossible to do, you can use *too* + adjective + infinitive. The infinitive does not always have to be stated:
Why don't they grow anything?
Because the land is too poor.

B. Situation

Make excuses by explaining why these things can't be done.

Example: Why aren't those people working? (tired)
They're *too tired to work*.

1. Why isn't that tractor being used? (old)
2. Why isn't the other tractor doing the job? (small)
3. Why aren't those women working in the fields? (sick)
4. Why aren't those children working? (young)
5. Why don't those people save any money? (poor)
6. Why aren't you listening to me? (busy)

C. Transfer

Make a list of things you have to do as a student (do homework, come to class, etc.). You are a student and you are talking to your teacher. Make excuses for all the things you did not do last week.

Example:
The homework was *too hard to do*. I was *too busy to do it*.

D. Situation

Two students are talking. Respond as *B* does. Notice the position of the preposition at the end of the sentence.

A: Why didn't you *listen to* the speech? Was it too boring?
B: Yes, exactly. It was *too boring to listen to*.

1. Why didn't you sit through the lecture? Was it too long?
2. Why didn't you read that book? Was it too boring?
3. Why didn't you sit in that desk? Was it too small?
4. Why didn't you sit on the floor? Was it too dirty?
5. Was the parade too early? Is that why you didn't go to it?
6. Why didn't you talk to the professor? Was she too busy?

E. Situation

The problem is *too big for one country* to solve.
   Notice the use of *for* + noun to indicate the person or thing which finds something impossible.

A husband and wife have checked into a room in a very bad hotel. Respond as *B* does.

   A: It's hot in here. Will you be able to sleep?
   B: No, it's *too hot for me* to sleep.

1. The picture on the television is very dark. Will you be able to watch it?
2. The people in the next room are having a noisy party. Will you be able to sleep?
3. This closet is very small. Will you be able to hang up your clothes?
4. The water in the shower is quite cold. Will you be able to take a shower?
5. This bed is very soft. Will you be comfortable?

F. Transfer

You are looking at a small house in the country for you and your family of four. The owner is showing you the rooms. There is something wrong with each of them.

Example:
OWNER: This is the dining room.
YOU: It's very small. It's really *too small for five people to eat in*.

What do you say about:

1. a small bedroom?
2. a cold bedroom for the children?
3. a small kitchen?
4. a dark study?
5. a very, very small garage?
6. a tiny backyard?

Think of other things that might be wrong with the house and what you would say about them.

2 Modal with passive

The land *can be improved*.

A. Comment

The passive modal is formed with the modal (*can, could, have to*, etc.) + *be* + past participle.

36

B. Situation

A government official is questioning an expert on world problems. Respond as the expert does.

OFFICIAL: Can you improve this land?
EXPERT: Yes, *the land can be improved.*

1. Can we solve this problem?
2. Should we give help?
3. Can you find water?
4. Do we have to spend a lot of money?
5. Should we buy tractors?
6. Can you train these people?
7. Can we grow food here?
8. Will we have to build new roads?
9. Must we do something now?

3 Inseparable 2- and 3-word verbs

Most people *put up with* this.
They would rather *do without* some products.

A. Comment

Some verbs combine with one or two prepositions and have a meaning different from the verb used alone. Notice that you cannot separate the prepositions from these verbs. Therefore, the object *(this, some products)* goes after the preposition.

B. Situation

Pretend that you went into a large department store yesterday to do some shopping. The store was very crowded and as you walked through the crowd of shoppers, you overheard the bits of conversation given below. Using the cues, complete the unfinished sentences you heard.

Example:
A: She explained it to John ten times before he finally understood her.
B: So she finally _____. (get through to)
   So she finally got through to him.

1. A: I happened to see George the other day.
   B: Do you mean you just _____? (run into)
2. A: He says Mr. Scott is sick in bed. Poor thing, he's all alone!
   B: Do you mean there's nobody _____? (look after)
3. A: She thinks he's a genius.
   B: I know. She's always _____. (look up to)
4. A: Joyce wanted to go out dancing tonight. She begged and begged and begged, so I finally said yes.

B: But she's only 15! You shouldn't have _____. (give in to)
5. A: What are you planning to do with your old couch?
   B: Well, I guess I'll _____. (get rid of)

4 *Make + Someone/Something + Adjective*

It is often those things which *make them rich* that also *make them unpleasant.*

The products that *make the country* rich also pollute the air.

A. Comment

In these sentences, the adjective modifies the direct object *(them, the country)*. Notice that the adjective goes after the direct object.

B. Practice

Make sentences about yourself or someone in the class by matching the word or phrase in column *A* with an adjective from column *B*.

Something make(s) someone adjective.

Examples:
Flying makes *Marta* nervous.
Rainy days make *me* sad.

A	B
high places	sleepy
lack of money	tired
horror movies	sick
walking	nervous
too much work	anxious
too little rest	angry
holidays	happy
rain	sad
lack of sleep	silly
	dizzy
	unhappy

C. Transfer

You and an architect are discussing the house that you want built for you. Tell the architect how you want various things, for example, the windows, the staircases, the rooms, the roof, the floors, etc.

Example:
Make the windows very large.

UNIT 5 Dialog/Communication Practice

DIALOG 📼

Listen to the dialog and complete the secretary's part.

SECRETARY: May I help you?

MARSHA: Yes. I'm here to see Professor Daniels. I have a two o'clock appointment.

SECRETARY: Professor Daniels (1) *won't be back until* next Tuesday morning. He's (2) *gone to Chicago*

MARSHA: Oh, no, I'm sorry . . . Perhaps he didn't tell you about our appointment. We arranged to meet here this afternoon. His flight isn't until six o'clock and he said he wouldn't have to leave here until four o'clock.

SECRETARY: Well, (3) *I'm terribly* sorry, but (4) *he changed his plans at the last minute*. He (5) *asked me to get him on* a three o'clock flight (6) *to Chicago* and he (7) *left here about* (8) *once*. It's too late (9) *to reach him at* home—he's (10) *probably on his way to the airport now*.

MARSHA: He's taking a three o'clock flight to Chicago? Are you sure?

SECRETARY: Yes. Oh, (11) *I'm sorry*! I hope this has not been an inconvenience (12) *for you* too much. He (13) *was interviewed for a TV* program and since (14) *that was finished earlier than he expected, he (15) *decided to leave on an earlier flight*.

MARSHA: I—I don't understand. You say he was interviewed for a television program?

SECRETARY: Yes. Oh, my. It was (16) *exciting*. It's usually *pretty boring* (17) *around* here, you know. But (18) *not today*! We had (19) *bright lights & cameras*. I (20) *was fascinated*. Looked like a regular (21) *T.V. studio*. And *the program* (22) *me be shown on* on TV next week! Hmm. Give (23) *me your name* why (24) *don't you*? I'll (25) *leave a note on Prof. Daniels's desk* to let him know (26) *you were here*.

MARSHA: My name is Marsha Nelson. I'm with WNYN-TV. I . . . still don't understand. You say—?

SECRETARY: WNYN-TV? Well, then, (27) *you must know* David Denton! He's (28) *the one who did* the interview (29) *with the prof. Daniels* Nice (30) *young* man!

MARSHA: David was here?

SECRETARY: Yes. He (31) *was a very capable young* man. I'm sure *the station* (32) *couldn't do without him*. But (33) *he really needs an assistant* (34) *to operate the* *camera* It's (35) *really too complicated* for one person (36) *to do—set up lights, run (37) the camera do (38) the interviewing besides*.

MARSHA: Yes, . . . tell me, what time did David get here anyway?

SECRETARY: Well, (39) *he called at* at nine thirty—wanted to know (40) *if it could be* at eleven o'clock (41) *instead of* later (42) *in the day*

MARSHA: I see . . . So he came . . . over at eleven o'clock?

SECRETARY: (43) *that's right* (44) *thank you very*

MARSHA: Well, . . . thank you very much.

SECRETARY: Oh, (45) *you're welcome*. And again, I'm *awfully sorry* *about your* (46) *appointment* I'm sure (47) *this mix up can be explained some-how*

MARSHA: Yes. Yes, I'm sure it can. I think I'm beginning to understand what might have happened. Well, goodbye.

SECRETARY: Goodbye, Ms. Nelson. It's (48) *been nice talking with you*.

Oh, and (49) *when you get back to* WNYN, I hope (50) *you will have a chance to see David Denton*.

MARSHA: Yes. Well, I'm sure I'll be running into him very soon.

COMMUNICATION PRACTICE

Describing Feelings and Causes of Feelings

Professor Daniels' secretary was enthusiastic about the TV interview. She said:
It was exciting!
I was fascinated!

Feelings		*Causes of Feelings*
I was excited		the movie was exciting.
I was fascinated	(because)	the lecture was fascinating.
I'm bored		this book is boring.
I'm frightened		those dogs are frightening.

Some verbs that express feelings have participial forms (*-ed* and *-ing* forms) that function as adjectives to describe those feelings (*-ed* form) and the things that cause them (*-ing* form). The sentences in the boxes above show some verbs that work this way. Others include: *amaze, amuse, annoy, astonish, confuse, disappoint, disgust, horrify, interest* and *surprise*.

Practice

Fill in each blank with the correct adjective form of the verb given under the blank.

Renée and Peter visited New York City for the first time last month. They were 1. astonish by the size and pace of the city and at first they thought that so much activity was 2. confuse . They were 3. surprise , however, that they were able to familiarize themselves with the city so quickly. They saw two plays on Broadway and they thought that one of them was 4. amuse but that the other one was 5. disappoint . They found parts of the city beautiful, but they were 6. disgust by the dirty streets in some areas. In general, they were 7. fascinate by a 8. fascinate city.

Practice

Look at the illustrations given. Then make two sentences describing each illustration. Use adjectives based on the verbs given below the illustrations.

Example:

a. The ghost was frightening.
b. The boy was frightened.

frighten

1.

excite

2.

fascinate

3.

bore

Transfer

With a classmate, discuss movies or TV shows you have seen, using some of these words in your conversation: boring, exciting, fascinating, interesting, bored, excited, fascinated, interested.

LISTENING

A UNESCO official talks about the objectives of the organization.

Getting Ready to Listen

1. What is the United Nations?
2. Why was it created?
3. Based on its name, what do you think the goals of the United Nations Educational, Scientific and Cultural Organization (UNESCO) are?

Vocabulary

foster: promote the development of
eradicate: eliminate, get rid of
funding: money
grants: contributions or gifts of money
created an impact (on): had a strong effect (on)

Now listen to the interview.

Comprehension Checkup

Choose the phrase that correctly completes each statement, based on the interview.

1. The specific purpose of UNESCO is to
   a. support the aims of the United Nations.
   b. foster communication among nations.
2. UNESCO does distribute funds back to member nations in the form of grants,
   a. but most of its money is used to support its own work.
   b. and this has created a positive impact on the world.

Cross out the items on the following list which were *not* listed by the official as goals of UNESCO.

a. the promotion of cultural exchange between countries
b. the eradication of illiteracy
c. encouraging trade and commerce between countries
d. raising educational standards
e. helping settle international disputes
f. the distribution of food in areas where there is famine
g. providing technical assistance
h. teacher training and educational research
i. improving health facilities in developing countries
j. the setting up of cultural information agencies

Critical Listening

Listen again to the interviewer's last question and the official's response. Did the official give a satisfactory response to the question?

Situation

Work with a partner and do an interview similar to the one on the tape. One of you is the interviewer and the other is an executive from MARTS, a large corporation that sells its products throughout the world. Prepare the questions and answers in advance so that you'll be able to give the following information during the interview: what the letters in the company name stand for, what products the company sells, where and how the products are manufactured, what kind of impact the company has had on the world, etc.

"A Classier Set of Problems"

NEWSTIME Magazine
World Affairs Report

EXCLUSIVE INTERVIEW with
Peter O'Shea, Economist,
Watchworld Institute,
Washington, D.C.

(1) **Newstime:** Over the years we seem to have had the assumption that money could cure all of our ills. And yet today, many of the so-called wealthy nations of the world are facing critical economic problems.

(2) **O'Shea:** I once got a birthday card from a friend reminding me humorously that "Money won't buy you happiness . . . it will only buy you a classier set of problems!" If ever there was a phrase to describe world economics, that's it. In the mad scramble for wealth and power, we often overlook the problems that go with them.

(3) **Newstime:** Hasn't America lost a lot of its prestige on the international economic scene over the past few years?

(4) **O'Shea:** Let me put it this way. To many people, the American stereotype has been a big fellow with a fat cigar, driving around in his long Cadillac with the convertible top down. But America's position as a wealthy world leader is rapidly changing and a more accurate stereotype might be the same fellow with the big cigar, stuffed tightly into a foreign-made economy car with a sun roof. America no longer has the wealth of resources it once had to offer the world market and we are busily learning the art of cutting back, as our politicians call it.

(5) **Newstime:** We have been using up our natural resources at a rapid rate, haven't we?

(6) **O'Shea:** Indeed we have! Part of the problem is that people haven't been used to thinking in those terms. When you run out of something, the solution has always been to go out and get some more.

(7) **Newstime:** A great deal of the world, America included, is in a most uncomfortable position at the moment because of our dependence on a nonrenewable resource, petroleum.

(8) **O'Shea:** Yes, and that's a little scary to think about. As long as any nation is dependent upon another nation's resources, then the nation with the resources can exercise a certain power over the one without.

(9) **Newstime:** Are you suggesting that there is an alternative? Can any country be wholly independent?

(10) **O'Shea:** Absolutely not. No nation in the world is completely independent of the others. No national economy is strong enough to stay within its own borders. What I am suggesting is that the country with the most accumulated wealth can afford to pick and choose who it wishes to trade with. For decades now, America has enjoyed having a wealth of resources. Because of these resources, we've been able to trade all over the world. But now times have changed. America, as well as many other nations of the world, is finding its resources running short. And, as I was saying, dependence on other sources makes dependent nations vulnerable to political situations.

(11) **Newstime:** That raises the whole basic question of survival, doesn't it?

(12) **O'Shea:** Well, each nation is trying to use its resources to gain a more powerful position in the world market. And as the present resources that we know of are exhausted, the trading will become more and more heated. The bargaining then becomes more crucial to survival.

(13) **Newstime:** That's rather a grim view, isn't it?

(14) **O'Shea:** I suppose it is. Here we are with that "classy set of problems" that money has bought—on a worldwide scale. The "have-nots" of the world are eager to enter into the successful end of the bartering, and the "haves" are working hard to protect their wealth and develop new resources. The cycle is endless. One day a quiet nation with little to offer is ignored by the world market. The next day it finds it is sitting on a resource that is diminishing elsewhere in the world, and suddenly it is the center of world attention—often uncomfortably so. In a sense, it's the victim of its own wealth.

Words and Expressions

classier: more elegant
bracing: preparing
scary: frightening
"have-nots": poor nations, poor people, underdeveloped countries
"haves": wealthy nations, wealthy people, developed countries

Comprehension Checkup

Decide whether each sentence is *true* or *false* based on the interview.

_____ **1.** We have a tendency to believe that if a country has money, it also has a lot of problems.

_____ **2.** Americans are having to learn the art of cutting back because their government forces them to.

_____ **3.** Difficult times lie ahead because nonrenewable resources are diminishing.

_____ **4.** It is possible for a country to be economically independent in today's world.

_____ **5.** The "have-nots" of the world want to become economically successful.

_____ **6.** The "haves" of the world are eager to help the poorer countries develop their resources.

Scanning

Find the paragraph in which each of the following topics is mentioned or discussed. Write the paragraph number in the blank.

_____ **1.** "have-nots" and "haves"
_____ **2.** the American stereotype
_____ **3.** the art of cutting back
_____ **4.** petroleum

Vocabulary Building

Find the sentences in the interview that contain these words and phrases. Then choose the meaning that fits each one. The numbers in parentheses refer to the paragraphs where the words and phrases can be found.

1. overlook (2): **a.** view from above **b.** fail to see **c.** look at something very quickly
2. cutting back (4): **a.** starting out one way and then turning around and going the opposite way **b.** injuring one's back with a knife **c.** reducing spending and the consumption of products and resources
3. a most uncomfortable position (7): **a.** a certain way of standing that gives a great deal of discomfort **b.** a very difficult situation **c.** not a very comfortable way to sit

Discussion Topics

1. Do you agree or disagree with Mr. O'Shea that no country in the world is wholly independent economically? Can you think of specific examples?
2. Do you agree or disagree with Mr. O'Shea's idea of the stereotype many people have of Americans? Give your own ideas of what you believe the American stereotype is.
3. Mr. O'Shea pointed out that many countries are finding that their resources are running out. What kinds of resources was he referring to? Give examples of resources that are being exhausted.
4. Do you believe that money can buy happiness? Give specific examples to support your views.

Writing Topics

Choose one of the topics and write a composition of 300–350 words.

1. What I would do if I inherited a million dollars. (Explain what you would do with the money, what effect it would have on the way you live, what effect it would have on your personality, how it would change or affect your friends' attitudes toward you, etc.)
2. What people can do to conserve energy. (Give specific examples of practical things people can do and discuss the problems that would be faced in convincing people to do these things, etc.)
3. Rich problems and poor problems. (Describe the kinds of problems so-called wealthy nations have and the kinds of problems so-called poor nations have. Discuss the problems that money can solve and those that money cannot solve.)

UNIT 6 VACATIONS

WNYN interviewed people about their vacations.
They discussed the problems and pleasures of traveling.

Where are these people? Why are they there? | 1

These people are on a package tour. This kind of vacation is becoming more and more popular because it is usually fairly cheap. Package tours are arranged by wholesalers, but they are sold through travel agencies. This means that you have very little planning to do—someone else charters the plane you fly in, reserves the hotel rooms you stay in and even plans your day. But not everybody likes this kind of vacation. Some people say you don't see much of the country you are visiting.

Ask and Answer

You are interviewing a travel agent. Ask him/her:
1. if travel packages are becoming more and more popular; why
2. who arranges the package tours; who sells them
3. how much planning you have to do
4. what someone else does for you
5. why some people don't like them

2 | Where are these people? What do they have on their backs?

These people are traveling too, but they're not on a package tour. Their vacation won't be very expensive either. They will probably hitchhike most of the way. They will sleep at youth hostels. This is how a lot of young people travel today. They say it is the cheapest and most interesting way to see the world. But, of course, not everybody thinks this is the best way to travel.

Ask and Answer

You are talking to these people. Find out:
1. if they are on a package tour
2. if their trip will be very expensive
3. how they are traveling
4. where they will sleep
5. why they are traveling this way
6. if everybody thinks this is the best way to travel

Discussion

Give reasons for recommending one type of vacation to:
1. your Aunt Agatha, who is 55 and widowed (She likes fine art, but she does not like foreign food or being alone.)
2. a student with no money
3. a husband and wife and their two young children

Where are these people?
What are they doing? | 3

It's getting easier and easier to travel but harder and harder to get away from other people. These people thought camping would be a good idea. But they were not able to find a campsite they really liked. They managed to find a pleasant spot by the side of the road only after they had spent hours looking. The police will probably come by soon and tell them they cannot camp anywhere they want. They will probably have to go to a crowded campsite somewhere.

Ask and Answer
Interview these people. Find out:
1. why they went camping
2. if it was easy to find a campsite
3. how long it took them to find a pleasant spot by the roadside
4. if the police will come soon
5. what the police will tell them
6. where they will have to go

4 | Where are these people?
Why are they there?

This couple is taking a winter vacation in the Caribbean. The beach is getting more and more crowded and this couple is getting more and more annoyed. They came at the end of the winter season because they hoped to avoid the crowds and high prices. They've managed to avoid the high prices, but so has everyone else.

Ask and Answer
Interview this couple. Ask them:

1. what they are doing
2. what's happening on the beach
3. how they're feeling
4. why they came now
5. what they've managed to avoid
6. what they haven't managed to avoid

UNIT 6 Grammar

1 Position of the preposition

Someone else charters the plane you fly *in,* reserves the hotel rooms you stay *in* and even plans your day.

A. Comment

I stayed *in* that hotel.
That's the hotel (that) I stayed *in.*

When a preposition's object is a relative pronoun, the preposition often occurs at the end of a sentence. Note that the relative pronoun can be left out.

B. Situation

You are showing a friend the pictures you took on your last vacation. Some are not very clear. Your friend is asking you questions about them. Use the pattern given in the example.

Example:
A: what
   What's this?
B: I flew in that plane.
   That's the plane I flew *in*.

1. **A:** who
   B: I sat next to this man.
2. **A:** what
   B: I stayed at that hotel.
3. **A:** what
   B: I climbed up that church tower.
4. **A:** who
   B: I climbed it with this guide.
5. **A:** what
   B: I sailed on this boat.
6. **A:** what
   B: I fell into this hole.
7. **A:** what
   B: I was taken to this hospital

C. Discussion

Bring in pictures you took on your last trip and talk about them.

2 Superlatives

They say it is *the cheapest* and *the most interesting* way to see the world.

A. Comment

Note that the superlative form of one-syllable adjectives and adverbs is made by adding *est* to the simple form. For adjectives and adverbs with two or more syllables, we place *the most* before the simple form.

Exceptions:
1. If a two-syllable adjective ends in *y,* the superlative is made by changing the *y* to *i* and adding *est.*
2. Some adjectives have irregular superlatives, for example: *good–best; bad–worst.*

B. Situation

You are showing a friend more pictures of things you saw on your vacation. React to the cues as *A* does and respond as *B* does.

Example:
large museum
A: What a large museum!
B: Yes, it's *the largest* museum I've ever seen.
   or: Yes, it's *the largest* museum in Chicago/London/Japan.

1. beautiful street
2. tall building
3. old church
4. interesting architecture
5. high mountain
6. thick jungle
7. crowded beach
8. pretty restaurant

C. Discussion

Talk about the vacations you have taken. Which was the best, worst, most pleasant, shortest, longest, etc.? What things did you do that were the most difficult, boring, interesting, tiring, wonderful, etc.?

3 Comparatives

It's getting *easier and easier* to travel.

A. Comment

Note that the comparative form of one-syllable adjectives and adverbs is made by adding *er* to the simple form. For adjectives and adverbs with two or more syllables, we place *more* before the simple form.

Exceptions:
1. If a two-syllable adjective ends in *y,* the comparative is made by changing the *y* to *i* and adding *er.*
2. Some adjectives have irregular comparatives, for example: *good–better; bad–worse.*

B. Situation

You are lying on a crowded beach with a friend. Respond as *B* does.

Examples:
A: The beach is crowded.
B: Yes, and it's getting *more crowded.*
A: The wind is very strong.
B: Yes, and it's getting *stronger.*

1. The sun's bright.
2. Those children are noisy.
3. Look how blue the sky is!
4. The weather's good this morning.
5. It's difficult to find an empty beach, isn't it?
6. The ocean is very rough.
7. Your sunburn is bad.

C. Discussion

How is your neighborhood changing? Is it getting better, worse, safer, more dangerous, more pleasant, more crowded, noisier, more expensive, etc.?

D. Transfer

Imagine that you were born 100 years ago. Complain about how life has changed. Talk about:

1. young people
2. music
3. houses
4. the government
5. cars
6. food
7. television
8. the newspapers

4 Manage to

They *managed to* find a pleasant place by the side of the road.

A. Comment

Managed to . . . indicates that something was difficult to do but that you did it anyway.

B. Situation

You are talking about your vacation. You managed to do a lot of difficult things.

Example:
The sun didn't shine very much. You got a good suntan.
YOU: I *managed to get* a good suntan even though the sun didn't shine very much.

1. The town was full of tourists. You found a good, cheap hotel.
2. The beach was very crowded. You found an empty spot.
3. You had very little money. You had a good time.
4. There wasn't much time. You saw all the important sights.
5. You didn't speak the language very well. You understood directions.
6. There was a lot of rain. You got a lot of good photos.

C. Transfer

You had to travel to Chicago a few days ago on important business. You got on the midnight plane. You had three heavy suitcases. The plane was very crowded. When you arrived, it was very late and you were hungry. It was raining and so it was difficult to get a taxi. Think of all the things you managed to do.

Example:
I *managed to get* the last seat on the midnight plane.

UNIT 6 Dialog/Communication Practice

DIALOG 🔲

Listen to the dialog and complete Bob's part.

AGENT: Marsha Nelson? . . . No, there doesn't seem to be a ticket here for her. Wait a minute! Nelson. Here it is. What was the other name?

BOB: Uh . . . Denton. His (1) ▒▒▒ too.

AGENT: Denton? . . . Yes, it's here.
(David comes up to the counter)

DAVID: Morning, Bob. Sorry I wasn't able to get here a little earlier.

BOB: David! (2) ▒▒▒ ! (3) ▒▒▒ Marsha?

DAVID: Oh. Uh . . . Isn't she here yet?

BOB: No. And (4) ▒▒▒. I wonder (5) ▒▒▒. She knows (6) ▒▒▒ assignment (7) ▒▒▒ .

DAVID: I'd better check in. (to the ticket agent) Name's Denton. You should be holding a ticket for me. I'm on your nine thirty flight to Denver.

AGENT: Oh, yes, Mr. Denton. Uh . . . Do you have any baggage to check?

DAVID: Uh . . . yes. These two cases.

AGENT: All right . . . That'll be Gate 41. Seat assignment's at the gate. You might want to go right on down to the gate. We're boarding now. Here's your ticket.

DAVID: Thanks. (goes over to Bob) Well, I'm all set. We're supposed to go to the gate. They're boarding already.

BOB: (8) ▒▒▒ Marsha? She (9) ▒▒▒ ago!

DAVID: I don't know. Anyway, we'd better go. We don't want to miss the flight.

BOB: How (10) ▒▒▒ ? If (11) ▒▒▒ , I don't know (12) ▒▒▒ Denver!

DAVID: Anyway, we'd better not wait any longer. If she manages to get here in the next few minutes, she'll probably go straight to the gate.

BOB: I just (13) ▒▒▒ . We've (14) ▒▒▒ now. She's always been ▒▒▒ , but now . . . Lately, . . . I don't know. She's (15) ▒▒▒ .

DAVID: I . . . I know what you mean. It's getting harder and harder to talk to her about anything. Anyway, if we have to, we'll just manage this one without her.

BOB: Hmm! I (16) ▒▒▒ . She's (17) ▒▒▒ we've got. She's (18) ▒▒▒ on this and (19) ▒▒▒ . This is (20) ▒▒▒ .

DAVID: Don't worry. I'm sure I can handle it all right. I've spent some time studying the files . . . I know all the background.

BOB: You do? . . . But (21) ▒▒▒ Dr. Fisher? . . . And (22) ▒▒▒ research department? Those (23) ▒▒▒ information.

DAVID: No problem. I'm ready for them. Trust me! Ah, here we are . . . Gate 41. This is the flight we're going on. We seem to be the last ones.

AGENT: Smoking or non-smoking?

BOB: (24) ▒▒▒ .

AGENT: Uh . . . here you are . . . 26A and B. Uh . . . show these to the flight attendant and go right aboard.

DAVID: Thanks. Well, Marsha doesn't seem to be here.

BOB: David . . . Wait a minute. Maybe (25) ▒▒▒ . Are you (26) ▒▒▒ ?

DAVID: Absolutely. It's too bad Marsha couldn't come, but don't worry. It'll turn out all right.

BOB: Well, O.K. (27) ▒▒▒ tight spot. If (28) ▒▒▒ , we (29) ▒▒▒ job category (30) ▒▒▒ .

DAVID: You mean, . . . you might consider moving me into a job like Marsha's?

BOB: Possibly. All (31) ▒▒▒ is that you've (32) ▒▒▒ !

COMMUNICATION PRACTICE

Suppositions with *Should*

Bob Russo asked the airline agent to look for David's ticket. He said:

His ticket should be there too.

Comment

The agent located Marsha's ticket and Bob supposes that David's ticket is also there.

Situation

What would you say to express the following suppositions:

1. The ticket is in the Will Call section.
2. The other clerk knows where it is.
3. It is in the office somewhere.
4. The station manager has it.
5. It's in the office upstairs.
6. The agent at the gate has it already.

Making Apologies

David was late getting to the airport. He said:

Sorry I wasn't able to get here a little earlier.

Situation

How would David apologize to Bob if he hadn't done the following things:

1. finding the papers Bob wanted from his office
2. bringing an extra camera with him
3. stopping by the post office on the way to the airport
4. reading Bob's memorandum before he went to sleep last night
5. delivering Bob's message to the president's office

Expressing Tentative Conclusions with *Seem to/Not Seem to*

The airline agent is looking for Marsha's ticket. He says:

There doesn't seem to be a ticket here for her.

Comment

The airline agent thinks Marsha's ticket isn't in his files. He isn't positive about it, however.

Situation

What would the agent say to Bob if he thinks the following:

1. Bob does not understand.
2. Marsha Nelson does not have a reservation on the flight.
3. David Denton's ticket is missing.
4. There is a problem with the return flight.
5. Bob's ticket is in order.

LISTENING

This is an interview with a man who has just gone on a travel tour vacation.

Getting Ready to Listen

1. Have you ever gone on an overseas tour?
2. What are some of the problems that a tourist can have on such trips?
3. How do people feel when they run into problems while traveling in a foreign country?

Vocabulary

got started off on the wrong foot: got off to a bad start; things went wrong from the beginning
turn around and find out: suddenly discover
overbooked: oversold; sold more seats than they had
pocket money: money for various expenses
money's worth: what you get for the amount of money paid
come to find out: it turned out that; it was discovered that
made it home: got home

Now listen to the interview.

Comprehension Checkup

Choose the phrase that correctly completes each statement, based on the interview.

1. Because of his experience on the tour, the traveler
   a. is glad to be home.
   b. is happy to have taken a special tour package.
2. The tour got off on the wrong foot,
   a. but things got better after they got where they were going.
   b. and people found that the whole tour was nothing but frustration.
3. When he got to the airport, the traveler
   a. found that his flight had been overbooked.
   b. was told that he would have to wait for another flight.
4. When he got to the city he was going to, the traveler had to wait for his luggage, which
   a. arrived safely two days late.
   b. didn't arrive for three days.
5. The things on the tour that people enjoyed the most were
   a. the sightseeing trips included in the tour.
   b. the things they did themselves.
6. On the basis of the material he received before the tour, the traveler thinks
   a. the trip was probably worth the money in spite of the frustrations.
   b. the tour failed to live up to the claims that had been made.

Listening for Emotion

Listen to the interview again. How does the interviewer express his surprise at some of the things the traveler tells him?

Situation

Do an interview between an interviewer and an experienced traveler. Prepare questions and ideas about the traveler's experiences before you begin (where he's/she's traveled, his/her favorite place to visit, his/her most exciting travel experience, etc.).

Tour Hawaii

Hawaii—land of rumbling volcanoes and glistening white beaches. Home of hula dancers and surfers. Explore lush tropical jungles or fashionable shops. Come . . . to a paradise on earth.

Included in all Airworld Tours:
5 —All accommodations include air-conditioned rooms with private bath and color TV.
—All transfers between airports and hotels, except where indicated.
—Transfer and tipping for two pieces of luggage per passenger.
—Service charges and taxes.
10 **Special Airworld Tour Features:**
—Flower lei greeting on arrival.
—Welcoming cocktail party.
—Free hula lesson.
—Sightseeing tour of Honolulu.
15 —Road atlas to all the islands.
—Your own Airworld beach bag.
—Services of an Airworld tour guide.

Tour 1
WAIKIKI BEACH BUM $312

20 **First Day**

MAINLAND—HONOLULU
Depart by Airworld Airlines for Honolulu. Upon arrival in Honolulu, receive the traditional lei greeting and enjoy a welcoming cocktail party.

25 **Second Day**

HONOLULU
Free city tour. See the Iolani Palace, the only royal palace in the United States; The Punchbowl, an extinct volcano crater, now a national memorial cemetery; the
30 University of Hawaii and the Waioli Tea Room. Then return to your hotel for your hula lesson. You'll feel like a native in no time!

Third to Seventh Days

HONOLULU
35 Explore the island of Oahu. Cruise Pearl Harbor. Shop in our lovely stores. Experience a Hawaiian luau. Or just relax at Waikiki or any other beautiful beach.

Eighth Day

HONOLULU—MAINLAND

40 Transfer to the airport for your return flight. Aloha!
Come back soon. No one ever leaves Hawaii for good.

Tour 2
ISLAND HOPPER $549

First Day

45 MAINLAND—HONOLULU

Depart on an Airworld Airlines jet for Honolulu. On
arrival you will receive the traditional lei greeting,
then be whisked to your hotel on the beach. In the
evening enjoy your free cocktail party and meet your
50 Airworld guide.

Second and Third Days

HONOLULU

Tour the city of Honolulu. See the Iolani Palace, the
Punchbowl, the University of Hawaii and many other
55 intriguing sights. Swim in the Pacific, dine on native
foods. Enjoy . . .

Fourth to Seventh Days

HONOLULU—ISLAND OF YOUR CHOICE

Transfer to the airport for your short flight to one of
60 the neighboring islands. Pick up your rental car at the
airport when you land.

—HILO, "the City of Orchids." Enjoy the fascinating
Volcanoes National Park—view the huge Kilauea
Crater and see the Giant Tree Fern Forest.
65 —MAUI, "the Valley Island." Tour Heleakala
National Park, an enormous dormant volcano crater;
ride the 1890-style railroad into the old town of
Lahaina.
—KAUAI, "the Garden Island." Visit Waimea
70 Canyon—the Grand Canyon of the Pacific; cruise the
Wailua River; visit the famous Fern grotto.

Eighth Day

ISLAND OF YOUR CHOICE—MAINLAND

Depart for home. Return your car to the airport and fly
75 home via Honolulu. ALOHA!

Airfares: Midweek Thrift (Departure Tuesdays only)*

| Los Angeles | $310 | New York | $580 |
| San Francisco | $280 | Houston | $430 |

*Round-trip Coach to and from Honolulu.

Words and Expressions

lei: a circular bunch of flowers placed around the neck
hula: a Hawaiian dance
dormant: temporarily inactive

Comprehension Checkup

Choose the correct statement.

1. How many tours are described in the brochure?
   a. One. **b.** Two. **c.** Three.
2. The price of all the tours includes all of the following
   except one. It does not include the cost of
   a. hotel rooms.
   b. transportation between airports and hotels.
   c. meals.
   d. a tour guide.
3. If you take Tour 2, the Island Hopper, you visit
   a. all the islands.
   b. Honolulu and one neighboring island.
   c. Honolulu and two neighboring islands.
   d. Honolulu only.
4. Honolulu and Waikiki beach are on the island of
   a. Oahu. **c.** Maui.
   b. Hilo. **d.** Kauai.

Figuring Out Details

**Read the brochure quickly to get the information needed
to answer these questions.**

1. Is it cheaper to fly to Hawaii from Los Angeles or from
   San Francisco?
2. If you go alone on Tour 1 and travel from Houston, how
   much will it cost?
3. If you and a friend take Tour 2 from Los Angeles, how
   much will it cost for the two of you?
4. Can you arrive in Honolulu on Saturday for either of these
   tours?
5. What major expense is not included in either of these
   package tours?

Writing Topics

**Choose one of the topics and write a composition of 350–400
words.**

1. Describe your ideal vacation (where, what time of the
   year, with whom, what kind of transportation, etc.).
2. There are many national parks in Hawaii. What is a national park? Are there national parks in the area where you
   grew up? Do you think national parks are important? Why
   or why not?
3. Write an advertisement for a place you know well. Your
   ad should make tourists want to go there for a vacation.

DISASTER

A WNYN documentary examined the causes of disasters.

1 **What kind of ship is this?**
What's happening to this ship?

One night in April, 1912, a huge new ocean liner was crossing the Atlantic. The ship was carrying 2,224 passengers. It was going very fast, which was dangerous because there were icebergs around. The passengers were all having a good time when the ship suddenly struck one of these icebergs.

The ship began to sink and the passengers tried to escape, but there weren't enough lifeboats. Another ship was passing nearby. The *Titanic* fired rockets into the air in order to get the other ship's help, but it did not even stop. More than two-thirds of the passengers went down with the *Titanic*. It was one of the greatest sea disasters of all time.

Ask and Answer

You are interviewing someone who has written a book about the *Titanic* disaster. You want to know:

1. when the disaster happened
2. what kind of ship the *Titanic* was
3. how many passengers it was carrying
4. what caused the disaster
5. what the passengers were doing when the ship struck the iceberg
6. what they all tried to do
7. if there were enough lifeboats
8. if any other ships were passing by
9. what the *Titanic* did to get help
10. if the other ship stopped
11. how many passengers went down with the *Titanic*

Role Play

Do an interview between a reporter and a woman who was a girl at the time the *Titanic* sank and who was actually on the ship when it went down. Think of questions the reporter might ask and how the woman might answer. For example, the reporter might ask what she was doing at the time the disaster happened, how she got away, what the other passengers were doing when the ship finally went down, etc.

**What is this?
Is it alive?** 2

Some disasters, like the sinking of the *Titanic,* can be avoided. Others cannot. Nothing could have have prevented the disaster at Pompeii. Pompeii was a town near Naples, Italy, at the foot of Mount Vesuvius, an active volcano. In 79 A.D. the volcano suddenly erupted and buried the town and its people.

Recently the Italian government cleared away the ashes. If you visit the town, you can imagine exactly what they were doing when the volcano erupted. The person in this picture was probably trying to run away when he or she was buried alive.

Ask and answer:
1. what and where Pompeii was
2. what could have prevented the disaster there
3. what the disaster was
4. what you can imagine if you visit Pompeii
5. what the person in the picture was doing

Now imagine what these people were doing when the volcano erupted:
1. a baker
2. a farmer
3. a fisherman
4. a young mother with four children
5. the tax collector
6. a vendor in the marketplace

What do you think all these people did when the volcano started to erupt?

3 **What happened to this city?
Why?**

This was once a city. Here the question is not, "What caused the disaster?" but "Who caused it?" The city was destroyed by people. They knew exactly what they were doing. This type of disaster is called war.

Can wars be avoided? Could the destruction of this city have been avoided? Maybe not, but if the answer is no, we can ask another question. Can we avoid destroying ourselves?

Ask and Answer
Make questions for these answers:
1. It was once a city.
2. People did.
3. Yes, they knew exactly what they were doing.
4. War.
5. I don't know if they can be.
6. Yes, maybe it could have been.
7. I hope so.

UNIT 7 Grammar

1 | Past continuous

It *was carrying* 2,224 passengers.

A. Comment

The past continuous is often used for an action that had started at one past time and was still going on at another (later) past time.

B. Situation

People often have accidents when they daydream. Here is a man who daydreams all the time. Tell what he was doing, what he was thinking about and what happened to him.

Example:
a. He *was walking* down the street.
b. He *was thinking* about a beautiful woman.
c. He *ran* into a wall.

1.
a. _____
b. _____
c. _____

2.
a. _____
b. _____
c. _____

3.
a. _____
b. _____
c. _____

4.
a. _____
b. _____
c. _____

C. Transfer

All of these things have probably happened to you at one time or the other. Say what you were doing at the time.

Example:
You fell down.
I *was walking* down the street when I fell down. *or*
I *was ice-skating* when I fell down.

1. It started to rain.
2. The alarm went off.
3. A dog began to chase you.
4. You began to feel very cold.
5. Your boss/teacher came in and shouted, "What's going on in here?"
6. You broke your _____.

2 Which

The *Titanic* was going very fast, *which* was dangerous.

A. Comment

Which is used here to refer to the whole first part of the sentence.

B. Practice

Use *which* in this way to make these pairs into single sentences.

1. The ship was not carrying enough lifeboats. This was foolish.
2. The other ship did not stop. This surprised everybody.
3. Everybody was having a good time. This was only normal.
4. Some people gave their places in the lifeboats to other people. This was brave.
5. A lot of other people fought wildly to get into the boats. This is understandable.
6. Over a thousand lives were lost. This shocked the world.

3 Could have done

Nothing *could have prevented* the disaster at Pompeii.

A. Comment

Could have is used here to indicate that something was possible in the past, but it didn't happen.

B. Situation

Imagine you are talking to someone who has written a book about the *Titanic* disaster. The writer is telling you about many things that could have happened to prevent the *Titanic* disaster. Rephrase her sentences.

Example: The other ship didn't help. It just sailed away.

YOU: In other words, the other ship *could have helped*, but it didn't.

1. Some passengers didn't escape even though there was some room in the lifeboats.
2. The telegraph operator knew there were icebergs around. He didn't tell the captain.
3. The *Titanic* didn't avoid the iceberg even though it saw it in time.
4. For some reason, the other ship didn't stop and save the passengers.
5. And so, all those people weren't saved.

C. Transfer

You are thinking back on all the things you never did when you were younger. You're sure these things were possible and you're sorry you didn't do them.

Example:
I *could have become* rich, but I didn't. What a pity!

Think of some more things you might say. For example: you never learned Chinese, became a famous movie star, traveled around the world, etc.

UNIT 7 Dialog/Communication Practice

DIALOG

Listen to the dialog and complete Margaret's part.

JOHN: You look puzzled about something. . . . What is it? Is there something you don't understand?

MARGARET: No, . . . I was (1) ▨▨▨▨ tell . . . uh . . . uh . . .

JOHN: Tell what?

MARGARET: Well, we've . . . we've had (2) ▨▨▨▨ very good, . . . And now, (3) ▨▨▨▨ , we've (4) ▨▨▨▨ this month, . . . which (5) ▨▨▨▨

JOHN: What are you getting at?

MARGARET: Well, we (6) ▨▨▨▨ for some reason or another.

JOHN: Oh, I think I understand what you're trying to get at.

MARGARET: (7) ▨▨▨▨ I mean? We've (8) ▨▨▨▨ months—going (9) ▨▨▨▨ . And now, (10) ▨▨▨▨ . Is (11) ▨▨▨▨ be sure (12) ▨▨▨▨ ?

JOHN: No, I'm afraid not. All we really know is that something significant happened this month.

MARGARET: That's (13) ▨▨▨▨ ! . . . Trying to (14) ▨▨▨▨ we can make.

JOHN: O.K. Here's something. . . . Maybe it'll help. Look at this: if we compare this month with last month, we see something very interesting. Notice . . . that the audience for your daily news—both the six o'clock and the eleven o'clock programs—have almost doubled this month.

MARGARET: Yes, . . . up 94% (15) ▨▨▨▨ and 87% (16) ▨▨▨▨ .

JOHN: O.K. Now look at the news-feature category. You had twelve of them last month and ten this month.

MARGARET: They've (17) ▨▨▨▨ !

JOHN: Right! Now look at your specials . . . up an average of 110%. As I was saying, . . . this is very interesting. It's a consistent pattern. You've almost doubled your audience across the board!

MARGARET: (18) ▨▨▨▨ . . . .

JOHN: You could have had an increase in any one of the categories, and we'd say it had to do with interest in certain specific topics you presented on those programs.

MARGARET: (19) ▨▨▨▨ . . . !

JOHN: But when we see it across the board like this, in all your programming, then it seems to be a significant thing.

MARGARET: Which probably means (20) ▨▨▨▨ have led to (21) ▨▨▨▨ our programming!

JOHN: Exactly! So, I see it as something that should continue—providing you continue the same kind of programming.

MARGARET: This (22) ▨▨▨▨ , John. And (23) ▨▨▨▨ these observations. Now, (24) ▨▨▨▨ thing is . . . Well, uh . . . when (25) ▨▨▨▨ ?

JOHN: Next week. Mm . . . I should be able to have copies to you by Wednesday.

COMMUNICATION PRACTICE

Making Concessions

In talking to Margaret, John conceded that WNYN's success would continue, but he made one qualification. He said:

So, I see it as something that should continue, providing you continue the same kind of programming.

Comment

Note the use of *providing*, which sets up conditions under which the statement will apply. It is a statement with qualifications or "with strings attached."

Situation

You want to make concessions in all of the situations outlined below. However, you feel that you must set up certain conditions in each case. What statements would you make to each individual?

Example:
An employee wants a raise—but always gets to work late
YOU: I'll give you a raise, providing you come to work on time every day.

1. A boy wants a dog as a pet—doesn't want to feed it or take care of it
2. A friend wants to borrow $100—doesn't pay back loans on time
3. Your daughter wants to go to a dance—likes to stay out late
4. A child wants ice cream—hasn't eaten dinner
5. Your friend wants to play a new record—you don't like loud music
6. Your son wants to ride his bicycle—main roads are dangerous

Asking for Clarification

At one point, Margaret seemed to be introducing a point, but John didn't understand what it was. He said:
What are you getting at?

Comment

Sometimes a speaker does not go directly to the point because he/she is unsure of just what he/she wants to say or wishes to introduce the point carefully. The listener can ask the speaker to come to the point by using questions like these:

What are you getting at?
What are you trying to say?
What are you leading up to?

Practice

A starts to talk about something without coming directly to the point. B, using a question like those above, asks A for clarification. A then states his/her point.

Example:
(tired of working overtime; don't earn enough money; don't like your work much) (quit job)

A: You know, I'm getting tired of working overtime so much. And I don't ever seem to have enough money. In fact, I don't like my work very much these days.
B: What are you getting at?
A: Well, I'm going to quit my job.

1. (John always forgets everything; late for appointments; rude; hurts other people's feelings) (John shouldn't be manager of the company)
2. (your business has lost a lot of customers; new stores opening everywhere; expenses rising every day) (losing money in your business)
3. (house too small; don't like the kitchen; neighbors too noisy) (want to move)
4. (feeling tired; working too hard lately; not sleeping well at night) (need a vacation)
5. (things getting more and more expensive; can't afford new clothes for the children; wife/husband needs special medical treatment) (want a raise in pay)

Transfer

Make up a dialog between a patient and a doctor. The doctor talks about the patient's serious illness and the patient should ask for clarification when the doctor's point is not clear. The doctor will make statements about the patient's future health, but will qualify these statements with certain conditions.

LISTENING

This is an interview with an author who has written a book about the sinking of the *Titanic*.

Getting Ready to Listen

1. How does a novel differ from a work of historical non-fiction?
2. What is a historical novel?
3. What was the *Titanic* disaster?
4. Why has the *Titanic* disaster been so appealing to writers and filmmakers as well as to the general public?

Vocabulary

come out of your own life: be based on your own experience
in extremis: (Latin) at the moment of death
inexorably: without any hope
attendant to: concerning
provocative: challenging, stimulating
gone awry: working in the wrong way

Now listen to the interview.

Comprehension Checkup

Are these statements *true* or *false*, based on the information in the interview?

_____ 1. The writer thinks that factual research was more important than her imagination in writing about the *Titanic*.

_____ 2. To make a believable character, the writer should imagine things that do not come from his or her own experience.
_____ 3. There has been little creative effort devoted to the *Titanic* disaster.
_____ 4. The movie about the *Titanic* caused audiences to cry.
_____ 5. It is said that God sank the *Titanic*.
_____ 6. The passengers on the *Titanic* were all rich.
_____ 7. One reason the story of the *Titanic* interests people is that it touches on the theme of modern technology gone out of control.

Critical Listening

The author seems to have misunderstood the interviewer's last comment. Listen to the end of the interview again. What was the interviewer really referring to in his comment? What did the author *think* he was referring to?

Discussion

You have listened to a novelist talking about her work. If a publisher asked you to prepare a brief summary of a novel that you would like to write, what ideas would you have?

The Mountain's Fury

1 They were taking their chances, they knew. But on a fine morning like this it seemed impossible that anything serious could happen. They just wanted to see the mountain blow a little steam, that's all. They'd take some pictures, do a little sightseeing and then head for home. They wouldn't be gone more than four hours.

2 Cowlitz County Sheriff's patrol extended the "red zone" around Mt. St. Helens to twenty-five miles today. Residents of Cougar and other small towns within the red zone were evacuated and roadblocks were set up to discourage sightseers and tourists. The bulge on the north side of the mountain continues to grow at a rate of five feet per day and geologists warn that the mountain could have a major eruption at any moment.

3 Old Bill . . . he knew his way around the mountain pretty well, so it wasn't any trick for him to avoid the roadblocks and take the back roads up to Elk Meadow. "I wonder if there'll be any campers up there," Eileen said. But they never found out because they never got to Elk Meadow. First there was an earthquake and then there was a roar.

4 Mt. St. Helens erupted today in what scientists call the most violent volcanic explosion in the continental United States. Volcanic ash shot up to a height of 65,000 feet, blocking out the sun and turning daylight to darkness in Yakima, Washington, where up to three inches of ash is reported to have accumulated. Observers report that the north face of the mountain blew upward and outward, flattening trees for fifteen miles and sending floods of mud down the Toutle River. A giant log jam, picked up by the mudflow, destroyed five bridges and uncounted homes along the way. Fifty-four people are reported missing, but rescue workers are unable to approach the mountain while it is still in its violent, eruptive state. According to observers, the top 1,300 feet of the mountain have been blown away.

5 Eileen grabbed Bill's arm and shouted, "Oh, my God!" Ahead of them the mountain was literally blowing apart. An incredible cloud of black ashes was pouring straight down the side of the mountain toward them. "We'd better get out of here fast," Bill shouted at Eileen. Already, pebblesized bits of rock were pounding on the roof of the old pickup. "Roll up the windows, roll them up!" Bill screamed. They worked furiously to shut the windows and vents of the car before they suffocated in the hot dust. And then it hit them.

6 For five minutes or more, the truck rocked and banged as some unseen force tried to blow it off the mountain. A window exploded and hot gases poured into the cab, burning Eileen's back and right arm as she clung to Bill. They prayed aloud and wondered if they'd ever see their two children again. Then the roaring subsided and there was darkness outside the truck. Ashes fell like blackened snow around them.

7 After an hour or more, they decided they'd have to try to hike out. No one would be able to find them here and the ashes were building up around the fenders of the truck. They got out of the truck and started walking. Trees had fallen across the road and they had to scramble over and under them. The ashes were knee deep and where there had once been streams of water, hot mud streamed thickly. After an hour of plodding in the darkness, Eileen began to cry and protested she could not go farther. But Bill refused to leave her. "Either we both walk out of here alive, Eileen, or we die here together." After a few minutes Eileen got up and they continued their dismal journey.

8 They walked for three hours before they saw light breaking through the black clouds above them. And then they heard a helicopter and minutes later they were aboard. Eileen cried so hard out of sheer relief that she couldn't speak. When Bill finished telling their story to the rescuers, the young pilot shook his head and stared out at the barren gray terrain below.

9 "Man, you are lucky to be alive!" he said, nodding at the desolation left by the mountain's fury. "There isn't anything left down there."

10 "I know," Bill said as he comforted his exhausted wife.

Words and Expressions

discourage: keep out, stop
bulge: a swelling caused by pressure from within
protested: complained, declared
nodding: tilting his head (in order to point towards the desolation)

Comprehension Checkup

Decide whether these statements are *true* or *false*.

_____ **1.** Bill and Eileen knew that there was some danger in going up the mountain.
_____ **2.** Geologists thought that the mountain would erupt, but not soon.
_____ **3.** Bill and Eileen decided to walk out because they were afraid of another eruption.
_____ **4.** It was difficult to walk down the mountain because of the devastating results of the volcano.

Finding Facts

Read the two newspaper accounts at the beginning of the story to find answers to these questions. Give short answers.

1. How fast was the bulge on the mountain growing?
2. How high up did the volcanic ash go?
3. How much ash accumulated in Yakima, Washington?
4. For how far around the mountain were trees flattened?
5. How many bridges were destroyed?
6. How many people are missing?
7. How much of the mountain has been blown away?

Vocabulary Building

Find the sentences in the reading passage that contain the words and phrases below. Then choose the meaning that fits each one. The numbers in parentheses refer to the paragraphs where the words and phrases can be found.

1. taking their chances (1):
   a. carrying all their possessions
   b. getting a unique opportunity
   c. trying something despite danger
2. blow a little steam (1):
   a. relax for a few minutes
   b. release built-up pressure and gases
   c. release built-up anger and frustration
3. it wasn't any trick (3):
   a. it wasn't difficult
   b. it wasn't magic
   c. it wasn't a trap

4. subsided (6):
   a. divided up into two sides
   b. became heavier on one side
   c. quieted down
5. plodding (7):
   a. planning carefully
   b. moving with difficulty
   c. working with the soil

Making Inferences

1. What does the "red zone" refer to? (2)
2. What fact about the mountain tells geologists that it is dangerously close to eruption? (2)
3. "Eileen grabbed Bill's arm and shouted, 'Oh, my God!'" What emotion was she feeling? (5)
4. What words tell us that Bill and Eileen thought they might be killed? (6)
5. Why was the mud in the stream beds hot? (7)

Writing Topics

Choose one of the topics and write a composition of 350–400 words.

1. Describe a terrible experience you one had. (Try to include some element of suspense to arouse the curiosity of the reader.)
2. You are a reporter for the local newspaper and you have been asked to write an article about a plane crash a few miles from town. (Include short interviews with several people who survived the crash.)
3. You are a psychologist and you have been asked to write an article explaining why people do daring things that endanger their lives. (Include specific examples of several individuals and the things they have done, as well as your explanation of why they did them.)

UNIT 8 *ask Alice*

WNYN did a program on how people solve their personal problems. The news team talked to an expert on problems, Alice Mathews, a newspaper writer whose advice column, "Ask Alice," appears in daily papers throughout the country.

1

I've been writing "Ask Alice" for ten years now. I never get tired of it because people are so interesting. You never know what the day's mail will bring and the letters range from problems with love affairs to questions about manners. I also enjoy it because all sorts of people write to me—teachers, doctors, housewives, the old, the young, the in-between. I know that some people think that columns like "Ask Alice" are silly and don't reflect people's real problems. I disagree. It's always easy to say that another person's problem is silly or very simple to solve, but when the problem is your own, the solution isn't always so easy to see. The problems people write to me about are real and a column like mine offers help to people who have nowhere else to turn. I don't think, by the way, that I actually "solve" people's problems. All I can do is point out a direction or suggest a course of action. It's the letter writers themselves who have to work out the problem.

Interview Alice Mathews. Ask:
1. how long she's been writing "Ask Alice"
2. if she gets tired of it
3. what kinds of problems people write about
4. who writes to her
5. if she thinks her column helps people
6. who really "solves" the problem

2

Dear Alice,

I love my boyfriend very much, but there's a problem. He seems to love his mother more than me. Whenever we go out, she comes along. She's a widow and my boyfriend says he doesn't like to leave her home alone. So wherever we go, she goes too. Whatever we do, she does too. She's nice enough, but sometimes I'd like to be alone with my boyfriend.

We're going to get married soon. I'm afraid that when we do, his mother will come and live with us.

What should I do?

Blue Betty

Dear Blue,

You and your boyfriend can't sacrifice your lives to his mother. If he doesn't realize this, you'll both be very unhappy. Tell him how you feel. If he really loves you, he'll understand. If he calls off the wedding, you'll be better off in the long run. Whatever he does, it's better to settle it before the wedding, not after.

Ask and Answer
Ask Betty:
1. why she thinks her boyfriend loves his mother more than her
2. why her boyfriend likes his mother to come along
3. if she dislikes his mother
4. what she's afraid will happen

Ask Alice:
1. what Betty's boyfriend must realize
2. what will happen if he really loves Betty
3. what will happen to Betty if he calls off the wedding
4. when this problem should be settled

3

Dear Alice,

Last month I bought a used, reconditioned television set at a store in my neighborhood. The salesclerk told me that all their TVs carry a nine-month warranty for parts and labor. But I seem to have thrown out the sales slip and, of course, now the TV doesn't work. The store refuses to repair the TV without the receipt. Is there anything I can do?

Ripped-off Roland

Dear Ripped-off,

No. Learn from experience. If you don't protect yourself, no one else will. Whenever you buy something major or with a guarantee, keep both the sales slip and the guarantee.

Ask and Answer
Make questions for these answers.
For Roland:
  1. A used, reconditioned television set.
  2. The salesclerk.
  3. I threw it out.
  4. No, the store refuses to.

For Alice:
  1. No one will.
  2. Keep both the sales slip and the guarantee.

4

Dear Alice,

I am twenty and engaged. I love my fiancé very much. The problem is his father.

He is only forty. His wife is dead. He says he is in love with me and that he will kill himself unless I marry him. The situation is impossible. How can I marry my fiancé's father?

Unfortunately, I think I am in love with him as much as I am with his son.

I want to tell my fiancé about all this, but if I do, he will be hurt and angry. Whatever I do, it seems I'll hurt one of them. What would you do if you were me?

Fickle Franny

Dear Fickle,

You sound very confused to me. How can you possibly be in love with two men at the same time? If you really loved your fiancé, you would not be in love with his father.

If I were you, I'd tell my fiancé about it immediately. Of course he'll be hurt. But he would be more hurt if he found out about this from someone else. Unless you tell him yourself, he'll lose faith in you completely.

Ask and Answer
Imagine you are interviewing first Franny and then Alice. Make questions and have your partner answer them.

Find out:
  1. how old Franny is
  2. how she feels about her fiancé
  3. how old his father is
  4. what his father says he will do
  5. how she feels about the father
  6. if she has told her fiancé yet
  7. why not

Find out:
  1. what Alice thinks of Franny
  2. why she thinks Franny doesn't really love either man
  3. what she would do if she were Franny
  4. why she would do this

UNIT 8 Grammar

1 Real conditions

Cancel

If he *calls off* the wedding, you*'ll be* better off.

A. Comment

The real conditional is used to express the possibility that an event will happen under certain conditions. It is formed in the following way:

If + subject + present tense, subject + future tense

or

subject + future tense + *if* + subject + present tense

B. Situation

Imagine Betty is talking to you. Reassure her about her future.

Example:
BETTY: Maybe I'll speak to my boyfriend. Do you think he'll understand?
YOU: If you speak to him, I'm sure he*'ll understand*.

1. Maybe I'll go to him now. I hope he'll listen.
   If you go to him, I think he'll listen.
2. Maybe I'll marry him anyway. I wonder if we'll be happy.
   If you marry him, I'm sure you'll be happy
3. Maybe I'll be nice to his mother. Do you think she'll like me more?
   If you are nice to his mother, I'm sure she'll like you more
4. Maybe we'll have lots of children. I wonder if he'll still miss his mother.
   If you have a lot of children, I'm sure he'll not miss his mother
5. Maybe his mother will start dating. Do you think she'll leave us alone?
   If his mother starts dating, I think she'll leave you alone
6. Maybe he won't marry me. I'll be miserable.
   If he doesn't marry you, I think you'll feel
7. Maybe he'll call off the wedding. I'll die.
   If he calls off, I'm sure you'll die. If you tell him
8. Do you really think I should tell him? Will everything be O.K.?
   will be O.K.   I'm sure everything

C. Transfer

You have recently been offered a very good job in Houston, Texas. You live in California. The company wants you to start immediately—they won't wait. Say what will happen if you do these things:

1. go to Houston by plane, train or car *If I ... I'm sure I'll be there in 2 days. I'm sure I'll get on time. I think it will take 24 hrs.*
2. take a vacation now, *I might loose the offer*
3. quit your present job right away, *I sure I won't be correct.*
4. ask them to wait, *I'm sure they will.*
5. don't quit your present job, *I might loose the other one*
6. don't move to Houston, *It will be difficult for me to*
7. don't decide soon, *accept the job, there. I'll probably loose this opportunity.*

D. Transfer

You belong to a group of government advisors. The mayor of a large city has called the group together to ask your advice about a number of pressing problems. Give the mayor your opinion about what will happen in these situations.

1. Taxes may be cut in half. *I'm sure we'll loose a lot of income*
2. The mayor may fire all the managers of the sanitation department. *he'll be involved in a big problem with the citizens.*
3. The teachers might go out on strike. *I'm sure, we'll have to increase their salaries.*
4. The police might refuse to give speeding tickets. *people will have more accidents.*
5. The five largest businesses in the city might move to another city. *he'll have to convence them to stay.*
6. The power company might raise its electricity rates by 50%. *he'll have to find a way to put them down.*

2 Unreal present conditional

If you really *loved* your fiancé, you *wouldn't be* in love with his father.

A. Comment

1. This is the present unreal conditional. Use the *if* clause (with the past tense verb form) when you think something is not true or unlikely. The other clause, *would (not)* + base form of verb, tells the result or consequence of the *if* clause. Compare:

   REAL CONDITIONAL:
   If Peter *has* a problem, he *will* write to Alice.
   (The speaker doesn't know whether or not Peter has a problem.)
   PRESENT UNREAL CONDITIONAL:
   If Peter *had* a problem, he *would write* to Alice.
   (The speaker thinks Peter does *not* have a problem.)

2. The verb in the *if* clause is the simple past verb form (*went, wanted, knew,* etc.) except with the verb *be,* when *were* is used for all persons in careful speech and in writing.

   If I *were* you, I'd tell my fiancé about it.
   If he/she *were* here, I'd tell him/her now.

   Was is sometimes used in informal speech with *I, he* and *she. ← no*

60

Present unreal:
if I studied, I would pass the exam.
if I were you, I would ...

B. Situation

I wish I were rich
he wished he had been elected president

Your friend is asking you about things you don't think are true. Answer your friend's questions using the unreal conditional.

Example:

A: Can this be a real diamond? It only costs $2.00.

B: I don't think so. If it *were* a real diamond, it *would cost* a lot more.

1. Does Franny really want to marry him? She says she loves his father. *if she really loved him, she wouldn't love his father.*
2. Are those people really English? They speak with French accents. *if they were English, they wouldn't speak with french accent.*
3. Do you think that man really has a lot of money? His clothes are very worn and old. *if he had a lot of money, he wouldn't wear those clothes.*
4. Is this meat really fresh? It has a funny smell. *I don't know, but if it were fresh, it wouldn't have a funny smell.*
5. Do you believe those stories about a giant monster in the mountains of California? There are no photographs. *if they were true, there would be some photographs.*
6. Does that country really want peace? They keep buying arms. *I don't think so. If they were peaceful, they wouldn't buy arms.*
7. Is Mr. O'Brian really poor? He owns a very expensive car. *I don't think so. if he were poor, he wouldn't have an exp. car.*
8. Do you think that dog likes people? He always growls when people walk by. *I don't think so. if he liked people, he wouldn't growl when people walk by.*

C. Transfer

Think of all the things you'd have to do and all the things you'd be able to do if you lived in the following places (skip any place you live now):

Example:

New York

If I *lived* in New York, *I'd have to* travel in crowded buses, but *I'd be able to* see a lot of good plays.

1. San Francisco
2. Hawaii
3. Japan
4. a farm in the country
5. Peru
6. Egypt
7. Kenya
8. Germany

past unreal:
if he were here, he would answer the questions.
if you had studied you'd have passed.

3 Unless

A. Comment

1. *Unless* expresses a negative condition; it means *if not.* So the sentence "He will kill himself *unless I marry him*" means the same as "He will kill himself *if I don't marry him.*"

2. Note the form of the verb in the *unless* clause: it is affirmative and simple present. The verb in the main clause can be negative or affirmative future tense.

3. When the *if* or *unless* clause begins a sentence, put a comma between the two clauses. "Unless you tell him yourself, he'll lose faith in you completely." However, when the *if* or *unless* clause is at the end of the sentence, don't use a comma. "He'll lose faith in you unless you tell him."

B. Situation

Imagine you are talking to a doctor. She is telling you what will happen if you don't do certain things. Rephrase her advice using *unless*.

Example:

DOCTOR: Get some rest. Or do you want to have a nervous breakdown?

YOU: You mean, *unless* I *get* some rest, I'*ll have* a nervous breakdown?

1. Find another job. Or do you want to have a heart attack? *unless I find*
2. Take these pills. Or do you want to get sicker?
3. Stop eating so much. Or do you want to die?
4. See me tomorrow. If you don't, you'll get worse.
5. Stop eating salt. Or do you want to suffer from hypertension?
6. Stop eating high cholesterol foods. Or do you want to have a heart attack?
7. Learn to relax. Or do you want to die young?
8. Start doing exercises every day. Or do you want to get worse?

C. Transfer

You have a gardener. You're going to fire him unless he does certain things. Warn him using *unless*. You want him to:

1. take shorter coffee breaks
2. come to work on time
3. stop drinking your beer
4. trim the hedges more neatly
5. mow the lawn more frequently

Now think of some more examples.

future possible:
if you study, you will pass

UNIT 8 Dialog/Communication Practice

DIALOG

Listen to the dialog and complete Bob's part.

GRACE: What is it, Bob? You sounded pretty serious on the phone. Have we still got a budget problem?

BOB: I don't know. I (1) ▨▨▨▨. The (2) ▨▨▨▨. But (3) ▨▨▨▨ talk to (4) ▨▨▨▨. Uh . . . close (5) ▨▨▨▨, (6) ▨▨▨▨ you? (Grace closes the door.) It's Marsha. . . .

GRACE: Marsha? . . . What about her?

BOB: I'm (7) ▨▨▨▨. I (8) ▨▨▨▨. She's (9) ▨▨▨▨. We (10) ▨▨▨▨ let her go.

GRACE: Fire her? . . . She's been with us a long time, Bob. If she leaves, it'll be a big loss to the station. She's done really excellent work.

BOB: Yes, but lately, . . . the (11) ▨▨▨▨, in fact— there've (12) ▨▨▨▨. She's (13) ▨▨▨▨, Grace. Not only (14) ▨▨▨▨, but (15) ▨▨▨▨, doesn't (16) ▨▨▨▨, and (17) ▨▨▨▨ the last minute.

GRACE: Hmm. Did she ever explain why she didn't show up for the Denver trip?

BOB: No. She (18) ▨▨▨▨, and that (19) ▨▨▨▨ again—something about (20) ▨▨▨▨ airport. Now, whenever (21) ▨▨▨▨ her, (22) ▨▨▨▨ clams up. I don't know. Thank goodness (23) ▨▨▨▨ hole (24) ▨▨▨▨!

GRACE: Yes. He did a really fine job—filling in for Marsha like that at the last minute.

BOB: I (25) ▨▨▨▨ that. If (26) ▨▨▨▨ facts, I think (27) ▨▨▨▨ covering for Marsha (28) ▨▨▨▨ projects.

GRACE: Well, I know at least one other case. . . .

BOB: (29) ▨▨▨▨?

GRACE: Uh-huh. I just looked at the material for the space exploration special. It looks really good, by the way. But guess who did the interviewing?

BOB: (30) ▨▨▨▨?

GRACE: Right. Apparently, Marsha made the arrangements with Professor Daniels, . . . and then she didn't show up at the university for the interview. David had to do it by himself.

BOB: (31) ▨▨▨▨ explanation?

GRACE: Well, I talked to David about it and he was pretty evasive. Whatever the problem was, he didn't want to talk about it. Uh . . . I think he was trying to cover up to protect Marsha. He asked me not to make an issue out of it and uh . . . upset her.

BOB: Well, that does it! I (32) ▨▨▨▨. We (33) ▨▨▨▨ keep (34) ▨▨▨▨. I guess (35) ▨▨▨▨ and (36) ▨▨▨▨ cameraman. What (37) ▨▨▨▨?

GRACE: I don't know. I sure don't like the idea of losing Marsha. There must be something troubling her. Never before have we had a problem like this. Uh . . . Why don't we hold off for a few days? And . . . let me try to talk with her and see if I can't find out what the problem is.

BOB: Well, all right. Do (38) ▨▨▨▨. I (39) ▨▨▨▨ unless (40) ▨▨▨▨ necessary, but . . .

COMMUNICATION PRACTICE

Using *Not Only . . . , But . . .* for Emphasis

Not only does she have a tendency to be moody all the time, but she misses appointments.

Notice the inverted order of subject and auxiliary verb: *Not only does she have . . .* The use of *not only . . . but* in the sentence above puts strong emphasis on both *being late* and *missing appointments*. But the second fact is more emphasized than the first.

Compare:
  She was *an excellent student* and she became *a champion* (Equal emphasis.)
  Not only was she *an excellent student*, but she became *a champion athlete*.
  (More emphasis on becoming a champion athlete.)

Practice

Combine these pairs of sentences using *not only . . . , but. . . .*

Example:
I lost my umbrella. I lost my raincoat too.
Not only did I lose my umbrella, but I lost my raincoat too.

1. I met Mr. Avesian. I met his four brothers too.
2. He told me about his job. His brothers told me about their jobs.
3. I missed my train. I also missed my plane.
4. I saw the palace. I also met the Queen.
5. She spoke to me. She also invited me in.
6. I was interviewed by newspaper reporters. I appeared on national TV.

Using *Never Before* for Emphasis

Never before have we had a problem like this.

Notice the inverted order of auxiliary verb and subject following *never*. The less emphatic form is: *We have never had a problem like this before.*

Situation

Suppose the things listed below have just been done for the first time. Imagine that you are a reporter and that you are reporting each event. Use *never before* at the beginning of each statement.

Example:
A woman has run a four-minute mile.
Never before has a woman run a four-minute mile.

1. A man has eaten 50 pancakes in 15 minutes.
2. A woman has been elected president of the United States.
3. A young child has been sent into space in a rocket.
4. Ten people have crowded into a telephone booth.
5. A cat has given birth to 20 kittens.

LISTENING

A psychotherapist talks about his work.

Getting Ready to Listen

1. What do psychotherapists do?
2. What advantages are there to going to a psychotherapist if you have personal problems?

Vocabulary

psychotherapy: the science of investigating and treating mental disorders by use of special counseling techniques
dealing (with): solving, handling
patterns of behavior: usual or customary (habitual) ways of acting and responding
perspective: viewpoint

Now listen to the interview.

Comprehension Checkup

Choose the paragraph which you think is the best summary of the interview and explain why you think so.

A. Psychotherapists help people to understand and deal with recurring problems in their lives. Although some people are able to help themselves quickly, others have to be taught to do so through psychotherapy. Depending on the nature of the problem, a person can be referred to different kinds of psychotherapists by a doctor or a hospital. Two advantages of going to a psychotherapist are getting an outside perspective on your problem and getting professional help.

B. Psychotherapy is a self-help program that teaches people to become independent of others. The average person who has problems can be referred to a psychotherapist to get a new perspective on his or her problem and get professional help.

C. Psychotherapy is defined as helping people to change their minds about the way they deal with problems and their lives in general. People who go to psychotherapists tend

to repeat patterns of behavior and psychotherapists show them how this repetition causes problems for them. In other words, it is a self-help program. Some people can help themselves, of course, but others must be taught to do this through a long process called psychotherapy. Sometimes it is even necessary to treat all the members of a family. The average person goes to a psychotherapist after being referred by a doctor, hospital or someone who knows the therapist. There are different kinds of therapists. The one being interviewed here is a family therapist. He feels that the advantages of going to a psychotherapist are that, first, you get an outside perspective on a problem

Critical Listening

In the middle of the interview, the interviewer asked why an average person with a problem would go to a psychotherapist. He wanted to know why a psychotherapist would "be the best place for him to place his confidence and/or money." Listen to the interview again from that point to the end. Do you think the psychotherapist's answer to this question satisfied the interviewer? Why did the interviewer ask his last question?

Discussion

1. List the kinds of professionals who deal directly with people and their problems. (Start with psychotherapists.)
2. List the kinds of non-professionals who deal in some way (directly or indirectly) with people and offer advice on their problems. (Start with family members.)
3. If you needed advice or help with a big problem, would you turn to a non-professional (for example, an advice column in the newspaper or a family member) or a professional (for example, a psychotherapist or a member of the clergy)? Why?
4. What different help might you get from a psychologist than from a close friend?

A RUDE AWAKENING

1 When Natalie was offered the position of private secretary for Dan Tyson, she accepted immediately. Although her salary wasn't nearly what she had hoped it would be, it was still an improvement over her last job, and they had assured her that there would be raises. She had a mahogany desk in an office shared with two other secretaries. Also, she had a private phone line. The other two secretaries were quiet and courteous. But best of all, she liked her new boss, Dan Tyson.

2 Dan was in his forties, a tall, attractive man with blue eyes and a broad grin. He was patient and went to great pains to help her learn her new duties. Natalie was personable and courteous and soon became a favorite with the out-of-town customers that came to call on Dan. Dan began to invite her along on the various dinner meetings and luncheons that he had with his customers, and she felt flattered that he included her in these business meetings.

3 Although Dan's business meetings were always held in nice restaurants where the atmosphere was casual, Natalie soon discovered that her secretarial duties followed her even there. She was asked to make lists of orders, take dictation and make phone calls to get information when it was needed. She began to carry file folders and writing pads with her to the restaurants.

4 Dan was always kind to her, complimenting her on her looks and efficiency. But after a while, he began to make requests of her that she was sure her duties did not include. On one occasion, Dan was expecting an important visitor from Chicago and, as Natalie was getting ready to go home, he called her into his office.

5 "Natalie, Jim Roberts and his wife will be coming in on the two o'clock flight tomorrow, Midwestern Airlines. I have a board meeting. Would you please meet them at the airport, take them to their hotel and, once they're settled, drive Jim here to the office? I'd really appreciate it. Oh, and wear that blue wool dress you have . . . it's very attractive on you."

6 Natalie was burning. She knew she was being dangled like a pretty toy to keep these customers interested in Dan's business propositions. On more than one occasion, these agents had made a play for her when Dan wasn't around. Jim Roberts was one of them.

7 "Dan, I don't want to pick up Jim Roberts tomorrow, even if his wife is with him. Frankly, I don't want to be alone with him. Besides, I can't afford to go running out to the airport every time you want me to. The company doesn't reimburse me for my expenses and gas is expensive."

8 Dan looked surprised. "Are you asking for a raise?"

9 It hadn't occurred to Natalie how much it bothered her that she had not gotten a raise in the seven months she had worked for Dan. Suddenly she realized that she did want a raise. "That would be nice," she answered. Then she added, "I certainly think I deserve one."

10 "No doubt about it," Dan said. "You're extremely valuable to me. Tell you what, once I get this contract with Jim Roberts settled and I have a little time to breathe again, we'll talk about a raise."

Words and Expressions

duties . . . followed her: duties . . . went with her (she was expected to work)

a little time to breathe again: some free time

Comprehension Checkup

Choose the correct statement.

1. Natalie accepted the job of private secretary for Dan Tyson because
   a. she found out the salary was very good.
   b. she thought it was better than her last job.
   c. she liked her new office.
   d. she wanted to have a private phone line.

2. In her new job as Dan Tyson's private secretary, Natalie found that
   a. the other people in the office gossiped all the time.
   b. her boss was patient and helpful.
   c. her boss's customers didn't like her very much.
   d. the work was boring most of the time.

3. In time, Natalie became unhappy with her new job because she had to work evenings, for which she wasn't paid, and also because
   a. she wasn't invited to her boss's meetings in nice restaurants.
   b. her boss never complimented her on her looks and efficiency.
   c. she wasn't allowed to do all of the things her duties included.
   d. she was asked to do a lot of things her duties didn't include.

4. Natalie's rude awakening came when Dan Tyson became vice-president and chose somebody else as his new secretary. It was then that Natalie realized that
   a. she was never going to get a raise.
   b. Dan's replacement would not be as good a boss as Dan had been.
   c. Dan had used her all that time to further his own career.
   d. she should become an office manager.

Finding Specific Information

At the beginning of her job as Dan Tyson's secretary, Natalie saw several advantages to the job. List them.

Later, before Dan's promotion, some things had begun to bother her. List the disadvantages that developed.

11 But Jim Roberts and dozens of other customers came and went, and Natalie was still earning the same salary a year later. The only difference was that she was working twice as hard and her social life, as well as her working life, revolved around Dan Tyson's career. And then the final blow came.

12 One day Dan went into an executive board meeting and came out as vice-president in charge of sales. Natalie was thrilled for Dan, knowing how hard he had worked for the position. She was also excited by the new opportunities this would mean for her. She'd have a private office and a substantial raise as well. It would be a promotion for both of them. But when Dan called her into his office two days later, she knew something had gone wrong.

13 "Natalie, I'll be moving into my new office next week. I just wanted you to know how much I appreciate the work you've done for me. I'll see to it that the guy taking over this job realizes how valuable you are."

14 Natalie was stunned. Her face dropped and she stared at him, not fully comprehending what he had said. He smiled at her.

15 "I can see that you were expecting to continue working for me."

16 She could only nod her head.

17 "That isn't possible, Natalie. I already have an executive secretary who will be helping me learn the responsibilities of my new job. She's had a lot of experience. Besides, you're going to be needed here to help my replacement."

18 The full realization of what had happened hit her. Dan apparently read the change in her mood and began to busy himself with his papers. "I . . . I haven't forgotten about that raise, Natalie. I'll be sure to recommend a raise for you as soon as my replacement is hired."

19 Natalie turned and walked to the door. She slammed it shut and turned around to face him, her eyes blazing. Dan swung around in his swivel chair, startled by the bang of the door. Natalie spoke softly and slowly.

20 "You can forget about the raise, Dan. I'm quitting. I can see now that I will be used again and again to further some executive's career. And I refuse to be used by another ambitious, unscrupulous person like you." Then she pulled the door open and gently shut it behind her.

21 It didn't take long for Natalie to locate another job, even without a recommendation from Dan. She found a job as an office manager and at night she took classes to help further her career. But she never forgot her experience with Dan Tyson. She was resolved that it would never happen again.

Vocabulary Building

What would you have done in Natalie's place to reduce the list of disadvantages and add to the list of advantages?

Vocabulary Building

Find the sentences in the reading that contain the words and phrases listed below. Then choose the meaning that fits each one. The numbers in parentheses refer to the paragraphs where the words and phrases can be found.

1. burning (6): **a.** happy   **b.** embarrassed   **c.** angry
2. made a play for her (6): **a.** took her to the theater **b.** made advances to her   **c.** tried to get her to influence Dan
3. stunned (14): **a.** astonished   **b.** relieved   **c.** sad
4. read the change in her mood (18): **a.** realized she was feeling different from before   **b.** changed his mind about her   **c.** thought she was angry
5. unscrupulous (20): **a.** successful   **b.** dishonest **c.** handsome

Discussion Topics

1. Where are your sympathies—with Natalie or with Dan?
2. Have you, or has anyone you know, ever been in a situation like this, either as an employee or as the boss? Tell about the experience.

Writing Topics

Choose one of the topics and write a composition of 350–400 words.

1. The best job I ever had. (Tell what kind of job it was, what your duties were, why you like it, why you left the job, etc.)
2. The strangest letter I ever received. (Pretend that you write an advice column in the newspaper and that you receive a lot of letters from people who have problems of all kinds.)
3. A rude awakening. (Tell about a bad or unpleasant experience you had and what you learned from the experience.)

UNIT 9
life in the future

WNYN asked a panel of experts to predict what life will
be like in the next century.

Where was this photo taken? Do you think these chickens have enough room? 1

What will life be like 100 years from now? Some experts
are optimistic. Others are far more pessimistic. They think
that by then the population will have doubled. We will have
run out of essential materials like oil and coal. We may
even have run out of water to drink. They believe that we
will be living like these chickens. We will be living in little
boxes and eating artificial food.

Ask and Answer
Imagine you are interviewing an expert who is very pessimistic
about the future. Find out:
1. how much larger the population of the world will be
2. if we will have run out of some materials
3. if there are other things we may have run out of
4. how we may be living
5. what we may be eating

2 What do you see in this picture? Would you like to live here? Why or why not?

But those who are more optimistic say that life in the future
will be far better than it is today. We may be living in
communities like this. We may be getting more sunlight,
breathing fresher air, living in a better environment and
leading far more pleasant lives than we are today.

Ask and Answer
Imagine you are interviewing a more optimistic expert. Ask
questions using these phrases:

1. better than it is today?
2. in communities like this?
3. getting more sunlight?
4. breathing fresher air?
5. in a better environment?
6. leading more pleasant lives?

What is happening here?
Does the man look happy?
Why does he feel this way?

What is the man doing?

How does the man feel now?
Why?

Life will certainly have become far more mechanized by the year 2100. It may even have become *too* mechanized. Mechanization has already caused quite a few problems and will cause still more. For example, many jobs will have been "automated." That is, machines will be doing many jobs that people do today. People will no longer be able to learn only one job in their lifetime. They will have to learn several. Many of the jobs that young people are doing today will have become unnecessary by the time they are forty.

Ask and Answer

Ask the expert questions beginning, "Do you think . . . " using these words:

1. life/more mechanized in the future?
2. *too* mechanized?
3. mechanization/already cause problems?
4. mechanization/cause still more?
5. machines/jobs that people do today?
6. only one job in their lifetime?
7. some jobs/become unnecessary?

Discussion

1. Industrial robots are already used in some factories. What kinds of things are they doing for us?
2. What are some of the things you think robots may be doing for us 100 years from now?

UNIT 9 Grammar

1 Future continuous

We'*ll be living* in little boxes 100 years from now.

We $\begin{Bmatrix} may \\ might \end{Bmatrix}$ *be living* in better cities.

A. Comment

1. The future continuous (*will* + *be* + *-ing* verb) can be used to focus on an action going on at a given future time. The action can start before that time and end after it.

   At six o'clock, I'll be cooking dinner.

   (The cooking will start before six o'clock and finish after six o'clock, but at six o'clock, the cooking will be going on.)

2. *May/might be doing* is used here for what may *possibly* be going on at some time in the future. You do not know for certain whether or not it will be going on.

B. Situation

Imagine you are talking to a friend. He/She is going to begin something as soon as you leave. You are going to come back in about two hours. Ask questions, and have your partner answer, about what he'll/she'll be doing when you get back.

Example:
FRIEND: I'm going to type these letters now.
YOU: *Will* you *be typing* them when I get back?
FRIEND: Probably./I might be.

1. I'm going to watch television.
2. I'm going to clean this room.
3. I think I'll wash these clothes.
4. I'll just sit here and listen to some records.
5. I'll watch those children playing.
6. I'll write a letter to my mother.

C. Transfer

A friend wants to come visit you tomorrow. He/She is trying to find out when would be a good time to come. You really don't want to see him/her, but you don't want to say so. Think of other things you can tell your friend that you will or may be doing at certain times tomorrow so that he/she won't come.

Example:
6:00 P.M.
FRIEND: I'll come at six in the evening. Will that be all right?
YOU: No. Six isn't good. I'*ll be eating* dinner then.

1. 8:00 A.M.
2. 10:00 A.M.
3. 12 noon
4. 3:00 P.M.
5. 9:00 P.M.

D. Practice

You can't know for certain, but describe where you *may/might* be working, what you *may/might* be doing, where you *may/might* be living:

1. two years from now
2. when you're 65
3. this time next year
4. this time tomorrow
5. next Saturday at five in the afternoon

E. Discussion

Talk about what might be happening in the world or in your life in the year 1990, 2000, 2025, 2050.

2 Future perfect

The population of the world $\begin{Bmatrix} will \\ may \\ might \end{Bmatrix}$ *have doubled* by the year 2100.

A. Comment

1. The future perfect with *will* is used for actions that will be done before a certain point in the future is reached.
2. *May/might* in this form means that something will *possibly* have happened by the time a certain point in the future is reached.

B. Situation

Imagine your teacher is talking to you. She is telling you that certain things must be done before a point in the future. What would you say if your teacher tells you:

Example:

TEACHER: You're going to have a test next week. Learn all these words.

YOU: All right. I'*ll have learned* them by then.

1. Do this test now. It has to be done in an hour.
2. Finish this homework. I'll collect it in half an hour.
3. Read this book. But return it to me by the end of the week.
4. Write a composition about the future. It's due on Monday.
5. You must finish this textbook before the term ends.

C. Situation

You are an employee in a large office. People often come up to your desk and ask you to do things, but you are already busy with the work you have and you are not sure you can do the things the others want you to do. Reply to the requests as in the example.

Example:

Will you be able to meet with me in an hour?
(a lot of letters to write)
Well, I have a lot of letters to write, but I *may have finished/ written* them by then.

1. How about going out for a coffee break at 10:30?
   (a report to write)
2. I want to show you some sales figures. Can you come to my office in five minutes?
   (an important phone call to make)
3. Let's go out to lunch at one o'clock.
   (some meetings to attend).
4. Could I see you about your new project this afternoon?
   (a lot of people to see)
5. I can give you a lift home if you can leave in fifteen minutes.
   (a few memos to read)

D. Transfer

You cannot look into the future, but you can probably imagine many of the things you will have done or may have done in the next ten years. What are they? For example, people get married, get divorced, have children, get better jobs, move to different countries, learn languages, get degrees, travel, etc. What do you think you will have done?

3 | *May/Might have (done)*

A. Comment

May/Might have done can be used in the past too. It means, "Maybe this happened."

B. Situation

Margaret is talking to Bob Russo. His airline ticket is missing. What does she say if she thinks that maybe:

Example:
It got lost in the mail.
It *might have gotten lost* in the mail.

1. The letter carrier delivered it to another office.
2. The airline sent it to the wrong person.
3. The airline forgot to send it.
4. It came in this morning's mail.
5. She put it on his desk.
6. Someone has taken it by mistake.

C. Transfer

You have arranged to meet a friend in front of a coffee shop at 4:00. It's 4:15 and your friend isn't there yet. Think of possible explanations with *may/might have . . .*

Example:
He *may have forgotten* about it.
She *may have had* an accident.

UNIT 9 Dialog/Communication Practice

DIALOG 🔲

Listen to the dialog and complete George's part.

(Bob Russo is waiting in George Benson's office; George finally arrives)

GEORGE: Sorry (1) ▨▨▨▨, Bob. I've (2) ▨▨▨▨ auditors.

BOB: No problem. How's the audit coming?

GEORGE: O.K. They'll be (3) ▨▨▨▨. That means (4) ▨▨▨▨ the end of the month.

BOB: Good. Uh . . . uh . . . where's Steve?

GEORGE: He's (5) ▨▨▨▨. I guess (6) ▨▨▨▨ —do we?

BOB: Well, the only thing is, . . . I wanted to discuss our income projections. Did . . . did he show you the new advertising plan I worked out?

GEORGE: No, but he (7) ▨▨▨▨ .

BOB: Oh, . . . I went over my plan with him yesterday. Here's the revised budget.

GEORGE: (8) ▨▨▨▨ budget? Hmm . . . Wait a minute! I've (9) ▨▨▨▨, haven't I? Aren't (10) ▨▨▨▨ ?

BOB: Yes, but there have been—

GEORGE: (11) ▨▨▨▨? You (12) ▨▨▨▨ 20%.

BOB: I know you wanted me to cut the budget, but I've taken care of the problem in a different way. Uh . . . take a look at the income projections—Section II.

GEORGE: O.K. Uh . . . here we are—"Anticipated Revenue . . . Revenue, Advertisers" . . . Hmmm! Let's see, . . . your (13) ▨▨▨▨ $1,240,700. Uh-huh . . . and now, (14) ▨▨▨▨ $1,638,150 . . . That's (15) ▨▨▨▨, (16) ▨▨▨▨ ?

BOB: $394,024 . . . or, roughly, a 32% increase.

GEORGE: (17) ▨▨▨▨? What (18) ▨▨▨▨ these (19) ▨▨▨▨ ?

BOB: Current audience figures. We've had a dramatic change. We're up nearly 100%.

GEORGE: All the reports (20) ▨▨▨▨ have been going down!

BOB: The latest survey shows that we've reversed that trend now. Our audience—

GEORGE: (21) ▨▨▨▨! Hold on! I've (22) ▨▨▨▨ . Just, uh . . . I (23) ▨▨▨▨ —

BOB: You don't have the current one. Copies are due next week.

GEORGE: Oh. Uh-huh . . . and (24) ▨▨▨▨ —

BOB: Nearly a 100% increase in audience—in all categories! Daily news, features, specials—across the board!

GEORGE: Hmm . . . How (25) ▨▨▨▨ ?

BOB: Well, we've made a lot of changes in program format. We're simply getting better viewer acceptance because of these improvements—some new personalities, more "live" coverage in our news, more interesting features, more sports—

GEORGE: I realize (26) ▨▨▨▨ , but (27) ▨▨▨▨ "shift" wasn't just (28) ▨▨▨▨ last month?

BOB: Oh, no. We're sure that's not the explanation!

GEORGE: (29) ▨▨▨▨ shows (30) ▨▨▨▨ the downward trend then?

BOB: Absolutely!

GEORGE: Well, . . . it's (31) ▨▨▨▨ . You may be (32) ▨▨▨▨ . If you are, . . . and if (33) ▨▨▨▨ , then (34) ▨▨▨▨ necessary.

BOB: As you can see, even if we have an increase of only 20% in revenue, we'll have covered our operation without having to make any cuts.

GEORGE: Uh-huh . . . I see. Well, all right. I (35) ▨▨▨▨ . Uh . . . get me (36) ▨▨▨▨ as soon as (37) ▨▨▨▨ . I need (38) ▨▨▨▨ so (39) ▨▨▨▨ .

COMMUNICATION PRACTICE

Giving Reasons

I need the report $\left\{\begin{array}{l}\text{so I can}\\ \text{in order to}\\ \text{to}\end{array}\right\}$ show it to the budget committee.

Situation

You are a botany professor. Explain to your department chairperson why you need the items listed below. Use *so I can*, *in order to* or *to* in your explanations.

Example: money? build greenhouse
Why do you need the money?
I need it to/in order to/so I can build a greenhouse.

1. space? build greenhouse
2. assistant? further my research
3. time? do research
4. lights? grow plants
5. student aide? care for plants
6. vacation? relax
7. secretary? type up reports

Conceding a Point

a. I know you wanted me to cut the budget, but I've taken care of the problem in a different way.
b. I realize that's a possible explanation, but how do you know this audience shift wasn't just something unusual?

Comment

Often in arguing it helps to concede a point. After admitting that part of your opponent's argument is valid, you can continue with a stronger argument for your side. The fact that you have conceded a point makes you seem reasonable.

Situation

You are trying to persuade your husband/wife to spend money on things you believe you really need. He/She does not like to spend money. How would you concede and then argue for the purchases listed below?

Example: a dishwasher—more sanitary
I know a dishwasher is expensive, but it really is more sanitary.

1. washing machine—save time
2. new car—save money on repair bills
3. electric saw and electric drill—build your own furniture
4. camping gear—vacation
5. new house—room for kids
6. piano—children's music lessons
7. dog—guard house
8. new suit—interview

Debate

Have a debate with a partner on one of the following topics:

1. Nuclear energy—our doom or our salvation?
2. Solar energy—an impossible dream or our hope for the future?
3. Playing transistor radios should be permitted in public places.
4. Automobiles should be forbidden in our cities.

LISTENING

An economist is interviewed on the subject of automation.

Getting Ready to Listen

1. What are some of the advantages and disadvantages of automation?
2. How important is it for a worker to get satisfaction from his or her job?
3. What effect would a shorter workweek have on the economy?

Vocabulary

antithesis: opposite
alienation: separation of people's thinking from things in the real world
schizophrenically: without accepting the reality of things
glut: great overabundance, large surplus
step back (from): move away (from)

Now listen to the interview.

Comprehension Checkup

Choose the phrase that best completes each statement, based on the interview.

1. The woman being interviewed feels that she is different from most economists because
   a. most economists don't get much satisfaction from their jobs.
   b. she is concerned about the effects of automation on people.
2. She sees a need to continue to place emphasis on
   a. the quality of life.
   b. a higher production rate.
3. According to this economist, people are becoming
   a. less and less dependent on the mind.
   b. more and more accepting of computers.
4. She thinks that a shorter workweek
   a. would lead to lower productivity.
   b. is not likely to be adopted.
5. Computers might be paid not to work in order to
   a. prevent a glut of services in the economy.
   b. encourage people to work a shorter week.
6. The economist hopes that there will be a renewal of
   a. interaction between people and machines.
   b. the family unit.
7. As people have become better at business
   a. their families have prospered.
   b. they have lost interest in raising families.

Critical Listening

Listen to the interview again. The economist tries to present a balanced argument, taking a position neither strongly for nor against automation. How does she accomplish this?

Discussion

As the production of goods becomes more and more automated, do you think there will be a big change in our lives and attitudes? Are you as concerned about this possibility as the economist in the interview? Will it really have a bad effect on the people who work full time with machines?

UNIT 9 Reading

THE FINAL INTERVIEW

1 Rena got up and paced the room for the third time, staring at bright enamel paintings that broke up the monotony of the white walls. Why was it taking so long? She looked around her. The room was crowded with people, mostly women, waiting for the same interview she was waiting for. Rena reached for her makeup kit at the bottom of her purse and looked into its mirror. It was important to look healthy, she thought. She tossed the kit back into her purse. How much longer would they make her wait? She'd already been waiting six months for an answer.

2 A tall, slender woman came into the room and marched straight to the outer doors. Her face told everything. She had been denied a license. Rena watched her as the tinted glass doors slid open and she disappeared through the doorway. "What's she so upset about?" Rena wondered. "In six months she can try again. She's just a girl. She's got plenty of time to try for a license." Rena looked down at her own hands. She was thirty-four and her hands had lost their girlish prettiness. If she didn't get a license this time, she would not be allowed to apply again.

3 A man in a smartly tailored suit pushed the door open.

4 "Mrs. Rena Reddick?"

5 The man smiled at her. "This way, Mrs. Reddick." They walked down long, narrow corridors. As they passed doorway after doorway, Rena could hear the murmuring of voices inside. Question and answer, query and explanation. Rena did not look forward to this interview. She and her husband Brandon had passed the physical and psychiatric examinations with ease. But the final interview was the determining factor and she knew they would ask questions that might be painful to answer.

6 They stepped into a room whose broad, tinted windows opened out to the city panorama and gave the room a soft, comfortable glow. She was given a chair facing a long table. Two men and a woman sat at the table, sifting through piles of paper. Rena saw the woman press a button and knew that, as always, the conversation would be recorded.

7 "Mrs. Reddick, I am Glen Taylor. This is Jon Culbertson and this is

Linda Timms. Congratulations! Not many couples make it even this far. Your previous examinations seem to be in good order. However, there are a few questions we need to ask before the final determination can be made."

8 Rena swallowed hard. "I can understand that."

9 "Good. Then let's get started. This is your first application for a license, isn't it?"

10 "No, my second."

11 "Oh, your second . . ." Rena saw Ms. Timms lean across the table and point to a slip of paper. Mr. Taylor read it quickly. "Yes, I see. You applied for one six years ago and were denied. Is that right?"

12 Rena looked at her hands again. "Yes."

13 The interviewers murmured among themselves for some time. Then the woman spoke.

14 "Mrs. Reddick, it says here that your husband is presently piloting mission transports to Gamma III. Is that correct?"

15 Rena nodded.

16 "That must keep him away from home for long periods of time. How long is he usually gone?"

17 "Ten months, but he's been offered a moon shuttle position at the port. If we get the license, he plans to accept the job."

18 "And how long would he be gone then?"

19 "Three days at a time."

20 The woman nodded and made a note on the paper she held in her hand. Then she smiled at her. "I take it you wouldn't mind seeing more of him?"

21 Rena chuckled and began to relax a bit. "Not at all," she said emphatically.

22 Again, the interviewers conversed quietly among themselves. Rena watched their faces anxiously. The first man, Mr. Taylor, turned to her with a broad smile.

23 "Congratulations again, Mrs. Reddick. Your application has been approved. You can pick up your license at the computer station before you leave today. The computer will also give you the name of your attending physician for the term of your pregnancy. You understand, of course, that you will only be allowed to have one natural child because of your age, don't you?"

24 Rena fought back tears of relief. "Y-yes," she stammered.

25 "You should know, then, that having one natural child improves your chances of adopting another, if you're interested."

26 "Yes. Yes, thank you." Rena found her handkerchief and blotted her eyes before her makeup ran. The young man appeared silently at the door and Rena followed him out into the corridor. He showed her to the waiting room and then called out the name of another woman and disappeared through the inner doors again. Rena went to the computer station and punched her number into the machine. The machine did not respond for a minute, then rapidly began to print out her maternity license on the terminal.

27 "Congratulations. You're very lucky." A woman sitting near the terminal spoke to her.

28 "Thank you very much," she responded. Then, with her license carefully tucked into her wallet, she turned to the others in the room. "Good luck," she said happily. And then the silent doors slid open and she was gone.

Words and Expressions

sifting (through): looking carefully (through)
couples: married people, husbands and wives
it says here . . . : I see, according to these papers, it says in these papers . . .

Comprehension Checkup

Complete this summary of the story in your own words.

Rena had an appointment for an interview at an agency that . . . . She was very nervous because . . . . The three interviewers asked her about . . . and about her husband's job. They seemed concerned that he . . . , but Rena explained that . . . . Finally, the interviewers told Rena . . . . She picked up her license and left, feeling . . . .

Making Inferences

Which of the following statements can be inferred from the story? Write *right* or *wrong* for each one. The numbers in parentheses refer to the paragraphs where the inferences are made.

_____ 1. This is a fictional story that is supposed to take place sometime in the future.

_____ 2. When Rena was waiting for her interview, she was nervous and impatient. (1)

_____ 3. Rena had to wait in the room for over three hours before her interview began. (1)

_____ 4. Rena's husband, Brandon, is a spaceship pilot. (14)

_____ 5. Brandon's change of job did not affect the interviewers' decision. (17-20)

_____ 6. Glen Taylor, Jon Culbertson and Linda Timms are doctors. (6-7)

_____ 7. Rena wanted to have a baby very much. (24-28)

Vocabulary Building

For each word listed below, choose the best meaning. If you are not sure of the meaning, read the paragraph the word comes from again and try to guess the meaning from context. The numbers in parentheses refer to the paragraphs where the words can be found.

1. paced (1): **a.** left **b.** looked around **c.** walked around

2. murmuring (5): **a.** arguing **b.** singing **c.** quiet talking

3. query (5): **a.** question **b.** statement **c.** accusation

4. chuckled (21): **a.** sighed sadly **b.** frowned **c.** laughed lightly and quietly

Discussion Topics

1. Do you think the things suggested in the story about the future could actually happen?

2. Aside from the idea of population control, what other things might happen in the future that would be vastly different from our present way of life? Discuss your ideas.

3. Do you think people will have more choices or fewer choices in the future? Consider things such as jobs, transportation, housing, shopping, etc. Will life be simpler or more complex? Give your ideas.

Writing Topics

1. Make a list of ten important new developments (discoveries, inventions, new technology, etc.) that could take place between now and the year 2000. Use your imagination.

2. Make a list of some of the inventions and discoveries of the 20th century that would seem strange and unbelievable to someone who was alive in 1850.

3. Write a story describing a day in the life of a person who will be alive in the year 2100. Give the person a specific job or role in life (business executive, teacher, doctor, parent, student, etc.).

4. You are a history professor living in the year 2500 and you have been asked to write a short article about what life was like back in 1982. In your article, comment on what kind of transportation, communication and entertainment people had.

Unit 10

WNYN news investigated what happens to people accused of committing a crime.

CRIME AND

1 What is this a picture of?
What era is the picture from?
Are people ever hanged in your country?

2 Where was this picture taken?
Does this look like a comfortable room?

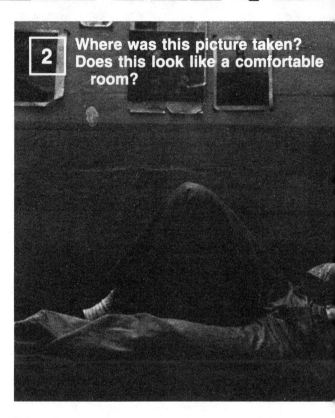

If you had been alive 200 years ago and had stolen a few loaves of bread, you would have gone to prison. If you had killed someone, something far worse would have happened to you. You would have been hanged in public. Life was hard and often brutal. So was the law. Maybe it had to be. If you had lived in a large city, and if you had walked through the streets at night, someone might have killed you just to get your money.

Ask and Answer

a. You are interviewing an expert on crime. You know that:
  1. people were hanged in public 200 years ago; ask why
  2. something happened to people who stole; ask why
  3. the law was hard; ask why
  4. things happened to people who walked through the streets at night; ask what

b. Now tell someone else what would have happened to them 200 years ago if:
  1. they had stolen some bread
  2. they had killed someone
  3. they had walked through the streets at night

Prisons have improved a great deal in the last 200 years. Most prisons used to have very low standards of health. If you had been a health inspector 150 years ago and had been sent out on an inspection tour of prisons, you would have been shocked by the lack of cleanliness in handling food. If, on your tour, you had dared to eat a meal in one of the prisons, you would probably have gotten a bad case of food poisoning. Worse than that, if you had entered some of the prison cells to talk to inmates, you would probably have become a victim of some terrible infection or disease. All that has changed now in most prisons and today there are regulations and controls to make sure that proper health standards are being met. But even with the many improvements, conditions in prisons are far from perfect. There are some people who say, "Why should criminals have such good treatment and be so comfortable? They shouldn't have broken the law in the first place!"

PUNISHMENT

Ask and Answer
Find out:

1. if prisons have improved any in the last 200 years
2. what kind of standards of cleanliness prisons used to have
3. what would probably have happened if you had been a health inspector
4. how all that has changed
5. if conditions are perfect now
6. what some people say about the treatment of prisoners

3 | Have you ever been in an automobile accident?

The driver of this car had been to a party before the accident happened. He had had a lot to drink. Driving home, he suddenly lost control of the car and ran into a bus stop and then a wall. Luckily, nobody was standing there. A bus had come by a minute earlier and picked up ten people. In other words, if the accident had happened only a minute before, the man might have killed ten people. Of course, if the driver had not drunk so much, the accident would not have happened at all.

The driver did not know the accident was going to happen or that he would hit the bus stop. But what should the law have done if he had killed someone? Would the man have been a murderer?

Ask and Answer

a. Interview a police officer who saw the accident. You know that:
   1. the man had been somewhere; ask where
   2. he had had something to drink; ask how much
   3. he was going somewhere; ask where
   4. he ran into the bus stop; ask why
   5. nobody was killed; ask why
   6. something might have happened if the bus hadn't come along; ask what

b. Ask the police officer:
   1. if ten people would definitely have been killed
   2. if the man knew what was going to happen

c. How would you answer the two questions about the law at the end of the reading?

Grammar

1 **...eal conditionals**

...loaves of bread, you would have gone

A. Comment

1. In the *if* clause, you use the past perfect (*had* + past participle) to talk about the past.
2. In the other clause, use *would have (done)* to talk about the past.
3. The *if* clause gives the reason for the event in the other clause.

B. Practice

Combine these pairs of sentences into one sentence using the past unreal conditional.

Example:
I got up late. Therefore, I missed the bus.
If I hadn't gotten up late, I wouldn't have missed the bus.

1. I missed the bus. Therefore, I was late for work.
2. I was late for work. My boss got angry.
3. My boss got angry. That's why he shouted at me.
4. He shouted at me. Then I shouted back at him.
5. I shouted back at him. Consequently, I lost my job.
6. I lost my job. Then I didn't have any money.
7. I didn't have any money. Therefore, I didn't pay the rent.
8. I got into a lot of trouble. Consequently, I came to see you.

C. Transfer

Two weeks ago you went out without an umbrella, got wet, caught a cold and stayed in bed for a week. One day when you were home, a burglar tried to break in. You called the police and they caught him. See how many sentences you can make from the story, beginning "If I hadn't . . . , I . . . " Can you think of a story of your own?

2 **Past with *might, may* or *should* have (done)**

They shouldn't have broken the law in the first place.
Someone might have killed you just to get your money.

A. Comment

1. In these sentences, *might have (done)* and *may have (done)* show that an action was possible in the past, but it did not happen.
2. *Should have (done)* is simply the past *should*. It makes a judgment. It means that the speaker thinks something would have been a good idea.

B. Practice

Make judgments about past actions using *should (not) have* and give your reasons using *may/might have*.

Example:
I drove very fast, but I didn't have an accident.
Yes, but you *might have had* an accident. That's why you *shouldn't have driven* so fast.

1. I ran out into the street without looking and nothing happened to me.
2. I didn't set the alarm clock and I didn't oversleep the next morning.
3. They built the house with very cheap materials, but it didn't fall down.
4. I didn't lock my car last night and it wasn't stolen.
5. I shouted at the boss, but she didn't fire me.
6. I ate a whole cake last night, but I didn't get sick.

C. Discussion

What things in your past do you think you should or should not have done? How might your life have changed if you had or hadn't done them?

wish — indirect command.
- Mr. Smith suggests that all leaves be cancelled.
  vacations

3 | Continuous conditional

He *was driving* so fast that he *lost* control of the car.

If he *hadn't been driving* so fast, he *wouldn't have lost* control of the car.

He *was* in a hurry; that's why he *was driving* so fast.

If he *hadn't been* in a hurry, he *wouldn't have been driving* so fast.

A. Practice

Transform these pairs of sentences into single sentences, using *if*. (See example above.)

1. I was standing there. That's why I saw the accident.
2. He was driving fast. That's why he had an accident.
3. He was drunk. That's why he was driving dangerously.
4. A police officer was driving by. She saw the accident.
5. She left work early. That's why she was driving by.
6. The man didn't know about the police officer. That's why he was driving fast.

B. Transfer

You saw the accident at the bus stop because you were standing on the corner buying flowers. You were on your way to your parents' house when you saw a man selling roses. It was your mother's birthday. She had invited you for dinner. The accident upset you and so you forgot to pick up her birthday present at the jewelry store.

See how many sentences you can make from this situation, beginning "If . . . hadn't . . . , . . . wouldn't have. . . ."

C. Discussion

Have you ever seen or been in a car accident? Describe what happened and tell how it would have been different if. . . .

4 | Future in the past

He didn't know the accident *was going* to happen or that he *would hit* the bus stop.

A. Comment

1. There is little difference in meaning between *was/were going to do* and *would do*.
2. *Was/were going to do* and *would do* are used as future in the past. "Future in the past" here means that, at the point in the past that we are referring to, the event is in the future; but looking back from the present, it is in the past. (If the man got into his car at 3:00 yesterday, and the accident was at 3:30, then at 3:00 yesterday the accident was still in the future—but now, it is in the past.)

B. Situation

Read this story:
The sun was shining when I got up that morning, so I decided to go for a walk in the country. I walked for about two miles. Then suddenly black clouds covered the sun. It began to rain. I stood under a tree. Suddenly lightning struck the tree. I was not hurt, but I was scared. I began to run. I ran across a small bridge over a stream. The bridge collapsed and I fell into the stream. I got terribly wet and muddy. I took a bus home and the bus broke down. I caught a cold and decided that I would never take a walk in the country again.

1. Make as many sentences as you can from this story, beginning, "I had no idea (or I didn't know) that . . . was going to (or would). . . ."
2. Now make sentences beginning, "If I had known that . . . was going to . . . , I would never have. . . ."

C. Discussion

Can you tell or write a story about a series of unfortunate things that happened to you? If you can, then use it to make a number of sentences beginning, "I didn't know . . . " or "If I'd known. . . ."

UNIT 10 Dialog/Communication Practice

DIALOG 📼

Listen to the dialog and complete Margaret's part.

MARGARET: Hi, Peggy. (1) ▒▒▒▒▒ ?

PEGGY: To tell you the truth, I'm not sure . . . How was the meeting?

MARGARET: Huh! Oh, (2) ▒▒▒▒▒ by satellite. If I'd known (3) ▒▒▒▒▒ , I (4) ▒▒▒▒▒ else. Actually, (5) ▒▒▒▒▒ .

PEGGY: Well, it sure wasn't boring around here!

MARGARET: (6) ▒▒▒▒▒ , huh?

PEGGY: Uh-huh. A lot of phone calls, your boss on the intercom, people in and out of the office all afternoon! You know, I recommend you ask for an assistant. I don't see how you handle it all by yourself.

MARGARET: Oh, it's (7) ▒▒▒▒▒ . Anything (8) ▒▒▒▒▒ ?

PEGGY: You've got a bunch of messages here. How about going over them together? I'm not sure you'd be able to figure out my notes.

MARGARET: (9) ▒▒▒▒▒ .

PEGGY: Boy! I'd sure like to know what's been going on in Mr. Russo's office!

MARGARET: Well, (10) ▒▒▒▒▒ ?

PEGGY: All the people he's been meeting with! Practically everybody on the staff!

MARGARET: You mean, . . . he (11) ▒▒▒▒▒ ?

PEGGY: Well, Grace Lee was in there—a long time . . . Then, Mr. Benson . . . And, let's see . . . Uh . . . Oh, yes! Tom Hackett from Personnel. He was in twice—once by himself, then later with his secretary.

MARGARET: Barbara?

PEGGY: Uh-huh. I guess she was taking dictation. I heard her tell Mr. Russo she'd get . . . whatever it was . . . typed up right away.

MARGARET: (12) ▒▒▒▒▒ . . .

PEGGY: Yeah. I could have done it for him. Why do you suppose he had Barbara come up?

MARGARET: (13) ▒▒▒▒▒ . . .

PEGGY: Anyway, later he called David Denton in and spent a long time with him. Then after he left, Grace Lee went in again. What do you suppose, uh . . .

MARGARET: Gosh, (14) ▒▒▒▒▒ .

PEGGY: I'm really curious now. Why don't you ask Grace about it? I would sure like to find out.

MARGARET: Hmm. Maybe (15) ▒▒▒▒▒ . Well, anyway, (16) ▒▒▒▒▒ . Anything (17) ▒▒▒▒▒ ?

(After Peggy leaves, Margaret goes to Grace Lee's office.)

MARGARET: Uh . . . Grace? (18) ▒▒▒▒▒ ?

GRACE: Oh, no. Come in, Margaret. How was the seminar?

MARGARET: It (19) ▒▒▒▒▒ . Sounds like (20) ▒▒▒▒▒ . Peggy (21) ▒▒▒▒▒ that—

GRACE: Oh, it's been quite an afternoon!

MARGARET: Grace? Uh . . . What's (22) ▒▒▒▒▒ ?

Peggy's (23) ▒▒▒▒▒ —

GRACE: Uh . . . Close the door, Margaret. Well, for one thing, David got a promotion. He really deserves it. He's now a full-fledged reporter.

MARGARET: (24) ▒▒▒▒▒ ? (25) ▒▒▒▒▒ !

GRACE: Wait. There's . . . there's something else. Uh, . . . well, it's not very pleasant. We had to make a very painful decision today. And uh . . . well, this is strictly confidential. I suggest you not discuss it with anybody—at least not for a few days. Uh . . . Bob, . . . that is, we, decided that . . . uh . . .

COMMUNICATION PRACTICE

Making Informal Suggestions

How about going over them together?
Why don't you ask Grace about it?
Let's get back to the phone messages.

Comment

In using *let's do* (something), the speaker also intends to do it *(let's = let us . . .)*. With the other two informal suggestion forms, the speaker may or may not intend to do it.

> Why *don't* (we, you, they)/Why *doesn't* (he, she) *do* (something)?
> How about (my, your, his, her, our, their) *doing* (something)?

Situation

You are on a trip with a friend. What suggestions could you make in the following cases:

1. your friend's back hurts
2. your friend's suitcase is lost
3. your friend is exhausted
4. your friend is hungry
5. your friend's passport is lost
6. your friend finds a very expensive gold watch

Transfer

You and your friends are going to have a party. Make suggestions about what to do for the party.

Making Formal Suggestions

I	recommend	you	(not) ask for an assistant.
	suggest	he	
		she	
		we	
		they	

Comment

Note that the verb in the dependent clause (. . . *you ask for* . . .) is the simple form for all persons and tenses. The negative is made with *not* + the simple form.

Situation

You are a doctor and you are making suggestions to someone whose wife/husband has been very ill. Using *I recommend* or *I suggest*, tell what his/her wife/husband should/ should not do.

Examples:
quit smoking
I strongly recommend that your husband quit smoking.

not get excited
I suggest that he not get excited.

1. not read the newspaper
2. sit in the sun every day
3. learn to swim
4. lose 20 pounds
5. make new friends
6. retire
7. do some work around the house
8. make out his will

Transfer

Your boss has asked for suggestions on how to improve work efficiency and morale on the job. Make some suggestions.

LISTENING

In this interview, a judge talks about a recent case that came before him.

Getting Ready to Listen

1. Why do people steal?
2. Should a person who has no job and steals to feed his or her family be punished?
3. Do you think that serving a prison term helps to "correct" criminals and make them good citizens?

Vocabulary

cases: [in a court of law] actions or suits involving legal proceedings
breaking into: entering illegally
muddied: unclear, confusing
brought testimony: presented evidence
sentence: declare a judgment against, pass judgment on, order someone to undergo punishment [the judge addresses the convicted person and says, "I sentence you to five years in prison."]

Now listen to the interview.

Comprehension Checkup

Choose the phrase that correctly completes each statement, based on the interview.

1. One of the judge's recent cases was that of a man who
   a. was accused of stealing some money.
   b. had broken into the judge's house.
2. The man admitted that he had committed the crime
   a. to get some money to feed his family.
   b. but there were no witnesses.

3. He had tried to get a job somewhere, but
   a. there weren't any.
   b. the employment agencies had too many other applicants.
4. The man had been in prison before
   a. because he was unemployed.
   b. for a different crime.
5. The judge thinks that some people
   a. should be put in prison for a long time to be kept away from society.
   b. need to go back to prison several times to learn a lesson.
6. The interviewer wonders what good it does to put the man in jail
   a. when he is in such need.
   b. since he committed only a minor crime.

Listening for Tone

Listen to the interview again. Pay particular attention to what the interviewer says. Is the interviewer convinced that the judge's argument and decision were correct?

Discussion

How do you feel about the case the judge was talking about? Do you think that the circumstances (needing money to feed his children, not being able to find a job, etc.) should have been taken into consideration more?

What about the Victims?

"Crime does not pay . . ."

1   That used to be the traditionally held view about breaking the law. It means that the consequences of crime are far worse than the benefits. But with all the laws set up to protect the criminal today, that's not the case anymore. Sometimes it seems that the only people who pay for crime are the victims.

A violent crime occurs every 31 seconds . . .

2   According to Federal Bureau of Investigation figures, in a twenty-four-hour period, there will be 53 murders, 1,400 assaults and 180 cases of rape in the United States. And the rate of these crimes continues to grow. Part of the reason these crime rates continue to grow is that the criminal justice system doesn't seem to be handing out justice.

3   "It's an old saying around here that the victim of a crime is actually victimized twice: once by the criminal and once by the criminal justice system," says the head of an agency that helps victims of crime. This agency has put together a book entitled *The Criminal Injustice System,* which notes that the criminal has only a 20-percent chance of being arrested.

4   If criminals are arrested, they are advised of their legal rights and given medical treatment if they require it. If they can't afford to hire their own attorney, one is given to them at the government's expense. They then get a hearing and bail is set. If their bail is paid, they are released and told to appear on the set trial date.

5   The trial itself offers a number of options to the criminal. The defense has the right to answer the charges that have been made, prove certain evidence to be inadmissible and postpone the trial's proceedings.

What about the victims?

6   The victims, on the other hand, are usually expected to pay their own medical bills or bills for any property damaged during the crime. They are often required to give up time at work to aid in the investigation and generally are not informed as to how the case is going.

7   The victims may be required to go through detailed, and often painful, descriptions of the crime and then face the cross-examination of the defense attorney. The victims are kept outside the courtroom until their testimony is called for. And should the victims dislike the decision of the court, they can make no protest. They have no right of appeal.

8   Many victims of crime are bitter about their experience in court. Said the mother of a 16-year-old murder victim, "The defense attorney was so much sharper than our district attorney. I felt I should have hired my own lawyer." In her case, the murderer of her daughter was given a reduced charge from second-degree murder to manslaughter, and was given a sentence of seven to twenty-one years in prison. He will be eligible for parole in six.

9   For the victims who survive the crimes, their suffering is often more than bitterness. A 50-year-old woman, who offered a ride to a teenage boy she knew, was raped and beaten with the butt of a gun. The incident nearly cost her one of her eyes and to this day she suffers headaches, dizziness and pain. She can no longer keep a job. The boy was sentenced to 11 to 23 months in prison.

10   It would be reassuring to think that these cases are rare. But it isn't that way at all. All too often, it seems, the criminal is afforded every loophole the law can provide. And the victim must live with the tragedy of the incident and the injustice of the outcome of the trial.

11   Clearly, major changes in the criminal justice system are needed and, with the support of the victim-witness advocate agencies, they are being demanded. These agencies help the victims of crime to cut through red tape and understand the proceedings of the system. They also offer counseling for victims of violent crime and their families. But even this is not enough to ensure that victims of crime will receive justice.

12   Judge Lois G. Forer of Philadelphia suggests that non-dangerous criminals be forced to make restitution of their victims. This would involve the court in deciding on a dollar amount that must be paid to the victim, and then forcing the criminal to take a job and make the necessary payment. "It has often been said that the wallet is the tenderest part of the anatomy," she commented.

Much of the problem lies in social attitudes . . .

13   It is the accepted belief that once an offender is caught, convicted and put in jail, that is enough. This is no longer proving to be an adequate answer. The simple knowledge that most criminals who serve time in prison will be released only to repeat the crime or go on to more serious crimes tells us clearly that the penal system is merely an expensive holding ground for criminals. It is inadequate in curbing criminal tendencies.

What can be done about the present system?

14   It is only through public demand that some protection will be afforded to the victims of crime. It is only through public demand that legal reforms will be made to ensure that criminals pay adequately and fairly for their crimes. Being silent and passive about the unfairness and persecution dealt to the victims of crime by the present criminal justice system may result in us all becoming victims one day.

Words and Expressions

Federal Bureau of Investigation: in the United States, the police department of the federal government, concerned with enforcement of federal laws and national security

handing out: giving, dispensing

gets a hearing: gets a chance to be heard (in a court of law)

inadmissible: not allowed, not acceptable for consideration

right of appeal: right to ask that a case be reviewed by a higher court of law

parole: release from prison before (one's) term is up, early release from prison

cut through the red tape: overcome obstacles created by complicated forms and regulations

wallet . . . tenderest part of the anatomy: (figurative) having to pay money (for damages) is the most painful thing

Comprehension Checkup

Are these statements *true* or *false*, based on the reading?

_____ **1.** Crime is on the increase because the criminal justice system isn't working very well.

_____ **2.** If a criminal doesn't have enough money to hire an attorney, he/she must represent himself/herself at the trial.

_____ **3.** In court, the victim seems to have more rights than the person accused of committing the crime.

_____ **4.** Some victims are bitter because the punishment given to criminals often seems light in comparison to the crime they committed.

_____ **5.** People have traditionally thought that catching criminals and putting them in prison is all society needs to do.

_____ **6.** People should be active in pursuing changes in the criminal justice system.

Finding Information

Find the paragraph(s) in which each of these topics is discussed. Write the paragraph numbers in the blanks.

_____ **1.** statistics on the crime rate
_____ **2.** the rights of criminals
_____ **3.** the responsibilities of victims
_____ **4.** help available to victims
_____ **5.** inadequacy of prisons as a solution

Vocabulary Building

Find a word in the reading to match each of the definitions below. The numbers in parentheses refer to the paragraphs where the answers can be found.

1. attacks (2)
2. money paid to a court to free a prisoner until his or her trial (4)
3. delay (5)
4. a formal statement that something is true (7)
5. filled with hate, anger or sorrow (8)
6. more intelligent (8)
7. a way of avoiding something (10)
8. payment for damage (12)
9. controlling (13)

Discussion Topics

1. In most countries of the world, including the United States, there is little or no crime in rural areas. How do you explain this? Why is there this difference between urban areas and rural areas?

2. What influence do you think television programs about crime and violence have on viewers, particularly younger viewers? Do you think the long-term effect of these programs is negative?

3. Some people believe that publicity in newspapers and on TV and radio about crime and criminals has the effect of encouraging more crime. For example, newspaper headlines and articles about airplane hijackings may encourage other individuals to do the same thing. Do you agree? Why or why not?

Writing Topics

1. Why I believe (or don't believe) in capital punishment. (Write several paragraphs giving reasons for your views on the question of the death penalty for criminals.)

2. What life in prison would be like. (Use your imagination and describe the thoughts and feelings you think a person would have in prison, what things you would miss about life outside, how your attitudes might change, etc.)

3. Crime doesn't pay. (Write a short story about somebody who breaks the law and gets into trouble; describe the effect this has on the person and the person's family and try to get across the point to your readers that "crime doesn't pay.")

THE WORLD OF ADVERTISING

1

Don't you want me to get that promotion? Don't you want my shirts to be whiter than anybody else's?

Of course I do, darling. Please don't shout at me! It isn't my fault I can't get your shirts any whiter!

2

I'd advise you to use new MIRACLE GLEEM. It's much better than ordinary laundry detergents.

3

I got that promotion today, darling, and all because of you!

(thinks) No, darling. All because of new GLEEM!

WNYN did a show on advertisements. Here is one of them. Is it typical?

A few months ago, Mr. and Mrs. Smith had a big problem. He had a chance to get a promotion at work. Naturally, she wanted him to get it. She wanted him to look his best and to make a really good impression at work. She worked very hard to make his clothes look clean, but in spite of all her hard work, she could never get his shirts as white as she wanted them to be.

Ask and Answer
a. Describe:
   1. the chance Mr. Smith had
   2. what Mrs. Smith wanted him to do
   3. their problem

b. Now ask questions beginning with "Did she want her husband to . . . ?" plus these phrases:

   1. that promotion
   2. his best at all times
   3. a good impression at work
   4. shirts that weren't really white
   5. shout at her

Then one day, a good friend happened to visit Mrs. Smith. She told her how to solve the problem. "I'd advise you to use new Miracle Gleem! It's much better than ordinary laundry detergents," she said.

Ask and Answer
Find out:
   1. who visited Mrs. Smith
   2. what she advised her to do
   3. why

So Mrs. Smith took her friend's advice. Now Mr. Smith's shirts are as white as he wants them to be and his company wants him to be their new sales manager. And now Mrs. Smith wants him to get an even better job. She wants him to become president of the company. She knows he can do it, with the help of Gleem.

Ask and Answer
Find out:
   1. if Mrs. Smith took her advice
   2. what Mr. Smith's shirts are like now
   3. what his company wants him to do
   4. what Mrs. Smith wants him to do
   5. if she thinks it's possible

4 | Is this man strong or weak?
Do you think he's attractive?

Hello. My name's Bill Pepper. Only a few years ago, I was a weakling. In spite of my pleasant personality and high intelligence, I was miserable. People laughed at me. But now, because of the Tom Buster Body-Building Course, my life has changed. Let me tell you about it; it could change your life too!

Ask and Answer

a. Working with a partner, ask and answer questions about each picture like, "What is happening here?" "Why is Bill angry?" or "What is . . . saying?"

b. Now tell the whole story in this advertisement. Begin with "One day Bill was lying on the beach with . . . when . . . "

UNIT 11 Grammar

1 Want + object + infinitive

Naturally, she *wanted him to get* the promotion

A. Comment

The verb *want* can be followed by an object and an infinitive (*to* + base form of verb).

B. Situation

For each picture below say what the little boy wants someone else to do.

Example: "I'm hungry."

He wants his mother to feed him.

1.

"Up."

2.

"Down."

3.

"Spoon."

4.

"Here, kitty."

5.

"Story."

6.

"Water."

7.

"Throw."

8.

"Kiss."

C. Discussion

Some of these verbs can be used in place of the verb *want* in sentences like the ones in 1B; some cannot. Make a list of those that can.

advise/suggest/beg/get/order/insist/expect/tell/ask/plan/hope/allow/demand/permit/force/suppose.

Answers:

advise, beg, get, order, expect, tell, ask, allow, permit, force.

Now make a sentence about you and your parents with each verb.

2 What + infinitive

Her friend *told* her what *to use*.

A. Pattern

Someone	told advised showed	me you him her it us them	what how when where which	to + verb

B. Situation

Suppose you are Mrs. Smith's friend and she asked you some questions. For each of Mrs. Smith's questions given below, say what you did.

A: Which laundry detergent should I use? Can you advise me?

B: I *advised* her *which* laundry detergent *to use*.

1. How can I get these shirts clean? Can you tell me?
2. Where can I get Gleem? Please tell me.
3. What should I do? Show me!
4. How long should I leave the shirts in the machine? Tell me.
5. Why should I use Gleem? Can you tell me?
6. Which iron should I buy? Please advise me.

C. Transfer

A friend from another country is visiting you. Yesterday he went into town alone. You couldn't go with him, so you told him how to get there, what to say if he got lost, advised him what to do in town, etc. Make more sentences on your own of the things you told him to do.

84

3 | Shouldn't have (done)
Shouldn't have been (doing)

What do you mean I *shouldn't have kicked* sand in your face?
You *shouldn't have been lying* there.

A. Comment

Should have done is used to express the speaker's opinion that a past action was a good idea. *Should have been doing* is used to express the opinion that an action going on at a particular past time was a good idea.

Compare:

I shouldn't kick sand in your face (at any time).
I shouldn't have kicked sand in your face (in the past).

You shouldn't lie there (at any time).
You shouldn't be lying there (right now).
You shouldn't have been lying there (at a particular moment in the past).

B. Practice

Answer as *B* does.

Examples:
A: I haven't finished the report yet.
B: Really? You *should have finished* it hours ago.

A: I've been working on something else!
B: But you *shouldn't have been working* on something else!

1. I haven't even started on it yet.
2. I haven't fixed my typewriter yet.
3. I was using your phone.
4. I used it yesterday too.
5. And I've been looking through your letters.
6. I've read them.
7. I wasn't listening to your instructions.

C. Transfer

You work in an office. Yesterday the office manager was away, so you, two secretaries and an accountant used her office to have a party without her permission. The office manager came back in the middle of it. You weren't working. You were dancing, eating and drinking. You didn't stop when she came in. Instead, you asked her if she wanted to dance as well. Naturally, she was furious. Describe all the things you should have done, shouldn't have been doing, etc.

4 | In spite of and because of

In spite of my pleasant personality and high intelligence, I was miserable.
Because of the Tom Buster Body-Building Course, my life was changed.

A. Comment

In spite of and *because of* are followed by noun phrases. *In spite of* shows an unexpected contrast between two facts. *Because of* indicates a cause-and-effect relationship between two facts. The *in spite of* and *because of* phrase can go at the beginning of the sentence or at the end. Use a comma if you put it at the beginning. Compare the sentences above with these:

I was miserable in spite of my pleasant personality and high intelligence.
My life was changed because of the Tom Buster Body-Building Course.

B. Practice

Make sentences with either *in spite of* or *because of*.

Examples:
They went out. The weather was bad.
They went out *in spite of* the bad weather.
They didn't go out. The weather was bad.
They didn't go out *because of* the bad weather.

1. His work was good. He didn't get a promotion.
2. His work was good. He got a large raise.
3. Everbody admires him. He has talent.
4. Nobody admires him. He has talent.

C. Transfer

You are telling someone that you like your job. Make sentences beginning with "I like my job because of/in spite of" plus the following:

1. The hours are long.
2. The people are pleasant.
3. The pay is low.
4. The work is interesting.
5. The management is efficient.
6. The benefits are good.
7. The work is demanding.
8. The vacations are long.
9. The chances for advancement are excellent.
10. The office is too crowded.

UNIT 11 Dialog/Communication Practice

DIALOG

Listen to the dialog and complete Margaret's part.

DAVID: Hey, why the long face? We're supposed to be celebrating, . . . remember? Aren't you happy about my promotion?

MARGARET: Yes, David . . . (1) ▨▨▨▨ that—

DAVID: Now I'm going to get a chance to do my own programs! I won't have some reporter telling me what to do. "I want this scene taken, David!" "I want this job done right away, David!"

MARGARET: Oh, David, (2) ▨▨▨▨! Marsha's (3) ▨▨▨▨! And (4) ▨▨▨▨ reporter—the (5) ▨▨▨▨! It (6) ▨▨▨▨!

DAVID: What do you mean "see her leave"?

MARGARET: I mean "leave"—lose (7) ▨▨▨▨! (8) ▨▨▨▨? They're (9) ▨▨▨▨!

DAVID: What? You're not serious!

MARGARET: (10) ▨▨▨▨ about it. I (11) ▨▨▨▨.

DAVID: I can't believe it! Why would she get fired?

MARGARET: (12) ▨▨▨▨, David!

DAVID: Me?! How should I know anything about it?

MARGARET: (13) ▨▨▨▨ wondering. What (14) ▨▨▨▨?

DAVID: What are you talking about?

MARGARET: Well, right after (15) ▨▨▨▨, she wanted (16) ▨▨▨▨ confirm (17) ▨▨▨▨.

DAVID: So?

MARGARET: So, I (18) ▨▨▨▨! The interview (19) ▨▨▨▨ that Friday. Marsha (20) ▨▨▨▨.

DAVID: She must have gotten mixed up. The time was changed to 11:00 A.M.

MARGARET: Really? And (21) ▨▨▨▨?

DAVID: Well, uh—

MARGARET: You did, (22) ▨▨▨▨? And (23) ▨▨▨▨!

DAVID: Well, what happened was—

MARGARET: I know. You (24) ▨▨▨▨ and moved (25) ▨▨▨▨ so you (26) ▨▨▨▨, didn't you?

DAVID: Oh, well, what if I did? That was the only way I could prove that I could do the interviewing—that I didn't need Marsha to tell me what to do.

MARGARET: Oh, David, how (27) ▨▨▨▨? What else (28) ▨▨▨▨? (29) ▨▨▨▨ Denver (30) ▨▨▨▨?

DAVID: What about it?

MARGARET: (31) ▨▨▨▨ sure . . . Was (32) ▨▨▨▨?

DAVID: I don't know what you're talking about . . .

MARGARET: (33) ▨▨▨▨ happen that (34) ▨▨▨▨ in time? Did (35) ▨▨▨▨ that?

DAVID: Me?

MARGARET: What did you do—tell (36) ▨▨▨▨, and then (37) ▨▨▨▨ apartment . . . so she (38) ▨▨▨▨?

DAVID: It wasn't like that at all! It was just—I just forgot to pick her up—that's all. It was as simple as that. I completely forgot!

MARGARET: Why (39) ▨▨▨▨? He (40) ▨▨▨▨ before you two (41) ▨▨▨▨! No, . . . I (42) ▨▨▨▨. I think (43) ▨▨▨▨ . . . But why? That's (44) ▨▨▨▨.

DAVID: It was my big chance! I knew I could do the job and I had to prove it.

MARGARET: (45) ▨▨▨▨ yourself! How does (46) ▨▨▨▨ that you're (47) ▨▨▨▨ job?

DAVID: I didn't mean any harm to Marsha. I certainly didn't want her to lose her job! I just wanted a chance to show Bob what I could do!

MARGARET: (48) ▨▨▨▨, . . . (49) ▨▨▨▨!

COMMUNICATION PRACTICE

Asking for More Details

Margaret wasn't satisfied with David's explanation about the Denver trip. She wanted more information. She asked:

> How did it happen that Marsha didn't get to the airport in time?

Comment

Margaret was suspicious. She thought David might have had something to do with Marsha's missing the plane to Denver. When she asked "How did it happen that . . . ?" she was trying to get to the bottom of the airport incident. Speakers use a number of different ways of getting more information, depending on the circumstances; for example:

> How did it happen that . . .?
> How was it that . . . ?
> What reason did he have for . . . ?
> How do you account for the fact that . . . ?
> Why did . . . , in the first place?
> What I don't understand is why . . .

Situation

Listed below are statements made by a number of speakers. Hearing these explanations, you simply can't understand how these things could possibly have happened. What would you say to get a better explanation and clearer understanding?

1. My little boy was hit by a car on the freeway. His bicycle was ruined.
2. He was feeding a lion and it bit him.
3. My aunt broke her leg when she fell off the roof of our house.
4. The wind was so strong that Sarah was nearly blown off the ladder.
5. After missing my flight, I had to wait ten hours for the next one.

Listening UNIT 11

Expressing Surprise or Disbelief

David was surprised when he heard Marsha was losing her job. He said:

> What? You're not serious!
> I can't believe it! Why would she get fired?

Comment

In addition to the expressions used by David, there is a variety of others frequently used to express surprise or disbelief, such as:

> You must be kidding!
> You're kidding!

I (just) can't believe it!
Really?
You can't be serious!
You're joking!

Situation

Talk to someone about what he or she has done in the last few years. If you want more information about certain things, ask for it. If you are surprised by some of the things the person says, express your surprise or disbelief. Then switch roles.

LISTENING

A man from an advertising agency talks about his work.

Getting Ready to Listen

1. Do advertisers tell lies to get people to buy their products?
2. Should the government put pressure on advertisers to keep them honest?
3. Why is so much money spent nowadays producing advertisements? What is their purpose?

Vocabulary

get away with: do (something) one is not supposed to do without suffering any consequences
jump on them: [informal] bring pressure on them
called down: criticized, reprimanded
recant: say in public that one has abandoned a position or opinion
amenities: extra things that bring pleasure, (the) more pleasant things
find its own place: establish itself
staying power: ability to remain (on the market)

Now listen to the interview.

Comprehension Checkup

Choose the phrase that correctly completes each statement, based on the interview.

1. The ad man doesn't think that
   a. advertising is a form of lying.
   b. he has to present evidence to back up advertising claims.

2. Because of the Federal Trade Commission, advertisers
   a. are always honest in their ads.
   b. must often justify the claims they make.
3. In an advertisement, a movie star may say that she uses a certain kind of soap,
   a. and advertisers make sure that she really does use it.
   b. but that doesn't mean she really uses it.
4. The ad man most enjoys
   a. developing new advertisements for old products that people like.
   b. educating people about new products that will make their lives better.
5. We take many amenities for granted now
   a. because advertising encouraged people to try them out.
   b. although we don't really need them.
6. Advertising brings products to people's attention,
   a. but they won't continue to buy the products if they aren't good.
   b. and they will continue to buy the products if the advertising is good.

Critical Listening

Listen to the interview again. Do the interviewer and the advertising man finally agree about lying in advertising?

Discussion

How would you plan and write an advertisement persuading people to buy a new product? Decide on a particular product, such as soap, toothpaste, food, a car, etc., and say what you would do to interest potential buyers.

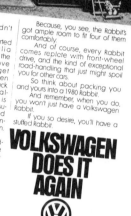

Words and Expressions

skeptical: doubtful, disbelieving
paraphernalia: personal belongings
steamer trunk: a chest for storing or transporting clothes, etc.
bric-a-brac: small objects, miscellaneous things
"knick-a-knack": a toy, something small (The word is actually knickknack. In the ad, it is used as "knick-a-knack" to rhyme with "bric-a-brac.")
in that department: on that subject [informal]
rack and pinion steering: mechanism used to steer and turn the wheels of a car
short-throw: moving a very short distance
stick: gearshift lever [informal]
wide-profile tires: tires with wide treads
front air dam: outside air intake vent

Comprehension Checkup

Check the ad that is designed to appeal to:

	Rabbit	MGB
1. people who want to impress their friends	_____	_____
2. a person with two children	_____	_____
3. a person who is concerned about saving money	_____	_____
4. a mother who often has a lot of shopping to do	_____	_____
5. a man who needs a new car and is depressed about getting older and not enjoying life	_____	_____

Finding Specific Information

Advertisements often present both *objective* and *subjective* qualities of their products. An *objective* quality is one that everyone can agree upon. It is a fact, not a matter of opinion. A *subjective* characteristic reflects the opinion of the advertiser. People may not all agree that it is true.

For example, the Volkswagen Rabbit ad implies that the car is very roomy and that it will hold a lot of things. This is a *subjective* characteristic. A car that is very roomy to one person may seem quite small to another. Another example of subjectivity in the Rabbit ad is the phrase "stylishly compact." People do not agree on what is "stylish," or even on what is "compact." An example of an *objective* characteristic in the Rabbit ad is the statement that the car is large enough to hold a steamer trunk. This is *objective* because we can all try to put a steamer trunk into a Rabbit and see whether the statement is true or not.

Both ads use both subjective and objective qualities. Read both ads and make a list of the *objective facts* in each one.

Rabbit	MGB
_____	_____
_____	_____
_____	_____
_____	_____
_____	_____
_____	_____
_____	_____

Discussion Topics

1. One of the ads presents more objective information than the other. Which one? (Use the information you found in the exercise above.) Why do you think this advertiser chose to present so much objective information?
2. Why do you think advertisers use subjective statements in their ads? Do you think they should be forced to be more objective?

Writing Topics

1. Write an advertisement for a particular brand of soap. Try to appeal to people who are worried about whether people will like them or not.
2. Write a factual advertisement for a car. Compare the car to others that are available.
3. Some people believe that advertising is bad because it creates a need for a product where no need existed before. For example, nobody needs to drink soft drinks, yet many people buy them. Would people buy them if there were no advertising? Do you think this type of advertising is wrong? Why or why not?
4. Do you believe that professionals, such as lawyers, doctors and dentists, should advertise their services? Why or why not?
5. Describe how to make a choice when you buy an expensive product. What factors influence your decision? Do you do research first? To what extent does advertising affect your decision?

UNIT 12 WORK

WNYN interviewed people to find out
what they liked and didn't like about their jobs.

1 — What does this woman do? Do you think she makes a lot of money?

I'm a professional tennis player. Last year I earned $600,000. This year I plan on doing even better. Being a tennis pro isn't an easy life. Sometimes I can't stand having to get up early. And I hate spending so much time away from home. I miss being able to relax and do nothing on weekends. But I like practicing and I really enjoy playing in tournaments. As soon as I start losing too many tournaments, I'll retire. I'm thinking of opening a tennis club. I love helping younger players, but I sure hate losing to them.

Ask and Answer
Find out about:

1. her job
2. the money she earned last year
3. her plans for this year
4. things she can't stand or hates doing
5. things she likes or enjoys doing
6. when she'll retire and what she's thinking of doing

What is this man's job? Do you think he makes a lot of money? — 2

I'm a police officer. Some people don't like the police. They say we stop people from doing what they want. But I like my job. And I think it's very important. When I'm on vacation, I always look forward to getting back to work. A lot of my work is hard and boring, but, in spite of the hard work, I still enjoy being a policeman. I'd never think of doing anything else.

Ask and Answer
Find out:

1. how some people feel about police officers
2. why they feel this way
3. how this policeman feels about his work
4. if he looks forward to getting back to work when he's on vacation
5. if his job is always interesting
6. if he enjoys it
7. if he would like to do something else

What do you think this woman does?
Do you think she's rich?

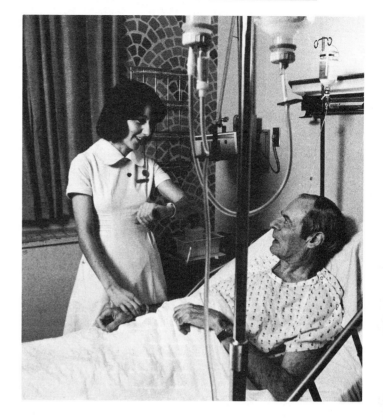

I'm a nurse and I don't earn very much money at all. In fact, I have a lot of difficulty just making ends meet. But I like being a nurse. I guess it's because I enjoy helping people. Being a nurse is hard work. It means working long hours. And sometimes it isn't very pleasant. There are all sorts of things I don't enjoy. For example, I don't enjoy seeing people in pain. It's true that my job is hard, but I'm used to working long hours and I don't mind the psychological pressure that my job puts on me. Being a nurse isn't much fun, but at least I know I'm doing something worthwhile.

Ask and Answer
Find out:
1. about this woman's job
2. about the money she earns
3. if she can make ends meet
4. about the things she likes or enjoys doing
5. if being a nurse is easy
6. about the hours she works
7. if it's always pleasant
8. about the things she doesn't enjoy
9. if she's used to working long hours
10. why she does this kind of work

Is this man rich?
What do you think he does?

I'm a millionaire. In fact, I'm one of the richest people in the world. My father was very poor. I remember his saying, "Someday you'll be a rich man." But now I am rich and people say I'm not a very happy man. I can understand their thinking that. I remember being happy only once in my life. That was just after I'd made my first million. I can still hear my wife saying, "Isn't life wonderful? We're rich!" But having money hasn't solved all our problems. In fact, sometimes I think being rich causes more problems than it solves.

Ask and Answer
Find out:
1. how rich this man is
2. if his father was rich too
3. what he remembers
4. what people say
5. if he understands why
6. if he is happy or can remember ever being happy
7. what he can still hear
8. if having money solves all their problems

UNIT 12 Grammar

1 Verb + gerund

I enjoy playing in tournaments.

A. Pattern

| enjoy
hate
can't stand
like
miss
remember
(don't) mind
stop
love
start | verb + *ing* |

B. Situation

You're a reporter. You're interviewing the tennis player. Ask questions combining the sentences below.

Example:
She met you last year. Ask if she remembers.
Do you remember meeting me last year?

1. She is popular. Ask if she enjoys it.
2. She gives interviews, but she can't stand it. Ask why.
3. In the past, she worried about money. Ask if she has stopped.
4. She doesn't teach yet. Ask when she's going to start.
5. She's recognized wherever she goes. Ask her if she likes that.
6. You want her to help you with your game. Ask if she would mind.

C. Discussion

Think about your childhood. What did you enjoy, hate, like, not like, mind, not mind, etc. doing? What have you stopped doing since then?

2 Gerund form of *can/could* and *must/have to/had to*

I miss being able to relax on weekends.
I hate having to get up early.

A. Comment

To express ability with a gerund form, use *being able to*. To express necessity or obligation with a gerund, use *having to*.

B. Practice

Change these modals to their gerund form when you combine these sentences.

Examples:
She has to give interviews. She can't stand it.
She *can't stand having* to give interviews.
She can do anything she likes. She enjoys this.
She *enjoys being able to* do anything she likes.

1. She has to sleep on planes. She minds this.
2. A long time ago she had to practice eight hours a day. She remembers that.
3. She can go to interesting places. She enjoys this.
4. She had to travel with her mother when she was younger. She didn't enjoy that.
5. She had to work in a drugstore on weekends. She didn't like that.
6. But she could go to the movies every Saturday night. She misses that.
7. She must sign hundreds of autographs every week. She doesn't mind this.
8. She must have her picture taken all the time. She hates this.

C. Discussion

What are some things you enjoy being able to do or don't like having to do?

3 Verb phrase + gerund

A. Comment

I'm used to working long hours.

Notice how verb phrases like *be used to, plan on, put off, think of, have difficulty, have something against, look forward to* and *object to* are followed by gerunds.

B. Practice

Combine these sentences using the gerund.

Example:
That woman is trying to get across the street. She is having difficulty.

That woman *is having difficulty getting* across the street.

1. I'll go back to work soon. I'm looking forward to it.
2. The tennis player doesn't like to talk to reporters. She has something against it.
3. Those students should study for the test right now. They're putting it off.
4. I'm trying to concentrate. I'm having difficulty.
5. I don't want to eat dinner so early. I object to it!
6. Police officers often stand in the same street for hours. They're used to it.

4 Gerunds as subject clauses

Having money hasn't solved all our problems.

A. Comment

Notice how an action can be the subject of a sentence.

B. Practice

Combine these sentences using a gerund phrase for the subject.

Example:
She assists doctors in surgery. It's interesting.
Assisting doctors in surgery is interesting.

1. She sees people die. It isn't pleasant.
2. She is a nurse in a large city hospital. It's good experience.
3. She works long hours without a break. It's very tiring.
4. She comforts the relatives of sick patients. It isn't easy.
5. She works on the maternity ward. It's usually fun.
6. She does all these things. It's worthwhile.

C. Transfer

Now talk about some of the things students do. Say whether you think these things are boring, interesting, tiring, useful, difficult, etc.

Example:
Studying foreign languages is useful.

5 Subject of the gerund

I can understand their thinking that.

A. Comment

The subject of a gerund is usually a possessive noun or pronoun, except after verbs of perception (see, feel, hear, etc.).

B. Pattern

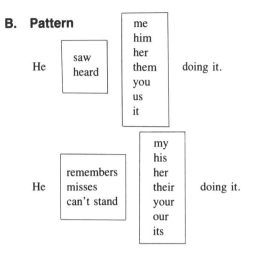

C. Practice

Combine these sentences using the patterns above.

Examples:
He took the time to come see us. We appreciate it.
We appreciate his taking the time to come see us.

I cooked breakfast at 7:00 A.M. They heard me.
They heard me cooking breakfast at 7:00 A.M.

1. I paid for the theater tickets. He objected to it.
2. She talks all the time. Don't you mind it?
3. He takes notes in class. The teacher never sees him.
4. We arrived an hour before the others. They didn't like it.
5. They felt bad about the accident. She understood.
6. She shouted to them from the fourth floor. They didn't hear.
7. The photographers snap pictures of her during tournaments. She can't stand it.

D. Transfer

Yesterday you happened to be in a bank when three people came in and robbed it. One of them hit you over the head so your memory isn't very clear. The police are trying to find out what you remember and don't remember happening. Make sentences using *I remember . . . -ing, . . . but I don't remember anyone . . .* For example, *I remember the robbers coming in . . .* What else do you say?

UNIT 12 Dialog/Communication Practice

DIALOG 🔊

Listen to the dialog and complete Rita's part.

MARSHA: What am I going to do now, Rita? I'll be lost without this job. I've really enjoyed working at WNYN.

RITA: I'll tell you (1) ░░░░! You're (2) ░░░░ and (3) ░░░░ whole story—

MARSHA: But there's nothing to tell. He says I'm not doing the job to their satisfaction. Now, how am I going to argue with that—tell them they're wrong?

RITA: (4) ░░░░ the reason (5) ░░░░ fired—and (6) ░░░░!

MARSHA: Wait a minute. Listen. This is what the letter says, uh . . . "We regret to inform you that after careful evaluation, . . ." and so forth, . . . and so forth, . . . uh . . . Listen . . . "the determination has been made that your job performance over the past 60 days has not been in accordance with the minimum performance standards established by WNYN-TV."

RITA: But, Marsha! (7) ░░░░? Uh . . . what's his name?

MARSHA: You mean, David?

RITA: Yeah, David! (8) ░░░░ interfering with (9) ░░░░! And (10) ░░░░! (11) ░░░░ sabotaging (12) ░░░░!

MARSHA: Now, that's a little strong, isn't it?

RITA: Well, I (13) ░░░░ call it. He's (14) ░░░░ look bad and (15) ░░░░ look good. He's (16) ░░░░, he's (17) ░░░░, he's (18) ░░░░, why, he's, he's just—

MARSHA: He just doesn't like being told what to do! He's a very ambitious young man and he's determined to get ahead as fast as he can. Unfortunately, I just happened to be in the way.

RITA: You've (19) ░░░░ to protect (20) ░░░░! Here's (21) ░░░░, he's (22) ░░░░, he's (23) ░░░░ . . . And (24) ░░░░ because of him. He (25) ░░░░! And (26) ░░░░ for him!

MARSHA: He's very good at his work. I've got to admit that!

RITA: (27) ░░░░! So (28) ░░░░! So what? That (29) ░░░░ all over you and (30) ░░░░! You're (31) ░░░░ too—remember? You're (32) ░░░░. Everybody (33) ░░░░!

MARSHA: Hmm . . . not quite everybody . . . The management at WNYN doesn't—

RITA: But (34) ░░░░! They think (35) ░░░░ job. And (36) ░░░░!

MARSHA: O.K. So what do you want me to do? Go to Bob Russo and say, "Bob, the reason my performance isn't acceptable to you is that David stopped me from doing my job! He just wouldn't let me do my job . . ."?

RITA: No. (37) ░░░░ the details! Tell him (38) ░░░░, saying (39) ░░░░ airport (40) ░░░░. Or, tell him (41) ░░░░ when (42) ░░░░ the appointment time!

And (43) ░░░░ City Hall (44) ░░░░? And (45) ░░░░? And (46) ░░░░ he (47) ░░░░ own?

MARSHA: Bob would just think that I was making excuses and trying to blame David for everything so I wouldn't lose my job. Besides, criticizing David behind his back wouldn't be right—

RITA: (48) ░░░░ back! Tell your boss (49) ░░░░ at the same time! Then (50) ░░░░ or not!

MARSHA: Oh, I'm sure David would be able to give very logical explanations for everything.

RITA: Sure, he'd (51) ░░░░. But (52) ░░░░ a long time and (53) ░░░░. Who (54) ░░░░ boss (55) ░░░░ believe—you (56) ░░░░? Oh, (57) ░░░░ sick! It's (58) ░░░░! That guy's (59) ░░░░!

COMMUNICATION PRACTICE

Giving Strong Advice

Marsha has lost her job and Rita gives her some strong advice:

MARSHA: What am I going to do now, Rita? I'll be lost without this job.

RITA: I'll tell you what you're going to do! You're going to go to your boss and tell him the whole story!

Comment

Marsha and Rita are close friends and, therefore, Rita uses very strong, direct expressions of advice to Marsha. It would not be appropriate for her to use formal expressions, such as "I suggest that . . ." or "I recommend that . . ." The following are other informal expressions that can be used in giving advice to a friend:

What you should do is . . .
What I'd do is . . .
You've got to . . .
You're a fool if you don't . . .

Practice

Have somebody take the role of a friend and make up sentences based on the cues given in the first column below. Then give strong advice based on the cues in the second column.

Example:

Friend	Advice
what do?/wallet/stolen/$100	go to police/report

What should I do? My wallet was stolen and it had $100 in it.

You've got to go to the police and report it.

	Friend	Advice		Friend	Advice
1.	but/already talk/police/do nothing	go to chief of police/complain	**3.**	can't do that/wait/Monday/better	fool/if you wait/never get/wallet
2.	already tried/but chief/not there/until Monday	get telephone number/home/call now	**4.**	not important enough/bother/chief/at home	go back/police station/demand action

LISTENING

Three people talk about their jobs.

Getting Ready to Listen

1. Would you prefer to work in an office under the supervision of somebody else or would you rather work for yourself? Why?
2. What are some of the advantages of working for yourself?
3. What responsibilities does someone in a management position have?
4. What do you think it would be like to work in a factory?

Vocabulary

if your muse is with you: if you are inspired [in Greek mythology, a Muse is a goddess that looks after artists, writers, etc.]

incorporated (into): mixed in (with), blended in (with)

evocation of place: bringing out the image of a particular scene, making up of a setting (for a story)

prestige: status, standing (in the community)

work with figures: deal with bookkeeping, work with records of money transactions

meet the public: deal directly with people (customers)

pretty dull: very boring

Now listen to the interview.

Comprehension Checkup

Choose the phrase that correctly completes each statement, based on the interview.

1. The interesting thing about the author's work is that she
   a. determines what she will write and when.
   b. is able to see her finished work published.
2. Since the author has a small child, she writes
   a. when she can find someone to take care of the child.
   b. when the child is sleeping.

3. The reason that this author doesn't write poetry very much anymore is that
   a. she incorporates poetic images into her writing.
   b. writing popular fiction pays more nowadays.
4. Mrs. Griffin likes her work as a supermarket manager
   a. because it's not too difficult, day-to-day work.
   b. even though it isn't very prestigious.
5. The most important part of her job involves
   a. keeping financial records and inventories.
   b. making sure her employees are happy and productive.
6. It's important for people working in a supermarket to be happy because
   a. if they are unhappy, they might quit.
   b. they won't do a good job otherwise.
7. The factory worker thinks his job is
   a. basically uninteresting.
   b. somewhat dangerous.
8. Once when he was working on the kick press, he
   a. became so tired that he fell asleep.
   b. accidentally put his hand under the press.
9. As a result, he
   a. was given five days off with pay.
   b. was suspended from work for five days.

Listening for Tone

Listen to the interview with the factory worker again. Does the factory worker take his job seriously? Was he upset about his accident?

Discussion

Which of the three jobs discussed in the interviews (author, supermarket manager or factory worker) sounds most interesting to you? What is it about the job that you find interesting?

THE RISE OF AMERICAN LABOR

1   Today, labor unions in the United States enjoy a considerable amount of power, but from colonial times until the 20th century, unions had very little influence. During the last quarter of the 19th century, the United States experienced a period of great industrial expansion, brought about in part by the establishment of large corporations that had political support and the favor of the courts. The workers in these corporations had none of the rights workers take for granted today—the right to organize into unions, the right to strike, the right to collective bargaining and the right to organize boycotts of a company's products. In addition, there were no effective laws establishing maximum working hours, a minimum wage or control over child labor. Labor unions existed in those days, but attempts to organize workers to press for expanded rights and protection under the law were generally unsuccessful. But with more and more people working in industry rather than agriculture, the pressure for change in labor rights grew and grew. As a result, the beginning decades of the 20th century saw an improved climate for changes in the country's labor policy, and within a few short years organized labor became an important force in the economic and political life of the United States.

2   In the early 1900s, unions were still weak. The courts generally supported employers in cases involving attempts by the unions to use strikes and boycotts against companies that employed nonunion workers. The economic and social reforms in these years were nevertheless important and affected all working people. By 1912, at least 38 states had adopted child labor laws, which put restrictions on the age at which children could be employed. Also by 1912, 28 states had enacted laws which afforded protection to women in industry by setting maximum work hours. By 1915, 35 states had adopted workmen's compensation laws and some 25 states had passed maximum-hour laws. Instead of pressing for legal limitation in hours, these laws provided for collective bargaining as the basis for unions to press for reduction of the workday.

3   In 1914, Congress passed the Clayton Act, which had important clauses that affected the rights of labor. It specifically stated that nothing in the antitrust laws could be interpreted as forbidding the existence of unions and preventing the unions from lawfully carrying out their objectives. Labor leaders welcomed the Clayton Act as a "final guarantee" of the workers' right to organize, to bargain collectively, to strike, to boycott and to picket. As it developed later, however, loopholes were discovered in the legislation and the "guarantees" of the Clayton Act turned out to be limited. In succeeding years, the unions pressed for new legislation that would eliminate these loopholes and in 1926 the Railway Labor Act was passed. It restated the right of unions to organize and reaffirmed the process of collective bargaining. Six years later, in 1932, the Norris-LaGuardia Act declared that it was public policy that labor should have full freedom of association, without interference by employers.

4   The Roosevelt administration, which began in 1933, marked a momentous change in the history of the labor movement in America. For the first time, the federal government made the welfare of workers its primary and direct concern. Rather than merely tolerating unions, the government urged all workers to join them. Greater gains by wage earners were made in this period than in any period of the nation's history. And in contrast to earlier periods, the government and the courts favored and supported labor interests.

5   Roosevelt's National Industrial Recovery Act of 1933, with its encouragement for workers to join a union, prompted companies to organize their own unions. Company unions, however, made it impossible for the national unions to recruit company employees as members. To redress this situation, the unions pressed for new legislation and succeeded in getting Congressional support. The Wagner Act, passed in 1935, was designed to prohibit company unions and uphold the national unions' rights to organize. In addition to the Wagner Act, two other significant pieces of legislation supporting labor interests were enacted. In 1935, the Social Security Act was passed and in 1938 the Fair Labor Standards Act was passed. The Social Security Act provided for unemployment compensation and a wide range of assistance programs. The Fair Labor Standards Act fixed a minimum hourly wage, established the 40-hour work week and set down prohibitions against the employment of children under 16 years old.

6   Labor legislation of the 1930s was admittedly one-sided and nearly ten years passed before the balance was restored by the Taft-Hartley Act, passed by Congress in 1947. Its declared purpose was to restore bargaining power between employees and employers. The Wagner Act, in guaranteeing basic rights to labor, had concentrated on unfair employer practices. The new law dealt with unfair labor union practices as well.

7   In the 1950s, Congressional investigations uncovered numerous cases of corruption in organized labor unions and, as a result of these disclosures, Congress passed the first legislation in ten years significantly curbing the powers of unions. The Landrum-Griffin Act of 1959 sharply limited the economic powers of all unions and established safeguards for ensuring democratic procedures within unions.

8   As a result of all this legislation, both unions and employers must comply with laws designed to maintain a fair balance of power between the two. Of course, conflict often arises between these two groups, but there is never conflict over the rights of unions to represent employees collectively on issues such as wages, working hours, benefits, safety and many other concerns of workers. These rights were established and written into law during three decades of this century—three decades that brought about fundamental changes in the relationship between employees and their employers.

Words and Expressions

collective bargaining: negotiations between a union and an employer (to agree on wages, hours and conditions)

boycotts: refusal to do business with or buy the products of (a company)

antitrust laws: laws that prohibit acts (by companies or individuals) that are designed to prevent competition in business

picket: (of workers on strike) to demonstrate outside a place of business in order to express complaints against the owner of the business

redress: correct, make right

curbing: limiting

Comprehension Checkup

Cross out the sentences below that *do not* state achievements of the labor movement in the United States.

1. Workers have the right to organize themselves into unions.
2. Companies cannot form their own unions.
3. All workers must join a union.
4. Workers have the right to strike.
5. Unions have the right to conduct their affairs in any way they wish.
6. A minimum hourly wage was established.

Finding Supporting Facts

The following statements can be made based on facts stated in the text. For each statement, find facts in the text that lend support to it. Sometimes the supporting facts will be found in different parts of the text.

1. In the first two decades of the 20th century, progress was made in bettering the lives of workers. (Find four facts.)
2. From 1926 to 1938, important basic workers' rights were established. (Find four facts.)
3. The labor unions have had to be controlled at times. (Find two facts.)

Vocabulary Building

Study the words below. If you do not know a word, look it up in your English-English dictionary.

Verb	Noun
protect	protection
adopt	adoption
boycott	boycott
recruit	recruitment
investigate	investigation

Read the pairs of sentences below and fill in the blanks with one of the words above.

1. The_____of child labor laws was an important goal. By 1912, 38 states had _____such laws.
2. Company unions made_____of employees into national unions impossible. It became impossible to_____employees into the national unions.
3. By 1912, 28 states had laws that_____women in industry. This_____afforded them maximum working hours.
4. Congressional_____discovered cases of corruption in labor unions. Congressional committees_____corruption in labor unions.
5. Early in this century, workers were not allowed to organize _____ . It was illegal to _____.

Discussion and Writing Topics

1. Do you think a person should have to join a particular labor union in order to get a job? Give reasons for your opinion.
2. If you were an employee in a big company, what do you think the advantages would be of having a union official negotiate with your employer, rather than dealing with your employer directly?
3. As an employer, what do you think the advantages and disadvantages would be of dealing with your employees indirectly through a union representative, rather than directly?
4. Describe what you consider the ideal job or career would be. Discuss details concerning work hours, pay, working conditions, etc.

UNIT 13
MEN and WOMEN

WNYN did a special program on the changing roles of men and women.
How do these changes affect a person's career and family?

What does this woman do? Do you think it's possible for a woman to have a career and a family?

1

Anne Conowitz has a very responsible job with an international oil company. Like most executives, she had to work very hard to reach her present position, but she thinks that her climb to success was especially difficult because she was a woman. "I wish men were more accepting of women in the business world," she said. "Too often, men assume a woman can't do a job as well as they can and so she often has to work twice as hard as a man to impress her boss and get more responsibility. And many men I've worked with resist promoting women because they think that we should just stay home and take care of a family." When asked if she would like a family of her own someday, Ms. Conowitz said, "I sometimes wish I had a family, but then it would be difficult for me to keep this job. I wish it were easier for women with children to work outside the home. But, unfortunately, for many women like me it's often a choice we have to make: a career or a family."

Ask and Answer
Find out:
1. what sort of job Anne has
2. if she had to work hard to reach her present position
3. why she thinks her climb to success was especially difficult
4. how she wishes men were different
5. what men often assume
6. why some men resist promoting women
7. what she sometimes wishes she had
8. why she doesn't have one
9. what else she wishes
10. what choice women often have to make

How old is this woman? Where is she? What is she doing here?

2

Pat Conowitz is Anne's mother. She has been a housewife for 35 years. Her youngest child has just left home so she has enrolled in a college to finish her degree. "When I was a young woman, there were very few opportunities for women. I wish the women's movement had started when I was a teenager and I wish I had finished college instead of quitting to get married. I'm glad I got married and had a family. It's very important to me. But I wish I had waited a little instead of rushing into it."

Ask and answer:
1. what Pat Conowitz does
2. why she is going to college
3. when she wishes the women's movement had started
4. what she wishes she hadn't done
5. if she wishes she hadn't had a family

Who is taking care of the baby here?
Is this usual?
Why?

Barry O'Brian is a teacher. His wife, Carolyn, is a computer programmer. She has to work evenings a lot. Barry often has to take care of the children. "Sometimes I wish I'd never said she could work. I mean, I wish she would stay home and take care of the children. That's a woman's job, isn't it? I wish teachers were paid more money. Then we could manage on my salary. But she says she would want to work even if we didn't need the money. What I don't understand is why she had to take such a demanding job."

Ask and Answer
Find out:
1. what Barry's wife does
2. if he often takes care of the children
3. what he wishes
4. what he doesn't understand

4

Carolyn O'Brian loves Barry, but her job is very important to her too. "I wish Barry would try to understand. He's a teacher because he likes to teach. I love what I do. I wish teachers were paid more too, but I wouldn't stop working even if he were a millionaire. I wish Barry would appreciate my contribution to our life style and income rather than complaining all the time. I wish we had talked more about what we expected before we got married."

Ask and Answer
Find out:
1. who and what Carolyn loves
2. what she wishes Barry would do
3. if she would ever stop working
4. what she wishes Barry wouldn't do
5. what she is sorry they didn't do before they got married

h—present

I *wish* men *were* more accepting of women.
I *wish* I *had* a family.

A. Comment

1. When *wish* is followed by a clause with an affirmative past tense verb, it means that the state or condition expressed in the clause does *not* exist in the *present*. When *wish* is followed by a clause with a negative past tense verb, it means that the state or condition expressed in the clause *does* exist in the *present*. Compare:

   Peter wishes he *had* the afternoon free. (He *doesn't* have the afternoon free, but he would like to.)
   He wishes he *didn't have* an appointment. (He *does* have an appointment, but he would prefer not to have one.)

2. The verb form after *wish* is the same as the simple past. Only *be* is different. Many people use *were* for all persons, and it is generally better to use *were* in writing. However, *I wish I was . . .* and *I wish he/she was . . .* are sometimes heard in speech.

3. The conjunction *that* is very often omitted after *wish*. This is correct in both speech and in writing.

B. Situation

Anne Conowitz likes her job, but there are many things she is dissatisfied with and wishes were different. The following things are true. What would she say if she wanted them changed?

Example:
She isn't president of her company.
I wish I were president of my company.

Now you do it. What does she say if she is sorry that:

1. her boss is so inefficient
2. her home is not near her office
3. she doesn't work abroad
4. her boyfriend works for an electric automobile company
5. she lives alone
6. her apartment is small
7. it doesn't have a garden
8. her clients are always surprised to find she is a woman

C. Transfer

A man is very dissatisfied with his life. What does he say?

Example:
   What does he say about his children? (they're not respectful)
   I wish my children weren't disrespectful. *or*
   I wish my children were respectful.

What does he say about:

1. his house (it has only one bathroom)
2. his lawn (it's brown)
3. his car (it's very old)
4. his job (it's boring)
5. his wife (she's dissatisfied too)
6. his friends (they talk about money all the time)

What else is he dissatisfied with?

D. Discussion

How do you wish your life were different now? Do you wish you looked different? How about your job? What's wrong with it? And your family and friends? What do you wish you had?

 2 | *Wish*—past

I *wish* I *had finished* college.

A. Comment

This pattern is often used when something happened in the past that you are sorry about.
   When *wish* is followed by a past perfect verb, a *past* action or state is referred to.

   I wish I *had bought* a new car last year. (I *didn't buy* one.)
   I wish I *hadn't spent* all my money on new clothes. (I *did spend* all my money on new clothes.)

B. Situation

A woman is complaining about her husband. The following things happened, but now she wishes they hadn't happened. What does she wish?

Example: She saw him.
She wishes she had never seen him.

1. She met him.
2. She eloped with him.
3. She listened to his promises.
4. She fell in love with him.
5. She married him.
6. She left home.
7. She gave up her career.
8. She didn't get her degree.

C. Discussion

There must be things you wish you'd never done or wish you had done but didn't. What are some of them?

 3 *Wish + would*

I *wish* she *would stay* home.

A. Comment

Compare these two sentences:

I wish she would stay home every night.
I wish she stayed home every night.

The two sentences have similar meanings, but the use of *would* indicates more possibility for change in the situation. The speaker seems to be saying "She could stay home if she wanted to." In the second sentence, the wish is neutral. There is no implication that a change is possible; the speaker is stating his wish that a fact (she doesn't stay home) were different.

Would + base form of verb can be used with this meaning to refer to present states and future actions. Compare:

I wish she would stay home every night. (regularly—present state)
I wish she would stay home tonight. (one future action)

Since *would* + base form of verb implies change, it cannot be used with present states that are seen as unchanging. Compare:

I wish the children *would be* good. (They aren't good, but they could start being good.)
I wish the children *were* tall. (They aren't tall and they can't start being tall. Therefore, we can't say "I wish the children would be tall.")

B. Situation

The people in the apartment above Marsha are having a noisy party. Marsha is getting angry. What does she say if she would like them to do the following:

Example:
stop making so much noise
I wish they would stop making so much noise.

1. turn down the stereo
2. keep their voices down
3. have their party somewhere else
4. stop slamming doors
5. let her sleep
6. be more considerate

C. Transfer

You are standing on a platform waiting for a train. What do you say if:

Example:
the train isn't going to come soon?
I wish the train would come soon.

1. people push and shove each other when the train comes?
2. they don't announce the trains clearly?
3. the city isn't planning on improving the service?
4. your boss won't let you come to work later in the morning?

DIALOG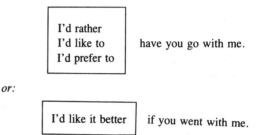

Listen to the dialog and complete Marsha's part.

(David rushes into the room.)

DAVID: Marsha! I wish you had told somebody where you were going to be! I've been looking all over for you! You've got to drop what you're doing right now! We don't have much time!

MARSHA: I (1)░░░░░░ —

DAVID: Come on! We've got to go! There's a four-alarm fire in a big apartment building on Second Avenue! We've got to get over there right away to cover it!

MARSHA: David, . . . (2)░░░░░░! The (3)░░░░░░ there. It's (4)░░░░░░, not (5)░░░░░░!

DAVID: No! It's our story—yours and mine! The news team is doing a story up in Danbury today. They couldn't possibly make it back in time. Come on!

MARSHA: (6)░░░░░░ Bob?

DAVID: Of course! He called me about it. He said to get over there right away!

MARSHA: (7)░░░░░░ cover it. You (8)░░░░░░! Haven't (9)░░░░░░? At the (10)░░░░░░ —

DAVID: Marsha! What I told Bob was that we'd do it together! You've got to go! Bob's counting on you.

MARSHA: (11)░░░░░░ you (12)░░░░░░, David. This is—

DAVID: I'd rather have you go with me. We're supposed to be a team—remember?

MARSHA: (13)░░░░░░, . . .

DAVID: Look, I wish we had time to argue about this, but we don't. We're wasting valuable time. Come on! I'll get the camera equipment and meet you at the van in five minutes. You'd better start trying to come up with some possible story angles! Let's go!

MARSHA: (14)░░░░░░ —

DAVID: Later, O.K.? Right now, let's do our job!

MARSHA: (15)░░░░░░ . . . I (16)░░░░░░ to get some things—then (17)░░░░░░.

COMMUNICATION PRACTICE

Stating Preferences

David wants Marsha to accompany him to the fire, but she doesn't want to. David expresses his preference by saying:

I'd rather have you go with me.

| I'd rather I'd like to I'd prefer to | have you go with me. |

or:

| I'd like it better | if you went with me. |

Situation

Joan and Peter are going to get married next month. Joan is becoming concerned over differences between them. Whatever she likes, Peter seems to prefer the opposite. Joan is telling her friend Barbara about some of these differences. What does she say about the following?

Example:
house—small/large

| He | would rather prefers to would like to | have a large house, but I'd prefer a small one. |

1. car—large/small
2. children—ten/two
3. children—right away/later
4. pet—dog/cat
5. wedding—informal/formal
6. ring—gold/silver
7. honeymoon—Bermuda/Canada
8. honeymoon—resort hotel/camping

Discussion

Using the patterns given above, state your preference (and the reason for it) in each of the following cases:

1. house or apartment
2. large car or small economy car
3. go to the mountains or to the beach
4. have children or not have any children

5. live in the country or live in the city
6. have a dog or a cat or other pet
7. go bowling or go see a movie
8. get married or not get married
9. eat at a restaurant or at home
10. go camping or stay in a hotel

Transfer

Create a dialog between two people who have decided to start a restaurant business. The two people have different ideas and different preferences. They have to decide on the type of food that will be served, the prices that will be charged, the location of the restaurant, the size of the restaurant and the design of the interior (furniture, arrangement, lights, paintings on the wall, etc.).

LISTENING

A young married woman is interviewed about her feelings toward women's liberation.

Getting Ready to Listen

1. Should women be able to do anything they want after they get married (for example, get a job)?
2. Do you think a woman should take her husband's name when she gets married?

Vocabulary

feminist: a person who believes that women should have equal rights with men

conventional: customary, in accordance with traditional customs

opens more doors: creates more opportunities

close doors: destroy opportunities

Now listen to the interview.

Comprehension Checkup

Choose the phrase that correctly completes each statement, based on the interview.

1. The woman in the interview considers herself to be
   a. a conventional wife with feminist ideas.
   b. an extreme feminist who thinks women should do anything they want.
2. If a woman wants to go out and get a job,
   a. that's her choice to do what she wants.
   b. she should do so after consulting her husband.

3. Even though this woman is a feminist, she
   a. took her husband's name when she was married.
   b. makes sure that her housework is taken care of.
4. She doesn't want to get involved in a protest movement,
   a. but she feels she has to speak out.
   b. but she does want to be equal and develop her potential.
5. Although she herself is not an extremist,
   a. she feels that extremists are good because they open doors.
   b. many of her friends are extreme feminists.

Listening for Restatements

Listen to the interview again, paying special attention to the interviewer's questions and comments. Find those that restate what the woman said before.

Discussion

1. The feminist movement has been in existence for quite a few years now. Has it had much of an impact?
2. Some jobs have traditionally been considered "women's" jobs and others have traditionally been considered "men's" jobs. Name some of them. Have these traditional attitudes changed very much?
3. Do you consider yourself conventional or not? Explain what "conventional" means to you.

Newstime Magazine A Biography
SUSAN B. ANTHONY

GUEST WRITER Marianne Wen is a historian specializing in feminist history

She discovered she had a talent for organizing . . .

1 The daughter of a cotton manufacturer, Susan Brownell Anthony was born in Adams, Massachusetts in 1820. From the very beginning, she enjoyed two privileges shared by few women of her time: she got a good education and her Quaker parents taught her that all men and women were equal before God. Her education led her to a career as a teacher, which was the only opportunity for independence open to women at that time and, also, the only alternative to marriage and motherhood that women had. She initially became involved in the temperance movement, the nationwide campaign to outlaw the sale and production of alcoholic beverages. She helped form the Women's State Temperance Society of New York and, in so doing, discovered that she had a great talent for organizing and getting support from others. She gradually began to turn these talents toward abolition, the movement to end the slavery of blacks in the United States.

She set out to fight for the right of women to vote . . .

2 After the Civil War, the Fourteenth and Fifteenth Amendments were proposed, extending civil rights and the vote to black males. Susan B. Anthony demanded the same privileges for women, but was ignored. However, she only became more determined than ever to see to it that all people, including women, could enjoy equality in the eyes of the law. She began her campaign by setting out to fight for women's suffrage, or the right to vote. Very quickly, she added two other demands to her public campaign: the first, the right for women to retain control of their own property after marriage, instead of having it become part of their husbands' property; and the second, the right for women to have guardianship of the children in the event of divorce.

". . . women, their rights, and nothing less."

3 From 1868 to 1870, she published a liberal newspaper, called *The Revolution*, in

which she voiced her demands to the men and women of New York. Her motto, printed at the top of the newspaper, was "The true republic: Men, their rights and nothing more; women, their rights and nothing less." In 1869, she organized the National Women's Suffrage Movement Association and thereafter traveled extensively across the nation, speaking to women from every walk of life, and fearlessly facing ridicule and even violence from those who opposed her views. Gradually, her support grew and the signatures on the petitions she circulated among her listeners began to number in the thousands. These she showered on the elected officials of Washington, forcing them to acknowledge the growing movement for women's suffrage.

She had hoped to force the court to make a decision . . .

4 Following passage of the Fourteenth Amendment to the Constitution, which gave the vote to all "male inhabitants," Susan B. Anthony registered and voted in the 1872 presidential election, in defiance of the exclusion of women from the amendment. She was arrested and tried for illegally casting a ballot and was to pay a fine of $100, which at the time, was a sizeable sum. In hopes of forcing the court to make a decision on the civil rights of women, she refused to pay the fine on the grounds that the law was wrong. The court, however, chose not to force her to pay, thus avoiding the otherwise inevitable confrontation on women's rights. She did not let this disappointing turn of events stop her, but instead she resumed a vigorous schedule of lectures, writing and travel.

She lived to see at least part of the progress that was made . . .

5 In 1888, she organized the International Council of Women and, in 1890, at the age of 80, retired from her post as president of the National American Women's Suffrage Association. But retirement was not made for women like Susan B. Anthony. In 1904 she traveled to Berlin, Germany to assist in the organization of the International Woman's Suffrage Alliance.

6 Susan B. Anthony died in Rochester, New York in 1906, at the age of 86. She lived long enough to see at least part of the progress that was eventually achieved because of her lifelong campaign for equality. By 1906, Wyoming, Utah, Colorado, Idaho, the Netherlands and Australia had granted women the right to vote. But it was not until 1920, fourteen years after her death, that the Nineteenth Amendment was finally adopted, giving women the right to vote in the United States.

7 Susan B. Anthony was a woman of high ideals and endless determination. She fought not just for the equality of women, but for the equality of all, so that both men and women, as she had been taught, would be equal before God. Her dedication to this ideal is best summed up in the message she gave women suffrage workers shortly before her death—"Failure is impossible."

Words and Expressions

Quaker: of or relating to the Quakers, a religious group that opposes violence
alternative: choice
civil rights: the nonpolitical rights such as freedom or equality which belong to people because they are citizens
liberal: favoring of some change in politics, religious affairs, etc.
ridicule: being laughed at
registered to vote: put one's name on an official list of voters

Comprehension Checkup

Are these statements true *or* false, *based on the information in the reading?*

_____ 1. Susan B. Anthony was a teacher before she became involved in various social causes.

_____ 2. Her campaign on women's rights was only about the right to vote.

_____ 3. The Fourteenth Amendment to the Constitution gave the right to vote to black men; the Fifteenth gave it to women.

_____ 4. Susan B. Anthony refused to pay the $100 fine because she wanted to force the court to decide whether it was right to deny the vote to women.

_____ 5. The movement for women's right to vote became international.

_____ 6. Susan B. Anthony lived to see the right to vote given to all women in the United States.

Finding Details

Find the details to complete these sentences.

1. Susan B. Anthony had three qualities that led her to take an active role in the women's movement. These were _____ , _____ and _____ .
2. In addition to the women's movement, Susan B. Anthony was involved in other social causes such as _____ , _____ and _____ .
3. After the Fourteenth and Fifteenth Amendments were proposed, Susan B. Anthony campaigned for basic rights of women such as _____ , _____ and _____ .
4. Susan B. Anthony worked with three organizations devoted to women's rights. They were _____ , _____ and _____ .

Vocabulary Building

Find a word in the reading to match each of the definitions below. The numbers in parentheses refer to the paragraphs where the answers can be found.

1. at first (1)
2. make illegal (1)
3. sent in great numbers (to) (3)
4. recognize; pay attention to (3)
5. help (5)

Discussion Topics

1. Why do you think it took so many years (and so much of a struggle) to get the right to vote for women? Why weren't women given the right to vote right from the beginning?
2. What does "women's liberation" mean to you? Explain your thoughts and views.
3. Do you believe that a husband and wife should share equally all the responsibilities of a home, including cleaning, doing the laundry, preparing meals, taking care of children, etc.? Give reasons to support your views.
4. What do you think will happen in the future regarding the roles of men and women? Give some specific examples.

Writing Topics

Choose one of the topics and write a composition of 350–400 words.

1. The most successful person I know. (Write about somebody you know who has become successful in his or her work in business, education, government, etc.)
2. What the roles of men and women will be in the future. (Write a composition giving your ideas about what different roles men and women will have in different walks of life.)
3. What the roles of men and women were 300 years ago. (Write a composition giving your ideas about what the different roles of men and women were in the 1700s, in government, politics, business, at home, etc.)
4. What women's liberation is all about. (Explain the purposes and objectives of the women's liberation movement; give examples.)
5. Why I am not in favor of the idea of women's liberation. (Explain your position; give examples.)

inflation unit 14

The cost of living is rising quickly.
WNYN-TV news focused on how people are coping with inflation.

1 What do you think these people are doing? Why are they angry?

These people are on strike. They are striking for higher wages. They were given a raise last year, but prices have gone up in the meantime. The raise has been wiped out by inflation. Some of these people are shouting, "Give us more money. Give it to us now!" An offer was made to them yesterday by their employer, but they didn't think it was good enough and so it was rejected. But even if a better offer is made to them, it will probably be wiped out by inflation too.

Ask and Answer
Interview one of these strikers. Ask the striker:

1. what they want
2. when they were last given a raise
3. what has happened to prices since then
4. what they are shouting
5. when an offer was last made to them
6. why it was rejected
7. what will happen to their next raise

2 Where are these people? What are they doing?

Jack Pérez is a teacher. He is explaining a grammar rule to a class of more than thirty students. Jack works very hard, but he feels that he has too many students in his class and that his salary is too low. In some cities, teachers have gone on strike to try and change these conditions. Jack thinks that teachers shouldn't go on strike. He says: "Personally, I'm against strikes, but many teachers disagree with me. I agree that teachers want and need a better standard of living. I can't make ends meet anymore. I can't afford new clothes. I can't even afford to have my old ones cleaned. But I don't think that going on strike is the way to solve our problems."

Ask and Answer
Ask and answer questions about Jack Pérez. Find out:

1. what he is doing in the picture
2. what he feels about his job
3. what has happened in some cities
4. if Jack thinks teachers should go on strike
5. what teachers want
6. if he can make ends meet
7. what he can't afford

Look at these headlines. What do they all have in common?

4

Food prices went up again by as much as three percent last month. Butter and other dairy products led the increase. Yesterday, food wholesalers were given a sharp warning by the president of AFSM (Association of Food Store Managers). "Don't be greedy!" he told them.

Ask and Answer
Make questions for these answers.
1. They went up.
2. By three percent.
3. Dairy products.
4. The president of AFSM.
5. The Association of Food Store Managers.
6. "Don't be greedy!"

3

The United Railworkers Union rejected the latest offer of eight percent from National Rail today. One of the union leaders described the offer as "ridiculous."

"Nothing under 20% will do. We've explained our position to National Rail time and again," he said.

Roland Chase, the spokesperson for National Rail, replied, "The union has been given a good offer. We can't do any better. This has been explained to the union again and again."

The real problem is inflation. The railroad cannot increase their offer without increasing the fares. Chase said, "We have a duty to fight inflation. So does the union."

Ask and Answer
Interview a union leader. Find out:
1. if they reject the eight-percent offer
2. what he thinks about the offer

Now interview Roland Chase. Find out:
1. why they can't make a better offer
2. how he feels about inflation

5

"Housewives are always given a bad deal. It's time we did something about it." These were the fighting words of Mrs. Laura Pasqual, who lives in Cincinnati, Ohio. "Everybody else gets more and more money. But we don't. Housewives should refuse to buy certain products. I'm organizing a shoppers' strike against dairy products. When no one buys them, then the prices will come down!"

Ask and Answer
Interview Mrs. Pasqual. Find out:
1. who is always given a bad deal
2. where she lives
3. who doesn't get more and more money
4. what housewives should do
5. what she is organizing
6. when the prices of dairy products will come down

UNIT 14 Grammar

1 Direct/Indirect object word order after verbs like *give*

Give us *more money*.
Give *it* to us now.

A. Comment

1. In the first sentence above, *us* is the indirect object and *more money* is the direct object.
2. Now look at the second sentence. The indirect object is expressed in a two-word phrase. What is it?
3. In the second sentence above, *more money* can be used instead of *it*.

   Give it to us now.
   Give more money to us now.

But in the first sentence, only a noun can be used as the direct object. "Give us it" is incorrect. When the direct object comes *after* the indirect object, a noun must be used. But when the direct object comes *before* the indirect object, either a noun or a pronoun can be used.

B. Practice

Here are the most common verbs with which the two indirect object patterns are possible. Make a pair of sentences for each. Think of the direct object and the indirect object yourself.

Example:
send   Please send me the information.
         Please send it to me soon.

teach/sell/bring/take/lend/write/hand/pay/show/tell/pass

C. Practice

The questions given below are all requests for decisions or advice about something. Read each question and make a decision. Use pronouns as indirect objects.

Example:
Should I just give the money to Mary? (lend)
   No. Lend it to her.

1. Should I throw you the book? (bring)
2. Should I take the book to Sarah? (mail)
3. Do you think I ought to sell Henry my car? (lend)
4. Do you think I should send Paula the report? (take)
5. Do you want me to bring you the paper? (throw)
6. Should I lend this tape to the student? (give)
7. Do you think I ought to show Michiko this letter? (read)

2 Direct/Indirect object word order after verbs like *explain*

He is explaining a grammar rule to his class.

A. Comment

There are some verbs in English which require the direct/indirect object pattern in the sentence above. The indirect object must have the preposition *to,* and the direct object comes first.

B. Practice

Some of the most common of these verbs are given in column *A*. Make sentences with them by combining them with words from columns *B* and *C*.

A	B	C
explain	good morning	to us
describe	the accident	to your father
mention	the classroom	to the police
report	my name	to me
introduce	a solution	
suggest	the problem	
say	that interesting woman	

3 *Have (something) done*

I can't afford to *have* my old clothes *cleaned*.

A. Comment

1. *Have (something) done* indicates that the action (of cleaning) is done by someone else.
2. Observe that in this pattern the object *(my old clothes)* always comes between *have* and the past participle (cleaned, done, etc.).

B. Situation

Frank and Laura only have a little money. Frank wants to have the house fixed up, but Laura has to keep reminding him that they can't afford it. Using the cues, say what he wants to do and give her response.

Example:
house—paint
A: We should have the house painted.
B: But we can't afford to *have* it *painted*. We'd better do it ourselves.

1. wall—painted
2. apple tree—cut down
3. electrical wiring—redo
4. garage—clean out
5. roof—fix
6. kitchen sink—repair
7. basement—clean up

C. Transfer

You have just inherited one million dollars and a castle in England. The castle is very old and not really livable. Naturally, you aren't going to fix it up yourself. What do you say about making changes if:

Example:
the bedrooms have never been painted
I'm going to have the bedrooms painted.

1. the bathrooms are outside
2. there is no electricity
3. there is a wood stove in the kitchen
4. the garden is full of weeds
5. there are mice in the dining room

What else has to be done before you can live there?

4 Passive voice with verbs like *give*

The union has been given a good offer.

A. Comment

There are two possible passive forms when verbs like *give* have an indirect object. Compare:

National Rail has given the union a good offer. (active voice)

1. *A good offer* has been given *to the union*. (passive voice)
2. *The union* has been given *a good offer*. (passive voice)

In the first passive sentence, the direct object of the active sentence has become the subject. This is the usual active-to-passive transformation. But in the second passive sentence, the *indirect object* of the active sentence has become the subject of the passive sentence. Both forms are equally correct. Choose the first if you wish to emphasize the "original" direct object; choose the second if you wish to emphasize the "original" indirect object.

B. Practice

Change these sentences to the passive using both forms.

Example:
Someone gave Lou a lot of money.
A lot of money was given to Lou.
Lou was given a lot of money.

1. Someone left her a beautiful house.
2. Someone offered her a good job.
3. Someone lent her a million dollars.
4. Someone sent her a diamond necklace.
5. Someone gave her a car.
6. Someone told me this stupid story.

5 Passive voice with verbs like *explain*

This has been explained *to the union* again and again.

A. Comment

When there is only one direct/indirect object word order, as with verbs like *explain,* there is also only one possible passive form. Only the direct object of an active sentence can become the subject of the passive sentence. You cannot say "The union has been explained this again and again."

B. Situation

Someone asks you to do something, but it has already been done. Say so.

Example:
You ought to explain this to the union.

YOU: It has already been explained to them.

1. You ought to explain this to the other students.
2. You should report the accident to the police.
3. Describe the thief to them.
4. Look at that good dancer. Introduce me to him.
5. Mention my name to your boss.
6. I can't find the answer to this problem. Couldn't you even suggest it to me?

UNIT 14 Dialog/Communication Practice

DIALOG

Listen to the dialog and complete Peggy's part.

(Margaret is just returning to her office.)

MARGARET: Hi, Peggy. I'm back. Thanks for covering the phones for me.

PEGGY: Boy! I (1)▦▦▦. Never (2)▦▦▦! Something's (3)▦▦▦ here. Except (4)▦▦▦.

MARGARET: Well, were there a lot of calls?

PEGGY: Not (5)▦▦▦. Four, (6)▦▦▦. Let's see . . . Steve called. He . . . (7)▦▦▦ take (8)▦▦▦ survey report (9)▦▦▦. He (10)▦▦▦.

MARGARET: O.K.

PEGGY: And uh . . . you (11)▦▦▦ a Mrs. Henderson. She's (12)▦▦▦ Friday and (13)▦▦▦ Tuesday. And . . . Let's see . . . Oh, yes! Mr. Fisher (14)▦▦▦ Research Institute. He (15)▦▦▦. He'll (16)▦▦▦. And uh . . .

MARGARET: Mr. Johnson didn't call?

PEGGY: Oh, (17)▦▦▦. Yeah . . . Now (18)▦▦▦? I remember. He said (19)▦▦▦. He'd (20)▦▦▦ next Thursday. I (21)▦▦▦ when David (22)▦▦▦ , . . . and (23)▦▦▦.

MARGARET: David . . . was here?

PEGGY: Yeah. But (24)▦▦▦.

MARGARET: Well, what do you mean?

PEGGY: Oh, (25)▦▦▦ he is—always joking (26)▦▦▦. But today he (27)▦▦▦. Different. He (28)▦▦▦ worried (29)▦▦▦. He was (30)▦▦▦ Mr. Russo.

MARGARET: Oh?

PEGGY: (31)▦▦▦ quite a while. I (32)▦▦▦ when (33)▦▦▦. He (34)▦▦▦ me . . . didn't (35)▦▦▦.

MARGARET: Hmm. Well, thanks, Peggy. I'd better get to work. I've got to get some reports typed up for Bob. I promised I'd have them finished by two o'clock.

PEGGY: Yeah. I've got to (36)▦▦▦. By the way, there's (37)▦▦▦ and (38)▦▦▦ disturbed.

MARGARET: Oh? Who's he meeting with?

PEGGY: (39)▦▦▦.

MARGARET: You mean, . . . Tom Hackett from Personnel?

PEGGY: (40)▦▦▦, never a dull moment (41)▦▦▦! Remember (42)▦▦▦? Marsha (43)▦▦▦. I wonder (44)▦▦▦ time . . . David?

MARGARET: No. Of course not.

PEGGY: (45)▦▦▦. He's (46)▦▦▦. It (47)▦▦▦. Well, (48)▦▦▦. I'll (49)▦▦▦ desk. See (50)▦▦▦.

MARGARET: Yeah. See you.

COMMUNICATION PRACTICE

Getting Estimates

| How long would it take | to *have* | ten copies of the survey |
| How much should it cost | to *get* | report *made*? |

Situation

Margaret needs some things done to her car. How would she ask for cost estimates for having the following things done?

1. washing the car
2. testing the brakes
3. checking the steering
4. balancing the front wheels
5. putting in a new engine
6. doing a new paint job
7. replacing a dented fender

How would she ask for time estimates for having these same things done? How would she ask why it takes so long or why it costs so much to have each thing done?

Transfer

Imagine yourself in the situations described below. What questions would you ask in each situation to get an idea of costs and estimated time to get things done?

1. You have taken some clothes (suit, dress, coat, etc.) to a dry cleaner's.
2. You have taken several packages to the office of a company that ships packages (by air, land or sea) to different parts of the world.
3. You have taken your broken TV set, portable radio, stereo and toaster to a repair shop to have them fixed.

Reporting What Has to be Done

She'd like to	*have*	the meeting *postponed* until next
I promised I'd		Tuesday.
I've got to	*get*	it *scheduled* for next Thursday.
		them *finished* by two o'clock.
		some reports *typed up* for Bob.

Situation

Pretend that you are the manager of the service department at a big car dealer. You discuss problems with customers

as they leave their cars and then you must tell a mechanic what each customer wants done. What would you say to the mechanic about each of the following customer requests?

Example:
CUSTOMER: I'd like someone to look at the engine.
MANAGER: This customer wants to have the engine looked at.

1. I'd like someone to adjust the brakes.
2. I'd like someone to change the oil.
3. I'd like someone to check the brakes.
4. I'd like someone to replace the oil filter.
5. I'd like to have you inspect the exhaust system.

Transfer

Pretend that you are staying at a luxury hotel. You want various things done (luggage taken to your room, room cleaned, meals served in your room, etc.). Talk to the desk clerk and make requests.

LISTENING

Four different people give their views on inflation.

Getting Ready to Listen

1. Why are so many unions today demanding higher wages and salaries for their members?
2. Has inflation caused any changes in your life style? Are there things that you used to buy or do that you now do without?
3. Do people buy too much on credit these days?

Vocabulary

clipping coupons: cutting discount coupons out of newspapers and magazines (these coupons entitle people to purchase merchandise at reduced prices)
frugally: watching expenditures carefully
show: movie
get by: get along, survive, make ends meet
staples: basic food items (flour, sugar, salt, etc.)
cuts into: takes (time) away from

Now listen to the interview.

Comprehension Checkup

Are these statements *true* or *false*, based on the information in the interview?

_____ 1. The teacher is involved in union activities in an effort to get a better salary.
_____ 2. Because his buying power is down, he and his wife try to avoid shopping whenever possible.
_____ 3. Food prices have increased more than those for housing and transportation.
_____ 4. They don't go out as much as they used to

because they have limited their budget for that kind of activity.
_____ 5. Mrs. Griffin, the supermarket manager, is getting by well because she is making more money than she was a few years ago.
_____ 6. People's buying habits at the supermarket have not changed in spite of inflation.
_____ 7. They're buying mainly essential items.
_____ 8. The economist thinks that inflation results from people spending a lot of money.
_____ 9. She believes that Americans buy too much on credit.
_____ 10. The way that inflation has affected the student is that she isn't able to go out often.
_____ 11. Because her parents can't afford to pay all of her tuition, she is taking fewer courses.
_____ 12. She claims that having to work and study at the same time has taught her to study more effectively.

Critical Listening

Listen to the interview again. Of the four people interviewed about inflation, only one talks about its causes. The others all comment on the effects of inflation. Which person talks about the *causes*?

Discussion

In the interviews, you listened to four different people talking about the problems of inflation. How do you feel about inflation? How does it affect you?

THE BIG MOVE

1   Joel came home from work on Friday feeling depressed. It was payday, but he wasn't even excited about having a full wallet. He knew that when he sat down and paid his bills and set aside money for groceries, gas for the car and a small deposit in his savings account, there wasn't going to be too much left over for having a good time. He had been earning a good salary since his last raise, but everything was becoming so expensive.

2   He thought about going out for dinner at his favorite restaurant with some friends, but he just wasn't in the mood. He wandered around his apartment for a while and ate a sandwich, but he couldn't stop himself from getting depressed about the money situation. Finally, he couldn't stand being in his apartment anymore so he got into his car and started driving. He didn't have a destination in mind, but he knew that he wanted to be far away from the city where he lived.

3   He drove on the turnpike for a while and then turned onto a quiet road. Being in the countryside made him feel better. He let his mind wander as he drove past the small farms and he began to imagine living on his own piece of land and becoming self-sufficient. It had always been a dream of his, but he had never done anything to make it a reality. Even as he was thinking, though, his logical side was scoffing at his impractical imaginings. He began debating in his mind the advantages and disadvantages of living in the country and growing his own food. He was mechanically inclined and was fascinated by the principle of solar energy. In high school, he had done a science fair project on solar energy and won first prize. He started to imagine his own farmhouse equipped with a solar energy panel on the roof to heat the house in winter and power a water heater. He envisioned fields of vegetables for canning and preserving to last through the winter. And if the crops had a good yield, maybe he could even sell some of the surplus and buy farming equipment with the extra money.

4   But Joel knew he couldn't do all of this alone. He wondered if he could get a job on a farm in the area until he learned how to get his own farm running. He was sure he could get some of his friends to help out with the work on weekends. They would probably be envious of his country life and would welcome the chance to get out of the city while they helped him get things going.

5   As he drove along the winding road, he began to think about how he would probably miss the excitement of the city. But he really wasn't moving too far away from his family and friends so he'd be able to see them often enough. And after a short period of adjustment, he knew he'd enjoy the slower pace of country life.

6   Suddenly, Joel stopped thinking and laughed out loud, "I'm really going to go through with this!" And then he couldn't wait to go and tell his friends about his new plans.

Words and Expressions

turnpike: a highway for fast-moving vehicles, especially one drivers pay to use

scoffing at: laughing at; ridiculing

solar: of or concerning the sun

Comprehension Checkup

Choose the correct statement.

1. Joel felt depressed because
   a. he didn't like living in the city.
   b. he had spent all his money.
   c. he didn't get a good raise last time.
   d. everything was getting more and more expensive.
2. For Joel, the main attraction of living in the country was
   a. experimenting with solar energy.
   b. becoming self-sufficient.
   c. selling his crops for profit.
   d. having his friends visit on weekends.
3. Joel thought that his friends
   a. would enjoy visiting him in the country.
   b. wouldn't understand his decision to move to the country.
   c. would be too far away.
   d. wouldn't be able to help him much.

Interpreting the Story

During his drive in the country, Joel starts out by fantasizing about living on a farm and finishes by deciding to do it. In fact, he seems to make the decision before he realizes it. Read paragraphs 3, 4 and 5 again and notice how Joel's *hypothetical* thinking ("What if I did this?") changes to *real* thinking ("This is what I'm going to do.").

Vocabulary Building

Find a word or phrase in the reading to match each of the definitions below. All of the words are in paragraph 3.

1. able to work easily with machinery
2. saw (in the mind)
3. the amount produced
4. the amount beyond what is needed

Now use the words you wrote above to complete the following sentences. It may be necessary to change the *form* of the words (past to present, singular to plural, etc.).

Being _____ , the farmer tried to figure out ways to use machinery to increase the _____ of his crops. He _____ a modern farm which would feed his family and give him plenty of _____ crops to sell for cash.

Discussion Topics

1. Do you think Joel's decision to move to a farm is realistic? What problems do you think he may encounter that he has not anticipated?
2. What would (do) you like and dislike about living in the country? About living in the city?

Writing Topics

1. Write a journal entry for a person who has recently moved from a city to a farm. Tell about the person's workday, the difficulties encountered and the person's feelings about farm life on that day. Is the person optimistic or pessimistic about his/her new life?
2. You are living on a farm in which you are trying to grow most of your own food. Write a letter to a friend of yours who you think would enjoy joining you on the farm. Try to convince your friend to come live on the farm and help you run it.
3. Not very many people are moving to working farms, but a lot of people are moving from cities to small towns in the countryside. Write a 300-word composition in which you give possible reasons for this trend.

unit 15

In a special news program, WNYN looked at modern life and the benefits and disadvantages of technology.

PROGRESS

This was a part of New York City almost 100 years ago. Life must have been difficult for the people living here. They had to put up with noise, smoke and dirt. The noise came from the elevated railway, and the smoke and dirt came from the trains and horses and thousands of chimneys all around them. Disease killed thousands of children. Families were large, but often five out of seven children would die before they were five years old.

Ask and Answer
You are interviewing a historian. Find out:

1. what people had to put up with in New York 100 years ago
2. where the noise came from
3. where the smoke and dirt came from
4. if disease was a problem
5. if many children died

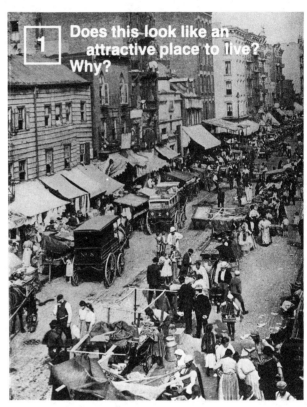

1 Does this look like an attractive place to live? Why?

2 What kind of airplane is this? Why is it special?

Is life really better than it was 100 years ago? It is certainly true that people live longer than they used to, travel faster than they could before and own more things than they did. We have made great progress in industry, science and medicine. But we still have to put up with noise, overcrowding and bad air. These things are still a basic part of modern life.

Ask and Answer
Ask:

1. in what ways life is better than it was
2. what we have made progress in
3. what we still have to put up with

Discussion
Are there any other ways that you think life is better for people now? Are there any ways in which life is worse now than 100 years ago?

Do you think this is a pretty scene? Why? | 3

There used to be a clear difference between town and country, but that is changing rapidly. The automobile has made it possible for people to live many miles from their jobs. Highways like this one have been built from every city into the surrounding countryside, and this has encouraged more and more people to move there and drive their cars into the city to work. Of course, as more people move to the countryside, it becomes more and more crowded. In some areas, small towns and farms are disappearing and turning into housing developments. And with the increased use of the automobile, pollution in the cities gets worse and worse.

Of course, cars are a basic part of modern life. Everyone wants one and the automobile industry employs thousands of people. The economy of a country like the United States depends on it a great deal. But what can we do about the problems the automobile creates?

Ask and answer:
You are interviewing a specialist in urban affairs. Find out:

1. if there used to be a clear difference between town and country
2. what the automobile has made it possible to do
3. what the highways have encouraged people to do
4. what is happening to farms and small towns
5. what is happening to pollution in the cities
6. in what ways cars are a basic part of modern life

Is this a pretty scene? Why? | 4

Industry and modern life do not have to be enemies of beauty. This is a picture of a modern power station. It proves that progress doesn't have to be ugly. It doesn't have to destroy the countryside around it. We can have beauty and progress if we really want to. We need clean rivers and open countryside just as much as people did 100 years ago. Perhaps, in some ways, we need them even more. Things like open land, clean water and good air are getting scarcer and scarcer.

Ask and Answer
Continue your interview above. Find out:

1. if industry and modern life have to be enemies of beauty
2. what this is a picture of
3. if it proves anything
4. if we really need clean rivers, open countryside and good air
5. what is getting scarcer and scarcer

UNIT 15 Grammar

1 Use and omission of *a, an* and *the*

We have made progress in industry and science.

A. Comment

We do not use *a, an* or *the* with nouns like these when they indicate the thing in general, the idea of the thing rather than a particular example of it.
Example:

I'm studying science. (science in general)
Physics is *an* exact science. (a particular example of a science)

B. Practice

Change the occupation to the general subject, as in the example.

Example:
A: I'd like to be *a* scientist.
B: Then you should study science.

1. I want to be an artist.
2. What do I have to do if I want to be a doctor?
3. What if I want to be an economist?
4. What do engineers study?
5. And chemists?
6. How about architects?
7. And musicians?
8. What's the subject called that deals with writers and their work?

C. Situation

You are talking with a friend about your likes and dislikes. Restate your friend's preferences.

Example:
A: I like wine, but it must be French.
B: In other words, you only like French wine.

1. I like jazz, particularly the old-fashioned type.
2. I like food, but not if it's English.
3. I enjoy music, especially classical.
4. I want to learn something about cooking. I want to make a Chinese dinner.
5. Sports are interesting to watch, particularly if they're played well.
6. I don't like architecture, particularly this modern type.
7. I'm fond of antiques, but they must be American.

D. Transfer

Imagine you are listing the subjects that can be studied at a very large adult education center. Choose the main subjects from group A and then add (an) appropriate adjective(s) from group B.

Examples:
Modern music; vegetarian cooking; Japanese flower arranging; ancient history.

Modern music; vegetarian cooking; Japanese flower arranging; ancient history.

A

architecture, music, literature, art, science, physics, chemistry, mathematics, cooking, history, literature, drawing, speaking, flower arranging, philosophy, psychology, religion, dance, broadcasting

B

classical, modern, English, American, organic, inorganic, French, nineteenth-century, baroque, vegetarian, commercial, radio, after-dinner, Japanese, oriental, twentieth-century, ancient, general

Now make up short conversations like this:

A: I'm thinking of taking a course at the Adult Education Center.
B: Really? What are you going to take?
A: I'm thinking about *modern music,* but the course in *vegetarian cooking* is also interesting.
B: What else do they offer?
A: Oh, lots of things. You might be interested in the course in *Japanese flower arranging* or *ancient history.*

2 *the* vs. no article

Modern industry
The car industry

A. Comment

The car industry is a specific example of a specific industry; the product is actually defined so we use *the. Modern industry,* however, is still a general category. It is not a specific industry.

B. Practice

Make sentences adding *the* when it is needed and omitting it when it is not.

Examples:
industry
   I want a job in industry.
heavy
   I want a job in heavy industry.
car
   I want a job in the car industry.

1. British
2. American
3. furniture
4. toy
5. modern
6. oil
7. clothing
8. textile
9. German

Now continue like this:

Life is full of surprises.
   city
   City life is full of surprises.

10. of a doctor
11. of a young child
12. modern
13. of a homemaker
14. twentieth-century
15. of a salesman
16. country

C. Transfer

You are going to give a lecture about noise. You say:

This evening I'm going to talk about noise.

You are also going to talk about one specific type of noise: noise from low-flying airplanes. You say:

I'm also going to talk about *the* noise made by low-flying airplanes.

Now make two such statements about each of these topics:

1. health (in general and that of old people)
2. industry (in general and that of this town)
3. progress (in general and that made in the last century)
4. music (in general and that which is popular now)
5. architecture (in general and that of this area)

3 | Reference signals

a. This is a picture of a modern power station. It proves that progress doesn't have to be ugly.

b. We need clean rivers and open countryside just as much as people did 100 years ago. Perhaps, in some ways, we need them even more.

What does *it* refer to in **a?** What does *them* refer to in **b?**

A. Comment

It and *them* are reference signals. They refer back to something that was mentioned earlier. In **a,** *It* refers to a modern power station. In **b,** *them* refers to clean rivers and open countryside. Some of the words that are used as reference signals are *it, they, them, this, that, these, those, he, him, she* and *her.* A reference signal can refer to a word (noun), to a phrase, to a whole sentence, to an entire paragraph and, sometimes, to an idea expressed earlier.

B. Practice

Fill in the blanks with the correct reference signals. Then tell what each one refers to.

A: I was looking for the pen that Tom and Ellen gave me for my birthday. I thought I had left _____ on the dining room table, but now I can't find _____. I'd sure hate to tell _____ that I lost _____. _____ was a nice thing for _____ to do, and I know _____ would be sad if I lost _____ so quickly. Promise you won't tell _____ about _____, O.K.?

B: Sorry, I haven't seen _____. Maybe _____'s in your coat pocket. _____'s over here in the closet if you want me to see if _____'s in _____.

UNIT 15 Dialog/Communication Practice

DIALOG 📼

Listen to the dialog and complete Bob's part.

(Bob Russo has asked Marsha to come to his office.)

MARSHA: Bob? Margaret said you wanted to see me?

BOB: (1) ▨▨▨▨! As a matter of fact, I've (2)▨▨▨▨ this morning (3)▨▨▨▨ .

MARSHA: Sorry. I was in the production room working on the final details for tomorrow's program.

BOB: Oh, yes. The (4) ▨▨▨▨. You've (5) ▨▨▨▨ , Marsha. (6) ▨▨▨▨ good program?

MARSHA: I hope so. Since it's going to be my last one, somehow I want it to be the best one I've ever done. Can you understand that?

BOB: Yes, of course. But (7)▨▨▨▨ . . . It's not (8) ▨▨▨▨ WNYN—

MARSHA: Oh? But, Bob, I'm leaving on Friday. I don't think there'd be enough time to do another prog—

BOB: Wait! (9)▨▨▨▨ on. In (10)▨▨▨▨ , I feel (11)▨▨▨▨ —

MARSHA: For what?

BOB: (12)▨▨▨▨ on the basis of (13)▨▨▨▨ —telling you (14)▨▨▨▨ . And for (15)▨▨▨▨ without (16)▨▨▨▨ case—

MARSHA: Bob, I—

BOB: (17)▨▨▨▨ minute. Let me finish. David (18)▨▨▨▨ and he (19)▨▨▨▨ everything—all the gruesome (20)▨▨▨▨ . I (21)▨▨▨▨ that (22)▨▨▨▨ . And of course, I (23)▨▨▨▨ . . . because of (24)▨▨▨▨ . Anyway, (25)▨▨▨▨ that I'm (26)▨▨▨▨ . We don't (27)▨▨▨▨ , Marsha! We (28)▨▨▨▨ job.

MARSHA: I . . . I . . . I don't know what to say. . . .

BOB: You (29)▨▨▨▨ anything—except (30)▨▨▨▨ . And (31)▨▨▨▨ unhappy thing.

MARSHA: Well, . . . well, of course I'll stay—if you want me to. But . . . but what about David?

BOB: (32)▨▨▨▨ about him yet. He (33)▨▨▨▨ yesterday.

MARSHA: Oh, Bob, don't let him go! He's a very talented person!

BOB: Yes, but (34)▨▨▨▨ . How could we (35)▨▨▨▨? He's (36)▨▨▨▨ , he's (37)▨▨▨▨ , he's—

MARSHA: But you know, Bob, I don't think there's anything malicious about David. Sure, he picked some peculiar ways to try to demonstrate his abilities—to get your attention. But maybe that's because he's young, and—Just think what it took for him to come to you and tell you what he's done!

BOB: (38)▨▨▨▨ , Marsha! You really do! You (39)▨▨▨▨ because (40)▨▨▨▨ . And (41)▨▨▨▨ , you (42)▨▨▨▨ , trying to (43)▨▨▨▨ .

MARSHA: I want him to stay, Bob. I know we can work together as a team—I think we proved that on the big

news story last week. Tell him he still has a job. . . .

BOB: Well, . . . it's (44)▨▨▨▨ . I am (45)▨▨▨▨ about it. That (46)▨▨▨▨ . But (47)▨▨▨▨ very carefully (48)▨▨▨▨ decision.

COMMUNICATION PRACTICE

Discouraging Interruptions

When Marsha interrupted something that Bob was saying, Bob said:

Wait! Let me go on . . .

Later, when Marsha tried to interrupt him again, Bob said:

Just a minute. Let me finish.

Situation

Working with a partner, have a conversation about the city or town you grew up in, the schools you went to, friends you had, things you used to do, your family, etc. The person you are talking to will constantly try to interrupt you to tell you about his/her own life. Each time your partner tries to interrupt, discourage the interruption by using phrases like those given above.

Discussion

Have a discussion with other members of the class. Together, as a class, choose any five topics for discussion. Then have somebody make a list of the topics on the blackboard and begin the discussion. During the discussion, try to use the communication items practiced in previous units, such as:

introducing a new subject (Unit 2)
describing feelings and causes of feelings (Unit 5)
suppositions with *should* (Unit 6)
expressing tentative conclusions with *seem to/not seem to* (Unit 6)
making concessions (Unit 7)
asking for clarification (Unit 7)
giving reasons (Unit 9)
conceding a point (Unit 9)
asking for more details (Unit 11)
stating preferences (Unit 13)
reporting what has to be done (Unit 14)
discouraging interruptions (Unit 15)

LISTENING

Two people are interviewed about the problem of noise pollution. One is a student who lives near an airport in New York and the other is an architect.

Getting Ready to Listen

1. What do you think it's like to live near an airport?
2. What kinds of noise pollution do people living in cities have to cope with?
3. Do people need to be protected against noise pollution?

Vocabulary Building

Find a word in the reading to match each of the definitions below. The numbers in parentheses refer to the paragraphs where the answers can be found.

rumbling: deep vibrating sound
protest: complain about
cushioning (it): reducing the effect of (it), cutting down the force of (it)
skylights: windows in roofs of houses or buildings
seclusion: privacy
touchy: sensitive, particular

Now listen to the interview.

Comprehension Checkup

Choose the phrase that correctly completes each statement, based on the interview.

1. The student is concerned about noise pollution because he is
    a. unable to concentrate on his studies.
    b. afraid of planes hitting his house.
2. He's been living in the same place all his life and he thinks that in recent years the problem
    a. seems to have gotten worse.
    b. has been controlled by technological improvements.
3. He has tried to protest to the city, but
    a. he's always given a bureaucratic runaround.
    b. they say they're meeting the legal noise standards.
4. The architect points out that noise comes from all directions and that architects
    a. cannot possibly prevent all noise pollution.
    b. are responsible for cushioning people from noise pollution.

5. According to the architect, people are bothered most by
    a. noise outside their homes that they cannot control.
    b. noise made by family members inside the house.
6. According to her, architects have to
    a. consider the personality of the people living in a building.
    b. take many factors into consideration.
7. Although you can easily tell someone in the family who is making noise to be quiet,
    a. it is much more difficult to approach a stranger.
    b. you should be careful not to offend the person.
8. When people are being bombarded by sound,
    a. they are unable to focus on what they are doing.
    b. they sometimes attack other people around them.
9. Having a space of your own is important because
    a. everyone needs to have a place to be alone.
    b. you can control the environment yourself.

Critical Listening

At one point in the interview, the architect and the interviewer laugh. Listen to the interview just before the laughter and explain what they were laughing at.

Discussion

1. We read and talk a lot about pollution of all kinds (air, noise, water, etc.). Is it a problem that you think about or worry about? Why or why not?
2. How do you feel about loud rock music?
3. How would it be to live near a constant source of noise (such as an airport, a train station, a factory, etc.)? Have you ever had to do this?

Is It Progress?

1 Everyone seems to be in favor of progress. But "progress" is a funny word. It doesn't necessarily mean that something has become stronger, wiser or better. It simply means changing it from being one thing to another and sometimes it turns out to be worse than before.

2 Consider medicine, for instance. No one can deny that medical progress has enriched our lives tremendously. Because of medical advancements, we eat better, live easier and are able to take care of ourselves more efficiently. We can cure disease with no more than one injection or a pill. If we have a serious accident, surgeons can put us back together again. If we are born with something defective, they can repair it. They can make us happy, restore our sanity, ease our pain, replace worn parts and give us children. They can even bring us back from the dead. These are wonderful achievements, but there is a price we have to pay.

3 Because medicine has reduced infant mortality and natural death so significantly, the population has been rising steadily, in spite of serious efforts to reduce the rate of population growth. Less than a century ago in the United States, infant mortality claimed more than half of the newborn within the first year of life. Medical advances, however, have now reduced that rate to nearly zero. A child born in the United States today has better than a 90% chance of survival. Furthermore, medical advances have ensured that most of those infants will live to be seventy years of age or more, and even that life expectancy increases every year. The result of this progress is an enormous population increase that threatens the quality of life, brought about by progress in the medical profession.

4 Or, consider the progress being made in agriculture. Here again, there are remarkable achievements. With the introduction of scientific farming, specialized machinery, highbred strains of stock and produce and intensive fertilization, American farmers are capable of producing annual yields that not only feed the population of the United States, but parts of Europe and Asia as well. They have learned to make barren lands fertile, marshlands dry and desert lands green. But could this advancement, this progress, have a negative side? Unfortunately, it does.

5 The specialized machinery and heavy equipment that intensive farming requires are, for the most part, powered by petroleum products. Oil dependency is a serious problem in most of the world today. And unless an alternative method of power for machinery is found, shortages of food may accompany the inevitable oil shortages.

6 Spraying crops for disease and insects has helped reduce crop failure, but it has also produced poison-resistant insects and a growing dependence on more and more sprays. As farmers selectively annihilate one form of pest, another species thrives as it finds its former enemy or competitor has been eliminated. Farmers are committed to endless spraying, as one insect succeeds another in the competition for food.

7 Intensive fertilization, perhaps the greatest contribution to high crop yields, is highly dependent upon imported minerals and chemical fertilizers. As the supply of these materials decreases, the cost increases and the availability of the products is lowered. Farmers may soon find it difficult to find the minerals and fertilizers they need to continue high-yield farming. Furthermore, it is being discovered that these fertilizers and pesticides have entered the food chain and aquifer, and are beginning to affect people in highly adverse ways. This poses a question concerning agricultural progress.

8 Perhaps the most often scrutinized area of progress is industry. Here, the side effects of progress are only too apparent. Initially, there was the growing concern that people were being replaced by machinery. It was economically advantageous to make machines that did what people could do. They were cheaper, more efficient and less demanding. However, they couldn't take care of themselves, so workers found themselves back on the job with a new direction of employment.

9 Today, we see the negative effects of industrial progress in the environment. Factories produce waste and for too many years this waste has been dumped into rivers, lakes and oceans. Now we are paying for this carelessness as valuable water resources become polluted by high toxic waste. Some rivers and lakes will never recover from this misuse and we are just beginning to discover what the effect on oceans has been.

10 The raw materials being used in factories are only now becoming the targets of protest. Coal mines emit a fine dust that is breathed by coal miners and can cause "black lung," a disease similar to emphysema. Asbestos, a mineral product that is highly resistant to heat, was lauded as one of the greatest contributions to industrial progress. However, recently it has been found to cause cancer. Paint fumes are toxic chemicals and can be extremely dangerous if mishandled. So as the long-term effects of factory work are being gradually isolated and identified, it is becoming evident that the factory is a very dangerous place to work.

11 It is true that the industrial revolution has made life easier, more comfortable and convenient and a lot more fun. But can this ease of living be justified at the expense of someone's health and, perhaps, the health of society as a whole?

12 No doubt, human beings have made remarkable progress in a great many directions. Some of these directions have benefited society greatly. Some have not. But we cannot hope to make positive progress in any direction without considering the welfare of the world as a whole. We need to slow down and consider the possible consequences of all of our options. It is clear to us today that there is a good deal of "progress" that we could have done without.

"You know, they say the bugs are becoming resistant to this insecticide."

Words and Expressions

highbred strains: varieties (of animals or plants) that are superior
barren land: land on which nothing will grow
shortages of food/oil shortages: conditions in which there is not enough food/oil
spraying: scattering liquid in small drops under pressure
scrutinized: looked at very carefully
fumes: strong-smelling air, like that given off by wet paint, gas, etc.

Comprehension Checkup

Are these statements *true* **or** *false,* **based on the reading?**

_____ 1. Progress always brings about an improvement.
_____ 2. Modern medicine has made our lives better in some ways.
_____ 3. The growth in population we have been experiencing is partly the result of medical progress.
_____ 4. An oil shortage would not affect modern farmers.
_____ 5. Fertilizers and pesticides do not present dangers to our health.
_____ 6. The negative effects of industry are easy to see.

Getting Essential Information

Read the text again and this time take notes to complete the outline below. It is not necessary to take down every detail. Write only enough to help you remember the general ideas.

General Statement: Progress may make some aspects of our lives better, but there is often a negative effect too.

Medicine
Positive effects:
Effect on life expectancy:
Result of change in life expectancy:

Agriculture
Positive effects:
Problem with using machinery:
Problem with using pesticides and fertilizers:

Industry
Positive effects:
Problems with waste from factories:
Problems with raw materials:

Vocabulary Building
Find a word in the reading to match each of the definitions below. The numbers in parentheses refer to the paragraphs where the answers can be found.

1. to destroy completely (6)
2. an animal or insect that harms or destroys food supplies (6)
3. to develop well and be healthy (6)
4. a poison that kills pests (7)
5. poisonous (9)
6. praised (10)

Discussion Topics

1. Do you think that life expectancy will be increased significantly in the future because of new medical discoveries? If life expectancy is 70 years now, what will it be 100 years from now?
2. Have you ever talked to an older person (grandparent, friend, etc.) about what life was like when he or she was young? Tell some of the things you found out about.
3. Older people sometimes say that things were better years ago. Do you think that people were better off without some of the things we have today (television, jets, computers, automobiles, etc.)?

Writing Topics

1. Write a composition telling what you think the most important invention or discovery has been in the 20th century. Give reasons to support your view.
2. Pretend that you are a reporter for a small newspaper in the year 1785. Write an article making predictions of what will happen in the next 200 years. Mention new forms of communication, transportation, etc.
3. Pretend that you are a reporter for a small present-day newspaper. Write an article making predictions of what will happen in the next 200 years. Do you think that we are heading for destruction or more progress?
4. Write a composition describing things you think should be designed or invented to make living easier or more convenient or to improve the quality of life for more people.

Tapescript for Dialogs

UNIT 1

(Robert Russo's assistant, Margaret Klein, is introducing David.)

MARGARET: Mr. Russo, this is David Denton.

MR. RUSSO: How do you do?

DAVID: Glad (1) *to meet you.*

RUSSO: Come in. Please . . . sit down.

DAVID: Sorry (2) *I'm late.* I—

RUSSO: That's all right.

DAVID: I (3) *usually try to* be pretty (4) *punctual,* but (5) *this morning*—

RUSSO: I understand. Don't worry about it. Go ahead . . . please sit down. Now, let's see. . . . I have your resume here. I would like to ask you a few questions.

DAVID: (6) *O.K.*

RUSSO: You haven't had a job in television before, have you?

DAVID: Well, no, . . . actually, I (7) *haven't.* But (8) *I've had a lot of* camera (9) *experience!* In college (10) *we had a TV station on campus.* I (11) *was chief of the* camera crew (12) *for nearly two* years.

RUSSO: I noticed that in your resume. Was your work confined to studio productions?

DAVID: Oh, no. We (13) *did* a lot of field production (14) *too.* I . . . went out on assignments (15) *all the time.* We (16) *did a weekly news program* that was (17) *pretty popular.* I'd (18) *like to* tell (19) *you* a little bit (20) *about it,* if (21) *I could.* It (22) *was called* "Odyssey." Maybe (23) *you've heard about* the (24) *program?*

RUSSO: No, I'm afraid I haven't.

DAVID: There (25) *was* quite a nice write-up (26) *about it in the paper* last year.

RUSSO: Well, . . . I . . . uh . . . see here that you graduated from college two years ago. You haven't been working since you graduated—is that right?

DAVID: Well, uh . . . I (27) *haven't had a paid job.* But (28) *I've kept on working* for (29) *the college.*

RUSSO: Well, let me tell you a little bit about the job. (Thirty minutes later. The interview is almost over.)

RUSSO: Well, I think that with the camera experience you've had, you should be able to do the work all right. But it's going to be a lot different than the kind of thing you've been used to.

DAVID: (30) *Different?*

RUSSO: Well, I'm thinking particularly about the question of handling responsibility.

DAVID: Oh, I (31) *don't mind* having (32) *a lot of responsibility!* In (33) *college,* I (34) *had to* produce shows (35) *all by myself.* I had (36) *full responsibility for everything.*

RUSSO: That's just the point I'm trying to make. Here at WNYN, a cameraman works as an assistant to a reporter.

DAVID: (37) *An assistant?*

RUSSO: Yes. And the reporter's the "boss," so to speak. And the reporter tells you what to do on each assignment.

DAVID: Oh . . . Well, uh . . . wouldn't be (38) *any problem for me* . . . I . . . I don't mind (39) *working with other people.*

RUSSO: Hmm. I'd like to set up an interview for you with Grace Lee, our chief program coordinator.

DAVID: You mean (40) *I'm going to get the job?*

RUSSO: I'd say there's a good chance. We need a cameraman right away. But I want you to talk with Ms. Lee before we make a final decision.

UNIT 2

GRACE: What did they say about the viewer survey report?

MARGARET: The information's being prepared now. They promised we'd have the complete report in a couple of weeks.

GRACE: Oh, what takes them so long with these things? They're not much good to us if we don't get them promptly. Well, . . . let's get started. This is going to be a very short meeting. Uh . . . Where's David?

MARGARET: I don't think he's come in yet. He does know about the meeting.

GRACE: Hmm . . . Well, we'll go ahead without him. I've got another appointment at eleven thirty. Now, . . . I want to go over plans for our special features this month. What have you got, Marsha?

MARSHA: First of all, there's (1) *the special on space exploration.*

GRACE: Right. How much have you done on that so far?

MARSHA: (2) *Quite a bit.* Oh! I finally (3) *managed to get in touch with Professor Daniels.* He said (4) *he'd be on the program.* And I'm (5) *just delighted!*

GRACE: Oh, good! We've scheduled that for the twenty-third. Are you going to be ready by that time?

MARSHA: Oh, (6) *no problem.*

MARGARET: Is that going to conflict with the dates for the Denver project?

GRACE: No, . . . No, the trip will be the week after that.

MARGARET: Bob's really excited about that one.

MARSHA: (7) *What are you two* talking about? (8) *What* trip? (9) *What's the "Denver Project"?*

GRACE: Well, . . . Bob wants to talk to you about that himself. All I can say is that it's going to be the biggest and most important assignment you've ever had at WNYN.

MARGARET: He just got the final O.K. this morning to go ahead with the project.

GRACE: Well, let's see . . . Any problems? Uh . . . How many other deadlines do we have? Uh . . . Are we all set for Friday's program on the airline strike?

MARSHA: Yes. And (10) *the other two programs* . . . the housing industry (11) *and* . . . noise pollution . . . They're (12) *both being* edited (13) *right now*.

MARGARET: Oh, it's eleven thirty, Grace. Time for your appointment.

GRACE: Oh, O.K. I'd better go. Uh . . . we'll get together again on Thursday.

(Marsha goes back to her office . . . She finds David there.)

MARSHA: David! You (14) *missed the meeting*.

DAVID: I just walked in. Got tied up this morning. You know the program you want to do on the new hospital?

MARSHA: Yes, of course. We're (15) *supposed to* go over there (16) *on Tuesday to do the story*.

DAVID: Yeah, I know. Well, I spent three hours with the people at the hospital this morning and planned the whole thing. I think they understand what they're supposed to do when we do the recording on Tuesday.

MARSHA: (17) *You went* over there (18) *this morning?*

DAVID: Yeah . . . Well, I was passing by and I thought I might as well stop in and set things up for Tuesday. I thought you'd be happy about . . .

MARSHA: David! (19) *What made you* do (20) *such a* thing? You (21) *didn't even know* what kind of (22) *story I wanted!*

DAVID: Oh, I think you'll like the story angle I came up with.

MARSHA: That's (23) *not the point!* (24) *We're supposed to be* a team. I'm (25) *responsible for the* story and (26) *you're responsible for* the video . . . (27) *remember?*

DAVID: Sorry. It won't happen again . . .

UNIT 3

DANIELS: Hello.

MARSHA: Is (1) *this 889–7654?*

DANIELS: Yes, it is.

MARSHA: I'd like to (2) *speak to Professor Daniels,* please.

DANIELS: Speaking.

MARSHA: (3) *Oh.* Professor Daniels, (4) *this is* Marsha Nelson.

DANIELS: Who?

MARSHA: Marsha Nelson. We're (5) *doing the special program on space exploration*. I (6) *spoke to you* about (7) *two weeks* ago. . . .

DANIELS: Are you with the Hartley Foundation?

MARSHA: No, I'm (8) *calling from* WNYN-TV. You (9) *asked me to call you* this week (10) *to arrange a definite time for our interview*. Do (11) *you remember?*

DANIELS: Oh, the television program! Yes. Yes, of course. Forgive me. Since we spoke the last time, I've been involved in two other projects.

MARSHA: Oh, (12) *that's all right*. I (13) *understand*.

DANIELS: Let me get my appointment book. Hold on for a minute, will you?

MARSHA: (14) *Certainly*.

DANIELS: Hmm. Now, let's see . . . uh . . . Are you planning to do the interview here at the university, or will I have to go into the studio?

MARSHA: Oh, (15) *there at the university,* if at all possible. (16) *You have* interesting things (17) *in your laboratory*. I think it (18) *would be important* to record (19) *the program there*.

DANIELS: Of course. Well, in that case, I could do it on Wednesday of next week, or . . . Hmm . . . How about this Friday?

MARSHA: (20) *Friday would be* perfect.

DANIELS: Friday's fine. There's just one thing—it'd have to be fairly early Friday afternoon. Since I'll be catching a six o'clock flight to Chicago, I'll have to leave here by around . . . four o'clock.

MARSHA: That's fine. How would it be . . . if (21) *we set it up for two o'clock,* then? It (22) *shouldn't take more than an hour* or so.

DANIELS: Good. Two o'clock, here at my office in Goddard Memorial Center. Will you be able to find it all right?

MARSHA: Oh, no problem. I (23) *used to* take courses (24) *at the university*.

DANIELS: Now, . . . Should I prepare a short lecture?

MARSHA: Oh, no. You (25) *don't have to do that*. We'd (26) *like to keep it* as (27) *informal* as (28) *possible*. I'll prepare (29) *a couple of questions* to (30) *ask you*.

DANIELS: Fine. See you on Friday then.

MARSHA: (31) *Wonderful!* Friday, (32) *at two o'clock*. Thank you, Professor Daniels.

DANIELS: Goodbye.

(Marsha hangs up, then buzzes David Denton on the intercom.)

DAVID: Extension 32.

MARSHA: David, I (33) *just talked with Professor Daniels*. The (34) *interview* is set for (35) *this Friday*.

DAVID: At the university?

MARSHA: Uh-huh. At (36) *his office at* Goddard Center. We're (37) *supposed to be there at two o'clock* sharp.

DAVID: O.K. Meet you at his office?

MARSHA: Well, . . . uh . . . all right, (38) *I guess that'd be* best. Since (39) *you'll need the van with the equipment*, I'll (40) *go in my car*. I'll (41) *meet you* there.

UNIT 4

MARGARET: I see you're working on something right now, Bob. As soon as you finish, I'd like to talk to you for a few minutes.

BOB: (1) *It's O.K.* Come on in . . .

MARGARET: Oh, no, I don't want to interrupt you. I can wait until you're finished.

BOB: (2) *You might have* a long wait! I'm (3) *working on budget figures*.

MARGARET: I thought you'd finished the budget. Didn't you turn it in on Friday?

BOB: Uh-huh. But the controller's office (4) *just sent it*

back to me. I've (5) *been given instructions to* cut it (6) *by 20%.*

MARGARET: They must be kidding! How can you do that?

BOB: That's (7) *what I'm trying to* figure out. I can't (8) *very well* cut down on (9) *our daily news programs. . . .*

MARGARET: No, . . . Well, what about the other departments?

BOB: We (10) *can't cut editorial.* And (11) *we've only got* 40 specials (12) *in the budget* for (13) *the whole* year. I (14) *don't dare cut out* any of those—we'd (15) *lose a lot of viewers.*

MARGARET: Well, what else is there?

BOB: (16) *Travel,* . . . (17) *equipment,* . . . (18) *staff salaries,* . . . I'd sure (19) *hate to have to cut* everybody's salary! Well, (20) *take* your case, for example. You've (21) *been employed here* for (22) *two years now.* It'd be (23) *pretty rough to have a 25%* salary cut, (24) *wouldn't it?*

MARGARET: A salary cut?

BOB: (25) *Even if I do that,* I can't (26) *make it come out right.*

MARGARET: Well, why do they want to cut our budget in the first place?

BOB: That's (27) *not hard to figure out.* Our (28) *ratings!* They've (29) *been going down,* . . . down.

MARGARET: Hmm . . . Well, would it help if we could show that we've had a big increase in number of viewers?

BOB: (30) *Of course it would!* But (31) *the last three reports have been* terrible. That's why (32) *they're making us cut back.*

MARGARET: Bob, listen! I got a call from John this morning. He told me he had some very good news for us.

BOB: The (33) *new viewer survey report?*

MARGARET: Well, he wouldn't tell me anything else. But he must be referring to the latest survey. He said he'd get back to me in a few days.

BOB: (34) *Would you mind calling him back* right away?

MARGARET: Now?

BOB: Sure. Find out if (35) *he's really got something good to report.* Tell him (36) *we can't wait.* We've (37) *got to know now.* Gee, if (38) *we could show that* our audience (39) *for the month* is up . . . by as much as 30%, . . . even 25%, it (40) *just might help.* But (41) *I can't talk to the controller* until (42) *I have something definite.*

MARGARET: Well, let me see what I can find out. I'll go call him right now.

BOB: (43) *Let me know* as soon as (44) *you find out anything.*

MARGARET: Oh, I will!

BOB: Thanks. Oh, Margaret? You said (45) *you wanted to talk to me about something.*

MARGARET: Oh, that . . . It can wait.

UNIT 5

SECRETARY: May I help you?

MARSHA: Yes. I'm here to see Professor Daniels. I have a two o'clock appointment.

SECRETARY: Professor Daniels (1) *won't be back until* next Tuesday morning. He's (2) *gone to Chicago.*

MARSHA: Oh, no, I'm sorry . . . Perhaps he didn't tell you about our appointment. We arranged to meet here this afternoon. His flight isn't until six o'clock and he said he wouldn't have to leave here until 4:00.

SECRETARY: Well, (3) *I'm terribly* sorry, but (4) *he changed his plans at the last minute.* He (5) *asked me to get him on* a three o'clock flight (6) *to Chicago* and he (7) *left here about* . . . (8) *1:00.* It's too late (9) *to reach him at* home—he's (10) *probably on his way to the airport now.*

MARSHA: He's taking a three o'clock flight to Chicago? Are you sure?

SECRETARY: Yes. Oh, (11) *I'm sorry!* I hope (12) *this hasn't inconvenienced you* too much. He (13) *was interviewed for a television* program and since (14) *that was finished earlier* than he expected, he (15) *decided to leave on an earlier flight.*

MARSHA: I—I don't understand. You say, he was interviewed for a television program?

SECRETARY: Yes. Oh, my. It was (16) *exciting.* It's usually (17) *pretty boring around* here, you know. But (18) *not today!* We had (19) *bright lights and cameras.* I (20) *was fascinated!* Looked like a regular (21) *TV studio.* And (22) *the program may be shown* on TV next week! Hmm. Give (23) *me your name,* why (24) *don't you?* I'll (25) *leave a note on Professor Daniels'* desk to let him know (26) *you were here.*

MARSHA: My name is Marsha Nelson. I'm with WNYN-TV. I . . . still don't understand. You say—?

SECRETARY: WNYN-TV? Well, then, (27) *you must know* David Denton! He's (28) *the one who did* the interview (29) *with Professor Daniels.* Nice (30) *young* man!

MARSHA: David was here?

SECRETARY: Yes. He (31) *was a very capable* young man. I'm sure (32) *the station couldn't do without him.* But (33) *he really needs* an assistant (34) *to operate the camera.* It's (35) *really too complicated* for one person (36) *to do it all*—set up lights, run (37) *the camera,* . . . do (38) *the interviewing besides!*

MARSHA: Yes, . . . tell me, what time did David get here anyway?

SECRETARY: Well, (39) *he called* at 9:30—wanted to know (40) *if Professor Daniels could be interviewed* at eleven o'clock (41) *instead of* later (42) *in the day.*

MARSHA: I see . . . So he came . . . over at 11:00?

SECRETARY: (43) *Yes,* (44) *that's right.*

MARSHA: Well, . . . thank you very much.

SECRETARY: Oh, (45) *you're welcome.* And again, I'm (46) *awfully sorry about your appointment.* I'm sure

(47) *this mix-up can be explained somehow.*

MARSHA: Yes. Yes. I'm sure it can. I think I'm beginning to understand what might have happened. Well, goodbye.

SECRETARY: Goodbye, Ms. Nelson. It's (48) *been nice talking with* you. Oh, and (49) *when you get back to* WNYN, I hope (50) *you will have a chance to run into David Denton.*

MARSHA: Yes. Well, I'm sure I'll be running into him very soon.

UNIT 6

AGENT: Marsha Nelson? . . . No, there doesn't seem to be a ticket here for her. Wait a minute! Nelson. Here it is. What was the other name?

BOB: Uh . . . Denton. His (1) *ticket should be there* too.

AGENT: Denton? . . . Yes, it's here.

(David comes up to the counter)

DAVID: Morning, Bob. Sorry I wasn't able to get here a little earlier.

BOB: David! (2) *Thank goodness!* (3) *Where's* Marsha?

DAVID: Oh. Uh . . . Isn't she here yet?

BOB: No. And (4) *it's almost flight time.* I wonder (5) *what's holding her up.* She knows (6) *this is the most important* assignment (7) *she's had.*

DAVID: I'd better check in. (to the ticket agent) Name's Denton. You should be holding a ticket for me. I'm on your nine thirty flight to Denver.

AGENT: Oh, yes, Mr. Denton. Uh . . . Do you have any baggage to check?

DAVID: Uh . . . yes. These two cases.

AGENT: All right . . . That'll be Gate 41. Seat assignment's at the gate. You might want to go right on down to the gate. We're boarding now. Here's your ticket.

DAVID: Thanks. (goes over to Bob) Well, I'm all set. We're supposed to go to the gate. They're boarding already.

BOB: (8) *Where in the world is* Marsha? She (9) *should have been here ten minutes ago!*

DAVID: I don't know. Anyway, we'd better go. We don't want to miss the flight.

BOB: How (10) *could she do this?* If (11) *she doesn't show up,* I don't know (12) *what we're going to do in* Denver!

DAVID: Anyway, we'd better not wait any longer. If she manages to get here in the next few minutes, she'll probably go straight to the gate.

BOB: I just (13) *don't understand it.* We've (14) *planned this thing for a couple of weeks* now. She's always been *more reliable than the others,* but now . . . Lately, . . . I don't know. She's (15) *been moody and different somehow.*

DAVID: I . . . I know what you mean. It's getting harder and harder to talk to her about anything. Anyway, if we have to, we'll just manage this one without her.

BOB: Hmm! I (16) *don't see how.* She's (17) *the most experienced interviewer* we've got. She's (18) *got all the background* on this and (19) *she's worked out the story angle.* This is (20) *the worst thing that's happened to us.*

DAVID: Don't worry. I'm sure I can handle it all right. I've spent some time studying the files . . . I know all the background.

BOB: You do? . . . But (21) *what about the special interview with* Dr. Fisher? . . . And (22) *the other one with the head of the* research department? Those (23) *involve a lot of technical* information.

DAVID: No problem. I'm ready for them. Trust me! Ah, here we are . . . Gate 41. This is the flight we're going on. We seem to be the last ones.

AGENT: Smoking or non-smoking?

BOB: (24) *Non-smoking.*

AGENT: Uh . . . here you are . . . 26A and B. Uh . . . show these to the flight attendant and go right aboard.

DAVID: Thanks. Well, Marsha doesn't seem to be here.

BOB: David! . . . Wait a minute. Maybe (25) *we should call this off.* Are you (26) *sure you can handle it?*

DAVID: Absolutely. It's too bad Marsha couldn't come, but don't worry. It'll turn out all right.

BOB: Well, O.K. (27) *I hope so! We are in a* tight spot. If (28) *you can pull this one off,* we (29) *might have to take another look at the* job category (30) *we have you in.*

DAVID: You mean, . . . you might consider moving me into a job like Marsha's?

BOB: Possibly. All (31) *I can say right now* is that you've (32) *got a real chance to show what you can do!*

UNIT 7

JOHN: You look puzzled about something. . . . What is it? Is there something you don't understand?

MARGARET: No, . . . I was (1) *just wondering how we could* tell . . . uh . . . uh . . .

JOHN: Tell what?

MARGARET: Well, we've . . . we've had (2) *several months that haven't been* very good, . . . And now, (3) *all of a sudden,* we've (4) *doubled our audience* this month, . . . which (5) *makes me think that these figures might be misleading.*

JOHN: What are you getting at?

MARGARET: Well, we (6) *could have had an unusual month* for some reason or another.

JOHN: Oh, I think I understand what you're trying to get at.

MARGARET: (7) *Do you see what* I mean? We've (8) *had this one trend for several* months—going (9) *down steadily.* And now, (10) *we had a really good month.* Is (11) *there any way we can* be sure (12) *that we've really reversed the trend?*

JOHN: No, I'm afraid not. All we really know is that something significant happened this month.

MARGARET: That's (13) *really the problem!* . . . Trying to (14) *figure out what kind of budget projections* we can make.

JOHN: O.K. Here's something . . . Maybe it'll help. Look at this: if we compare this month with last month, we see something very interesting. Notice . . . that the audience for your daily news—both the six o'clock and the eleven o'clock programs—have almost doubled this month.

MARGARET: Yes, . . . up 94% (15) *for the six o'clock* and 87% (16) *for the eleven o'clock.*

JOHN: O.K. Now look at the news-feature category. You had twelve of them last month and ten this month.

MARGARET: They've (17) *just about doubled too!*

JOHN: Right! Now look at your specials . . . up an average of 110%. As I was saying, . . . this is very interesting. It's a consistent pattern. You've almost doubled your audience—across the board!

MARGARET: (18) *I see what you're saying.* . . .

JOHN: You could have had an increase in any one of the categories, and we'd say it had to do with interest in certain specific topics you presented on those programs.

MARGARET: (19) *Yes, I see!*

JOHN: But when we see it across the board like this, in all your programming, then it seems to be a significant thing.

MARGARET: Which probably means (20) *that the changes we've made in all of our program formats* have led to (21) *greater viewer acceptance of all of* our programming!

JOHN: Exactly! So, I see it as something that should continue—providing you continue the same kind of programming.

MARGARET: This (22) *has been very helpful,* John. And (23) *I know that Bob'll be interested in* these observations. Now, (24) *the important* thing is . . . Well, uh . . . when (25) *can we have copies of the report?*

JOHN: Next week. Mm . . . I should be able to have copies to you by Wednesday.

UNIT 8

GRACE: What is it, Bob? You sounded pretty serious on the phone. Have we still got a budget problem?

BOB: I don't know. I (1) *hope not.* The (2) *meeting's on Friday.* But (3) *that's not what I want to* talk to (4) *you about.* Uh . . . close (5) *the door,* (6) *will you?* (Grace closes the door.) It's Marsha. . . .

GRACE: Marsha? . . . What about her?

BOB: I'm (7) *worried.* I (8) *don't know what to do.* She's (9) *just not performing.* We (10) *may have to* let her go.

GRACE: Fire her? . . . She's been with us a long time, Bob. If she leaves, it'll be a big loss to the station. She's done really excellent work.

BOB: Yes, but lately, . . . (11) *the last month or so,* in fact—there've (12) *been a lot of problems.* She's (13) *changed,* Grace. Not only (14) *does she have a tendency to be moody all the time,* but (15) *she misses appointments,* doesn't (16) *follow through on projects* and (17) *doesn't seem to plan anything till* the last minute.

GRACE: Hmm. Did she ever explain why she didn't show up for the Denver trip?

BOB: No. She (18) *said she was sorry* and that (19) *it wouldn't happen* again—something about (20) *a mix-up on arrangements to get to the* airport. Now, whenever (21) *anybody mentions the subject to* her, (22) *she just* clams up. I don't know. Thank goodness, (23) *David pulled us out of the* hole (24) *on that one!*

GRACE: Yes. He did a really fine job—filling in for Marsha like that at the last minute.

BOB: I (25) *don't think it was the first time he's had to do* that. If (26) *we knew all the* facts, I think (27) *we'd find that he's been* covering for Marsha (28) *on quite a few projects.*

GRACE: Well, I know at least one other case. . . .

BOB: (29) *Covering for Marsha?*

GRACE: Uh-huh. I just looked at the material for the space exploration special. It looks really good, by the way. But guess who did the interviewing?

BOB: (30) *David?*

GRACE: Right. Apparently, Marsha made the arrangements with Professor Daniels . . . and then she didn't show up at the university for the interview. David had to do it by himself.

BOB: (31) *Did you get any* explanation?

GRACE: Well, I talked to David about it and he was pretty evasive. Whatever the problem was, he didn't want to talk about it. Uh . . . I think he was trying to cover up to protect Marsha. He asked me not to make an issue out of it and uh . . . upset her.

BOB: Well, that does it! I (32) *don't think we have any choice.* We (33) *just can't afford to* keep (34) *Marsha on that job.* I guess (35) *the best thing to do is move David up* and (36) *hire another* cameraman. What (37) *do you think?*

GRACE: I don't know. I sure don't like the idea of losing Marsha. There must be something troubling her. Never before have we had a problem like this. Uh . . . Why don't we hold off for a few days? And . . . let me try to talk with her and see if I can't find out what the problem is.

BOB: Well, all right. Do (38) *what you can.* I (39) *don't want to fire her* unless (40) *it's absolutely* necessary, but . . .

UNIT 9

(Bob Russo is waiting in George Benson's office; George finally arrives)

GEORGE: Sorry (1) *to keep you waiting*, Bob. I've (2) *been meeting with the* auditors.

BOB: No problem. How's the audit coming?

GEORGE: O.K. They'll be (3) *finalizing their comments next week*. That means (4) *we may be getting the report by* the end of the month.

BOB: Good. Uh . . . uh . . . where's Steve?

GEORGE: He's (5) *not going to make it*. I guess (6) *we don't really need him*—do we?

BOB: Well, the only thing is, . . . I wanted to discuss our income projections. Did . . . did he show you the new advertising plan I worked out?

GEORGE: No, but he (7) *might have given a copy to my secretary*.

BOB: Oh, . . . I went over my plan with him yesterday. Here's the revised budget.

GEORGE: (8) *This is your revised* budget? Hmm . . . Wait a minute! I've (9) *already seen this*, haven't I? Aren't (10) *these your original figures?*

BOB: Yes, but there have been—

GEORGE: (11) *What about the reduction?* You (12) *were going to trim your budget by* 20%.

BOB: I know you wanted me to cut the budget, but I've taken care of the problem in a different way. Uh . . . take a look at the income projections—Section II.

GEORGE: O.K. Uh . . . here we are—"Anticipated Revenue . . . Revenue, Advertisers . . ." Hmmm! Let's see, . . . your (13) *original projection was*: $1,240,700. Uh-huh. . . . and now, (14) *you're showing*: $1,638,150 . . . That's (15) *quite a jump*, (16) *isn't it?*

BOB: $394,024 . . . or, roughly, a 32% increase.

GEORGE: (17) *What happened?* What (18) *are you basing* these (19) *new projections on?*

BOB: Current audience figures. We've had a dramatic change. We're up nearly 100%.

GEORGE: All the reports (20) *that I've seen show your ratings* have been going down!

BOB: The latest survey shows that we've reversed that trend now. Our audience—

GEORGE: (21) *Wait a minute!* Hold on! I've (22) *got all the reports right here*. Just, uh . . . I (23) *don't remember seeing anything like that*—

BOB: You don't have the current one. Copies are due next week.

GEORGE: Oh. Uh-huh . . . and (24) *you say it shows*—

BOB: Nearly a 100% increase in audience—in all categories! Daily news, features, specials—across the board!

GEORGE: Hmm . . . How (25) *do you explain that?*

BOB: Well, we've made a lot of changes in program format. We're simply getting better viewer acceptance because of these improvements—some new personalities, more "live" coverage in our news, more interesting features, more sports—

GEORGE: I realize (26) *that's a possible explanation*, but (27) *how do you know that this audience "shift" wasn't just* (28) *something unusual that happened* last month?

BOB: Oh, no. We're sure that's not the explanation!

GEORGE: (29) *You think it* shows (30) *that you've reversed the downward trend then?*

BOB: Absolutely!

GEORGE: Well, . . . it's (31) *a simple matter of economics*. You may be (32) *picking up bigger audiences with your new programs*. If you are, . . . and if (33) *you can generate this kind of advertising income*, then (34) *the cuts we've talked about shouldn't be* necessary.

BOB: As you can see, even if we have an increase of only 20% in revenue, we'll have covered our operation without having to make any cuts.

GEORGE: Uh-huh . . . I see. Well, all right. I (35) *don't have any problem with it*. Uh . . . get me (36) *a copy of that survey report* as soon as (37) *you can though*. I need (38) *the report* so (39) *I can show it to the budget committee*.

UNIT 10

MARGARET: Hi, Peggy. (1) *Everything all right?*

PEGGY: To tell you the truth, I'm not sure . . . How was the meeting?

MARGARET: Huh! Oh, (2) *it was all about TV programs* by satellite. If I'd known (3) *it was going to be so technical*, I (4) *would've asked Bob to send somebody* else. Actually, (5) *it was kind of boring*.

PEGGY: Well, it sure wasn't boring around here!

MARGARET: (6) *Busy*, huh?

PEGGY: Uh-huh. A lot of phone calls, your boss on the intercom, people in and out of the office all afternoon! You know, I recommend you ask for an assistant. I don't see how you handle it all by yourself.

MARGARET: Oh, it's (7) *usually not so bad*. Anything (8) *I should know about?*

PEGGY: You've got a bunch of messages here. How about going over them together? I'm not sure you'd be able to figure out my notes.

MARGARET: (9) *O.K.*

PEGGY: Boy! I'd sure like to know what's been going on in Mr. Russo's office!

MARGARET: Well, (10) *what do you mean?*

PEGGY: All the people he's been meeting with! Practically everybody on the staff!

MARGARET: You mean, . . . he (11) *called a staff meeting?*

PEGGY: Well, Grace Lee was in there—a long time . . . Then, Mr. Benson . . . And, let's see . . . Uh . . . Oh, yes! Tom Hackett from Personnel. He was in twice—once by himself, then later with his secretary.

MARGARET: Barbara?

PEGGY: Uh-huh. I guess she was taking dictation. I heard her tell Mr. Russo she'd get . . . whatever it was . . . typed up right away.

MARGARET: (12) *That's interesting . . .*

PEGGY: Yeah. I could have done it for him. Why do you suppose he had Barbara come up?

MARGARET: (13) *I . . . I don't know . . .*

PEGGY: Anyway, later he called David Denton in and spent a long time with him. Then after he left, Grace Lee went in again. What do you suppose, uh . . .

MARGARET: Gosh, (14) *I just have no idea.*

PEGGY: I'm really curious now. Why don't you ask Grace about it? I would sure like to find out.

MARGARET: Hmm. Maybe (15) *I will.* Well, anyway, (16) *let's get back to these phone messages.* Anything (17) *urgent?*

(After Peggy leaves, Margaret goes to Grace Lee's office.)

MARGARET: Uh . . . Grace? (18) *Are you busy?*

GRACE: Oh, no. Come in, Margaret. How was the seminar?

MARGARET: It (19) *was O.K.* Sounds like (20) *it's been pretty busy around here.* Peggy (21) *tells me* that—

GRACE: Oh, it's been quite an afternoon!

MARGARET: Grace? Uh . . . What's (22) *going on?* Peggy's (23) *telling me* that—

GRACE: Uh . . . Close the door, Margaret. Well, for one thing, David got a promotion. He really deserves it. He's now a full-fledged reporter.

MARGARET: (24) *Really?* (25) *That's wonderful!*

GRACE: Wait. There's . . . there's something else. Uh, . . . it's not very pleasant. We had to make a very painful decision today. And uh . . . well, this is strictly confidential. I suggest you not discuss it with anybody—at least not for a few days. Uh . . . Bob . . . , that is, we, decided that . . . uh . . .

UNIT 11

DAVID: Hey, why the long face? We're supposed to be celebrating, . . . remember? Aren't you happy about my promotion?

MARGARET: Yes, David . . . (1) *It's just* that—

DAVID: Now I'm going to get a chance to do my own programs! I won't have some reporter telling me what to do. "I want this scene taken, David!" "I want this job done right away, David!"

MARGARET: Oh, David, (2) *stop it!* Marsha's (3) *a sweet, lovely person!* And (4) *she's a top-notch* reporter—the (5) *very best!* It (6) *just breaks my heart to see her leave!*

DAVID: What do you mean "see her leave"?

MARGARET: I mean "leave"—lose (7) *her job!* (8) *Understand?* They're (9) *going to fire her!*

DAVID: What? You're not serious!

MARGARET: (10) *I shouldn't have told you* about it. I (11)

promised I wouldn't say anything.

DAVID: I can't believe it! Why would she get fired?

MARGARET: (12) *You tell me,* David!

DAVID: Me?! How should I know anything about it?

MARGARET: (13) *I've been* wondering. What (14) *really happened that day at the university?*

DAVID: What are you talking about?

MARGARET: Well, right after (15) *Marsha made arrangements with Professor Daniels,* she wanted (16) *a letter sent to him to* confirm (17) *their phone conversation.*

DAVID: So?

MARGARET: So, I (18) *typed the letter!* The interview (19) *was set up for two o'clock* that Friday. Marsha (20) *told me that you were supposed to meet her at the university.*

DAVID: She must have gotten mixed up. The time was changed to 11:00 A.M.

MARGARET: Really? And (21) *who changed the time of the interview?*

DAVID: Well, uh—

MARGARET: You did, (22) *didn't you?* And (23) *you didn't bother to tell Marsha about it!*

DAVID: Well, what happened was—

MARGARET: I know. You (24) *got in touch with Professor Daniels* and moved (25) *the interview up to eleven o'clock* so you (26) *could do it by yourself,* didn't you?

DAVID: Oh, well, what if I did? That was the only way I could prove that I could do the interviewing—that I didn't need Marsha to tell me what to do.

MARGARET: Oh, David, how (27) *could you have done such a rotten thing?* What else (28) *have you done?* (29) *What about the* Denver (30) *trip?*

DAVID: What about it?

MARGARET: (31) *I'm not* sure . . . Was (32) *that another one of your tricks?*

DAVID: I don't know what you're talking about . . .

MARGARET: (33) *How did it* happen that (34) *Marsha didn't get to the airport* in time? Did (35) *you have anything to do with* that?

DAVID: Me?

MARGARET: What did you do—tell (36) *Marsha you'd give her a ride* and then (37) *leave her waiting at her* apartment . . . so she (38) *couldn't get on that plane?*

DAVID: It wasn't like that at all! It was just—I just forgot to pick her up—that's all. It was as simple as that. I completely forgot!

MARGARET: Why (39) *didn't you tell Bob Russo that?* He (40) *should have known about it* before you two (41) *got on that flight!* No, . . . I (42) *don't believe you.* I think (43) *you did it deliberately* . . . But why? That's (44) *what I don't understand.*

DAVID: It was my big chance! I knew I could do the job and I had to prove it.

MARGARET: (45) *You must be very proud of yourself!* How does (46) *it make you feel to know* that you're

(47) *responsible for Marsha's losing her* job?

DAVID: I didn't mean any harm to Marsha. I certainly didn't want her to lose her job! I just wanted a chance to show Bob what I could do!

MARGARET: (48) *Yeah, . . .* (49) *at Marsha's expense!*

UNIT 12

MARSHA: What am I going to do now, Rita? I'll be lost without this job. I've really enjoyed working at WNYN.

RITA: I'll tell you (1) *what you're going to do!* You're (2) *going to go to your boss* and (3) *tell him the* whole story—

MARSHA: But there's nothing to tell. He says I'm not doing the job to their satisfaction. Now, how am I going to argue with that—tell them they're wrong?

RITA: (4) *That's not* the reason (5) *you're getting* fired—and (6) *you know it!*

MARSHA: Wait a minute. Listen. This is what the letter says, uh . . . "We regret to inform you that after careful evaluation, . . ." and so forth, . . . and so forth, . . . uh . . . Listen . . . "the determination has been made that your job performance over the past 60 days has not been in accordance with the minimum performance standards established by WNYN-TV."

RITA: But, Marsha! (7) *What's that young guy's name?* Uh . . . what's his name?

MARSHA: You mean, David?

RITA: Yeah, David! (8) *He's the one who's been* interfering with (9) *your job!* And (10) *with your job performance!* (11) *He's* been sabotaging (12) *you!*

MARSHA: Now, that's a little strong, isn't it?

RITA: Well, I (13) *don't know what else you'd call it.* He's (14) *been doing everything possible to make you* look bad and (15) *himself* look good. He's (16) *made you miss deadlines,* he's (17) *tricked you,* he's (18) *taken jobs away from you,* why, he's, he's just—

MARSHA: He just doesn't like being told what to do! He's a very ambitious young man and he's determined to get ahead as fast as he can. Unfortunately, I just happened to be in the way.

RITA: You've (19) *got to fight* to protect (20) *your own interests!* Here's (21) *this guy who's lied,* he's (22) *cheated,* he's (23) *played dirty tricks on you* . . . And (24) *now you're getting fired* because of him. He (25) *doesn't care about you!* And (26) *here you are making excuses* for him!

MARSHA: He's very good at his work. I've got to admit that!

RITA: (27) *All right, all right!* So (28) *he's terrific at his job!* So what? That (29) *doesn't entitle him to step* all over you and (30) *ruin your career!* You're (31) *very good* too—remember? You're (32) *at the top.* Everybody (33) *agrees with that!*

MARSHA: Hmm . . . not quite everybody . . . The management at WNYN doesn't—

RITA: But (34) *they don't know what's happened!* They think (35) *you're falling down on your* job. And (36) *you're not!*

MARSHA: O.K. So what do you want me to do? Go to Bob Russo and say, "Bob, the reason my performance isn't acceptable to you is that David stopped me from doing my job! He just wouldn't let me do my job . . ."?

RITA: No. (37) *Give him* the details! Tell him (38) *how David tricked you,* saying (39) *he'd pick you up and take you to the* airport (40) *that morning.* Or, tell him (41) *about that other time at the university* when (42) *David cut you out by changing* the appointment time! And (43) *what about that* City Hall (44) *interview?* And (45) *the hospital project?* And (46) *all those other times* he (47) *went out on his own?*

MARSHA: Bob would just think that I was making excuses and trying to blame David for everything so I wouldn't lose my job. Besides, criticizing David behind his back wouldn't be right—

RITA: (48) *Don't do it behind his* back! Tell your boss (49) *to have David come to his office* at the same time! Then (50) *have him ask David point-blank whether all those things are true* or not!

MARSHA: Oh, I'm sure David would be able to give very logical explanations for everything.

RITA: Sure, he'd (51) *probably deny everything.* But (52) *you've been with them* a long time and (53) *they know what kind of person you are.* Who (54) *do you think your* boss (55) *is going to* believe—you (56) *or him?* Oh, (57) *this thing makes me* sick! It's (58) *just all unfair!* That guy's (59) *getting away with murder!*

UNIT 13

(David rushes into the room.)

DAVID: Marsha! I wish you had told somebody where you were going to be! I've been looking all over for you! You've got to drop what you're doing right now! We don't have much time!

MARSHA: I (1) *don't know what you're talking about*—

DAVID: Come on! We've got to go. There's a four-alarm fire in a big apartment building on Second Avenue! We've got to get over there right away to cover it!

MARSHA: David, . . . (2) *you can't do that!* The (3) *news team is probably already* there. It's (4) *their story,* not (5) *yours!*

DAVID: No! It's our story—yours and mine! The news team is doing a story up in Danbury today. They couldn't possibly make it back in time. Come on!

MARSHA: (6) *Have you talked to* Bob?

DAVID: Of course! He called me about it. He said to get over there right away!

MARSHA: (7) *He wants you to* cover it. You (8) *don't need me, David!* Haven't (9) *you heard?* At the (10) *end of the month I'm*—

DAVID: Marsha! What I told Bob was that we'd do it

129

together! You've got to go! Bob's counting on you.

MARSHA: (11) *You know very well* you (12) *can handle it yourself*, David. This is—

DAVID: I'd rather have you go with me. We're supposed to be a team—remember?

MARSHA: (13) *But, David,* . . .

DAVID: Look, I wish we had time to argue about this, but we don't. We're wasting valuable time. Come on! I'll get the camera equipment and meet you at the van in five minutes. You'd better start trying to come up with some possible story angles! Let's go!

MARSHA: (14) *But, David—*

DAVID: Later, O.K.? Right now, let's do our job!

MARSHA: (15) *Well, O.K.* . . . I (16) *need to stop by my office* to get some things—then (17) *I'll meet you in the parking lot.*

UNIT 14

(Margaret is just returning to her office.)

MARGARET: Hi, Peggy. I'm back. Thanks for covering the phones for me.

PEGGY: Boy! I (1) *wish I had an office like this.* Never (2) *a dull moment!* Something's (3) *always going on* here. Except (4) *I don't see how you ever get any work done.*

MARGARET: Well, were there a lot of calls?

PEGGY: Not (5) *so many.* Four, (6) *I think.* Let's see . . . Steve called. He . . . (7) *wanted to know how long it would* take (8) *to have ten copies of the new* survey report (9) *made.* He (10) *said he'd call back this afternoon.*

MARGARET: O.K.

PEGGY: And uh . . . you (11) *had a call from* a Mrs. Henderson. She's (12) *supposed to have a meeting with Mr. Russo on* Friday and (13) *she'd like to have the meeting postponed until next* Tuesday.
And . . . Let's see . . . Oh, yes! Mr. Fisher (14) *called from the* Research Institute. He (15) *didn't say what he wanted.* He'll (16) *call back.* And uh . . .

MARGARET: Mr. Johnson didn't call?

PEGGY: Oh, (17) *I forgot.* Yeah . . . Now (18) *what did he call about?* I remember. He said (19) *he'd made the arrangements for the interview.* He'd (20) *like to have it scheduled for* next Thursday. I (21) *was talking to him* when David (22) *came in* . . . and (23) *I guess I forgot to write the message down.*

MARGARET: David . . . was here?

PEGGY: Yeah. But (24) *he wasn't in a very good mood.*

MARGARET: Well, what do you mean?

PEGGY: Oh, (25) *you know how he* is—always joking (26) *about everything.* But today he (27) *was really serious.* Different. He (28) *seemed like he was* worried (29) *about something.* He was (30) *in a big hurry to see* Mr. Russo.

MARGARET: Oh?

PEGGY: (31) *He was in there* quite a while. I (32) *was on*

the phone when (33) *he left.* He (34) *walked right by me* . . . didn't (35) *say a word.*

MARGARET: Hmm. Well, thanks, Peggy. I'd better get to work. I've got to get some reports typed up for Bob. I promised I'd have them finished by two o'clock.

PEGGY: Yeah. I've got to (36) *get back to my office.* By the way, there's (37) *a meeting going on in Mr. Russo's office* and (38) *he left word he didn't want to be* disturbed.

MARGARET: Oh? Who's he meeting with?

PEGGY: (39) *Grace and Tom.*

MARGARET: You mean, . . . Tom Hackett from Personnel?

PEGGY: (40) *Like I said,* never a dull moment (41) *around here!* Remember (42) *what happened the last time he was up here?* Marsha (43) *got fired.* I wonder (44) *who it's going to be this* time . . . David?

MARGARET: No. Of course not.

PEGGY: (45) *I hope not.* He's (46) *a good guy.* It (47) *would be too bad.* Well, (48) *I've got to go.* I'll (49) *leave your phone messages here on your* desk. See (50) *you later.*

MARGARET: Yeah. See you.

UNIT 15

(Bob Russo has asked Marsha to come to his office.)

MARSHA: Bob? Margaret said you wanted to see me?

BOB: (1) *Yes, I do!* As a matter of fact, I've (2) *been down to your office three or four times* this morning (3) *looking for you.*

MARSHA: Sorry. I was in the production room working on the final details for tomorrow's program.

BOB: Oh, yes. The (4) *special on Computers in Education.* You've (5) *worked hard on that project,* Marsha. (6) *Is it going to be a* good program?

MARSHA: I hope so. Since it's going to be my last one, somehow I want it to be the best one I've ever done. Can you understand that?

BOB: Yes, of course. But (7) *that's just what I want to talk to you about* . . . It's not (8) *going to be your last special for* WNYN—

MARSHA: Oh? But, Bob, I'm leaving on Friday. I don't think there'd be enough time to do another prog—

BOB: Wait! (9) *Let me go on.* In (10) *the first place,* I feel (11) *I owe you a big apology—*

MARSHA: For what?

BOB: (12) *For judging performance* on the basis of (13) *circumstantial evidence*—telling you (14) *that your work wasn't satisfactory.* And for (15) *taking action on terminating you* without (16) *looking into the facts of the* case—

MARSHA: Bob, I—

BOB: (17) *Just a* minute. Let me finish. David (18) *came to me* and he (19) *told me* everything—all the gruesome (20) *details.* I (21) *have to tell you* that (22) *I was shocked.* And of course, I (23) *was very* disappointed in David . . . because of (24) *the things he's done.* Anyway, (25) *what I'm trying to say is* that I'm (26) *sorry for the misunderstanding.* We don't (27) *want you to leave,* Marsha! We (28) *want you to stay on the* job.

MARSHA: I . . . I . . . I don't know what to say. . . .

BOB: You (29) *don't have to say* anything—except (30) *that you'll stay.* And (31) *that you'll forget this whole* unhappy thing.

MARSHA: Well, . . . well, of course I'll stay—if you want me to. But . . . but what about David?

BOB: (32) *I haven't made a decision* about him yet. He (33) *gave me a letter of resignation* yesterday.

MARSHA: Oh, Bob, don't let him go! He's a very talented person!

BOB: Yes, but (34) *he's done some terrible things.* How could we (35) *ever trust him again?* He's (36) *lied,* he's (37) *manipulated all of us,* he's—

MARSHA: But you know, Bob, I don't think there's anything malicious about David. Sure, he picked some peculiar ways to try to demonstrate his abilities—to get your attention. But maybe that's because he's young and—Just think what it took for him to come to you and tell you what he's done!

BOB: (38) *You really amaze me,* Marsha! You really do! You (39) *nearly lost your job* because (40) *of him.* And (41) *after all the things he's done,* you (42) *sit here making excuses for him,* trying to (43) *convince me not to fire him.*

MARSHA: I want him to stay, Bob. I know we can work together as a team—I think we proved that on the big news story last week. Tell him he still has a job. . . .

BOB: Well, . . . it's (44) *not quite that simple.* I am (45) *glad to know how you feel* about it. That (46) *helps a lot.* But (47) *I'm going to have to think it over* very carefully (48) *before I can make a* decision.

Tapescript for Listenings

UNIT 1

ADVISER: If you're nervous when you go for a job interview, I think one good thing that you might do is . . . uh . . . try turning that around, uh . . . to use the . . . the nervous energy . . . that you've got, to sell yourself. You know, you're the one that's on the line. So, if you're thinking about yourself, talk about that. Because that's what the purpose of the interview is.

STUDENT: Well, most times when I uh . . . go into uh . . . an office to apply for a job, I . . . get so nervous, anticipating what's going to happen, that I . . . practically forget everything I want to say and think about it when I leave, you know. . . .

ADVISER: Yeah. Uh . . . Have you ever tried practicing, uh . . . like with friends?

STUDENT: All the time—

ADVISER: . . . a mock interview?

STUDENT: . . . all the time. And it comes out just perfect in the practice session, . . . you know, so. . . . Then I get in the office and there I am. I freeze up, you know, . . . inwardly.

ADVISER: Sometimes it helps you to . . . uh . . . , you know, think a lot about what kind of a place it is that you're going to be going into and what kind of people you're going to encounter . . . uh . . . there. That might help to loosen it up a little bit, . . . you know, for you. Also, uh . . . if you try a tape recorder and listen to yourself talking about yourself, uh . . . that really helps. Do it cold. Do it uh . . . right off the top.

STUDENT: Most times I go in feeling that I'm going to have a relaxed . . . attitude about it and uh . . . just let it come off the top. Sometimes I wonder if . . . you can be too casual. Should you . . . uh . . . you know, discuss things outside of . . . the relevancy of the job and uh. . . .

ADVISER: I . . . I think that uh . . . you know, some degree of being casual is good, . . . as long as you're relevant. Uh . . . that, of course, is the central issue, you know, . . . are they going to give you the job? Uh . . . so, if you do bring in outside things, like your hobbies or interests, relate those to the job. Sell yourself.

STUDENT: The thing is, uh . . . what happens if you anticipate all the . . . wrong questions and . . . you're sitting there all primed and ready to go, with a whole—

ADVISER: Well, you know, there's some other things, like uh . . . uh . . . brief yourself on . . . on what your strong points are and . . . and what your history is and how it's relevant to . . . what you're looking for uh . . . in this job.

STUDENT: Well, this'd be, . . . you know, . . . it'd be my first time applying for a paid job and . . . that's another thing I worry about—whether or not I have enough experience, uh . . . I—

ADVISER: Well, I think—

STUDENT: . . . I feel like I'm qualified for the job . . . because I know the skills, but . . . I've never been paid to do them and I don't know if . . . I'm qualified enough . . . for what they're looking for.

ADVISER: Well, I think employers are often eager, you know, . . . to look for . . . uh . . . young men that are positive about themselves and have a strong attitude about their own success. So, I think that. . . uh . . . is in your favor, at least as much as . . . uh . . . some years of experience.

UNIT 2

MR. CAMPBELL: I think part of the problem of traffic is that, perhaps well-founded or not, planners and . . . architects . . . believe and are taught that those problems are solvable. And . . . that's—

INTERVIEWER: Do you think they're irreversible at this point?

MR. CAMPBELL: Well, it's the question that has to be decided upon —whether certain technological . . . aspects have made things irreversible. Maybe the car has to be eliminated. There certainly have been proponents for that.

INTERVIEWER: It dominates our life so much, especially in the cities. Uh . . . I'm sure that the major portion of a city's budget is directed towards uh . . . street maintenance.

MR. CAMPBELL: Well, it's interesting the . . . the way the car has a personal relationship to people —whether they park it around the corner, or they want it next to their house, or in their basement, or next to the living room—

INTERVIEWER: Do you think that —

MR. CAMPBELL: . . . Whether they spend their time on Saturday polishing it, or—

INTERVIEWER: It's revealing, psychologically—

MR. CAMPBELL: Uh-hmm . . .

INTERVIEWER: . . . I think you're saying. And that might be . . . a large part of the reason why it's so hard to make the change away from cars is because people have uh . . . put so much of their identity into it.

MR. CAMPBELL: Maybe we have to consider the implications of the problems we're having with cars in such a large collective sense—what they indicate about society, psychologically, maybe.

INTERVIEWER: What is the impact of the automobile on our cities?

MR. CAMPBELL: Well, the impact has resulted in a lot of congestion. We don't know . . . what to do with it, as well as where to put the car, now that so many people have it.

INTERVIEWER: How about environmentally, what's—you know, within the city?

MR. CAMPBELL: Well, there's some interesting things about that. Some plants actually seem to thrive on the exhaust fumes of cars, while people don't necessarily do that, but . . . plants certainly get off on some of the exhaust fumes.

INTERVIEWER: What about the environment for the people, . . . say, the buildings, and the—using, like, the sidewalks?

MR. CAMPBELL: Well, there has been attempts to . . . segregate the car more, . . . to . . . to put it in an area where it's not in such immediate contact with people as well as buildings and . . . one of the problems with its contact with buildings is that there has been observed an element of decay in the structure, . . . as

well as in the materials that make up the building.

INTERVIEWER: Do . . . do you mean to say that the buildings are beginning to crumble?

MR. CAMPBELL: Well, you can't . . . go outside and see this, obviously, but over a period of time, that seems to be the situation.

INTERVIEWER: So that, eventually, the cars . . . could destroy our cities. . . .

MR. CAMPBELL: Well, they certainly could destroy . . . the . . . materials in the buildings, they could affect the health of the people and maybe, in some way, they will actually destroy themselves.

UNIT 3

INTERVIEWER: What do you, as a space scientist, think of all the movies about space wars and . . . star wars and things like that, that we're having these days?

SCIENTIST: Well, I'm just like you. I enjoy them thoroughly. I don't see a lot of connection with my own work, necessarily. Uh . . . for example, when you see the spaceships battling in outer space, they behave like fighter planes—as though they had an atmosphere to fly in. And, of course, in space, there is no atmosphere and they would not be jockeying and jumping back and forth the way they are. Uh . . . another thing that I find fascinating is the way that they uh . . . deal with extraterrestrials—or "people," if you want to call them, from other planets. I think it tells us more about ourselves . . . as human beings and how we get along with races on this planet . . . the way we speculate about uh . . . "mookies" and uh . . . "chewbakki" and—

INTERVIEWER: Do you think we ever . . . really will encounter life from another planet?

SCIENTIST: I hope so. I think that would be very good for . . . for the race of mankind here on earth . . . for us to uh . . . have contact with uh . . .

INTERVIEWER: Are we presently making efforts to contact other . . . uh . . . species, I guess you'd call them?

SCIENTIST: Well, I'm not aware of any uh . . . uh . . . efforts to send a signal, other than uh . . . a few plaques sent out in . . . in orbit. But we're listening all the time. There are antennae that are trying to pick up signals from uh . . . other parts of the solar system—

INTERVIEWER: Are—Aren't those called radio telescopes?

SCIENTIST: Yes. Right. There's one in Puerto Rico that's quite large.

INTERVIEWER: Uh . . . Do they not uh . . . presently receive sig—regular kinds of signals from . . . outer space? . . . But those are just from stars, or something?

SCIENTIST: Well, they're listening to signals that are coming in from uh . . . from all over the . . . uh . . .

the galaxy, I gather. Uh . . . but there is nothing that can be interpreted as being an intelligent signal coming to us.

INTERVIEWER: I see. Uh . . . they're far more sensitive than optical telescopes, aren't they?

SCIENTIST: That's right.

INTERVIEWER: They can detect things that . . . we could not possibly see . . . uh . . . even with the Mount Palomar telescope. . . .

SCIENTIST: Well, th—those particular telescopes, uh . . . the radio telescopes, are not looking in the visible spectrum. They are looking in radio frequencies and uh . . . they—they listen to frequencies that we couldn't possibly see. But uh. . . . Th—there's something about astronomy and the study of the heavens that really, . . . Uh . . . we haven't changed all that much in four or five hundred years. Uh . . . half a thousand years ago, the men that looked through telescopes and who thought about the heavens were really philosophers. And when it comes right down to it, uh . . . the men and women that do that today have to have . . . a bit of that feeling in them too. There are so many things that we don't understand, . . . that we don't know about. We don't even have a language to talk about. And it—there's a —there's something almost a matter of faith—

INTERVIEWER: Yes, you—

SCIENTIST: . . . You have to be a philosopher almost—

INTERVIEWER: . . . must really be a pioneer, I suppose, to be in the field that you're in.

SCIENTIST: Every day, every week brings something new.

INTERVIEWER: And you have to find new ways to describe the new things.

SCIENTIST: Uh . . . the language problem is one of our difficulties. We have to coin new words and we have to uh . . . ''get our heads around,'' so to speak, . . . new concepts and then try to explain it to people who are also interested.

INTERVIEWER: So, in many ways, the problems that you face are quite similar to those faced by Galileo or Copernicus. . . .

SCIENTIST: Yes, I'd say so. There's a good deal of superstition even today about what uh . . . what should be done in space.

INTERVIEWER: I suppose that . . . is evidenced by the attitude that some of the movies take, at least. . . .

SCIENTIST: Well, the movies are uh . . . ar—are good, I think, for uh . . . for the space scientist. They may not be totally accurate, . . . but uh . . . they certainly popularize uh . . . some of the things that will be possible in the next fifty years, . . . hundred years, . . . two hundred years. . . .

UNIT 4

Part 1:   Man

INTERVIEWER: What are your viewpoints about continuing education?

MAN: What does that mean? Or, in other words. . .

INTERVIEWER: Oh. Oh, I mean, by continuing education, that you uh . . . go back to school after you've finished, for example, high school—

MAN: I wouldn't want to go back to school if I had to! I think that—

INTERVIEWER: Oh, well, why is that?

MAN: Well, I went to school for twelve years, . . . I finished high school, . . . it didn't do me a bit of good. I didn't get anything out of it and I . . . felt like I was a prisoner in school.

INTERVIEWER: Oh. How come you felt like you were a prisoner?

MAN: Oh, I had to be there at eight o'clock in the morning . . . They told me when I could eat lunch and uh . . . when I could leave and . . . and if they didn't like the way I was dressed, then they'd make me stay longer and it was just a terrible experience for me.

INTERVIEWER: I see. So—Well, what do you do now?

MAN: Well, I work in construction and uh . . . I'm pers—pretty free to uh . . . hammer nails and . . .

INTERVIEWER: I see. You—So, you do as you . . . like now and . . . and would see going back to school as a—

MAN: I think that it . . . it—school restricts my freedom.

Part 2:   Woman

Now listen to the woman.

INTERVIEWER: What are your views about continuing education?

WOMAN: I suppose it's a good thing. I've been taking some classes myself at night, trying to get—trying to get in control of my life, trying to learn some things that I need to know to—

INTERVIEWER: I see. I see. So—

WOMAN: . . . to take care of myself and my family.

INTERVIEWER: So, you are using continuing education right now—past the . . . high school kind of level or—

WOMAN: Yes, I've got a high school diploma and now I'm taking classes in . . . auto repair and—

INTERVIEWER: Ah . . . auto repair! Is that . . . uh . . . a necessary thing for you to have, do you feel?

WOMAN: I think it is. I'm single, I've got children and I need to know how to do those things for myself. I have no one else to rely on. So I think it's an important skill for me to have.

INTERVIEWER: Uh-huh. Uh . . . Is there anything else that you're . . . uh . . . studying or using continuing ed for?

WOMAN: Nothing else right now. I'm hoping next term

to take some courses in plumbing or electrical repair—something like that.

INTERVIEWER: So, you are using continuing education and th—and the way that you use it . . . is to . . . broaden your capabilities within your own life.

WOMAN: Right. On th—on the practical aspect, rather than . . . abstract courses that really won't help me on a day-to-day basis.

Part 3: Teacher

Now listen to the teacher.

INTERVIEWER: What is your occupation? What do you do?

TEACHER: Well, I teach G.E.D. to adults—that's people who haven't completed high school and would like—

INTERVIEWER: What does—

TEACHER: . . . to take a test—

INTERVIEWER: . . . What does G.E.D. stand for?

TEACHER: It stands for General Education Diploma and . . . it's for people who haven't finished high school and would like to take a test that . . . takes the place of a high school diploma.

INTERVIEWER: Well, what's your uh . . . opinion, then, of . . . continuing education past the high school . . . level?

TEACHER: Well, I don't think anyone has ever completed their education. I don't think anyone is ever too old to keep on going. Uh . . . so, I think continuing after high school is . . . a very important thing for many people.

INTERVIEWER: Uh. . . . It's a tool, then, for them to kind of shape their lives—to extend uh . . . and use their desires, huh? More—

TEACHER: Sure. It's a . . . a chance to choose what it is that you really want to pursue with your life and to uh . . . zero in on the . . . the things that are most important to you.

INTERVIEWER: Well—well, do you think there are limits on that sort of thing? I mean, a person could . . . conceivably follow . . . different alleyways uh—

TEACHER: Well, . . . of course. I mean, there are certain things that people can't do. . . . As you get older, for instance, you become physically limited. Uh. . . . But there's always . . . some area of education that a person can pursue. I don't think we ever get too old or uh . . . too limited to pursue something. I think it's a—it's a way to . . . pull things into focus in your life and to . . . better yourself in the ways that are most important to the individual.

UNIT 5

OFFICIAL: UNESCO is an organization that's part of the United Nations and the letters in UNESCO mean United Nations Educational, Scientific and Cultural Organization.

INTERVIEWER: What kind of things . . . uh . . . does it do uh . . . in the world—I imagine—it's . . . uh . . . it's a United Nations organ, so it must operate uh . . . internationally?

OFFICIAL: Oh, yes . . . yes, it . . . it operates within the member nations of the United Nations. Its aims are pretty much those of the United Nations, . . . but the specific purpose of it is to . . . uh . . . foster communication among nations.

INTERVIEWER: Well, could you tell me some of the ways in which UNESCO accomplishes . . . uh . . . its goals within the United Nations?

OFFICIAL: O.K. . . . We're working to eradicate illiteracy, raise educational standards of countries, . . . uh promote cultural exchange between different countries. We uh . . . provide technical assistance programs and research and teacher training, admin— educational administration . . . uh . . . cooperate in the setting up of informa—cultural information centers. Uh . . . we cooperate with other agencies . . . of the United Nations, the FAO, the Food and Agricultural Organization, the World Health Organization and cooperate with other international non-governmental agencies in these areas. Uh . . . we . . . receive our funding from the member nations. Uh . . . this funding is based on uh . . . national—

INTERVIEWER: Do you—

OFFICIAL: . . . income.

INTERVIEWER: . . . distribute funds to . . . uh . . . back to member nations, or uh . . . in the form of grants?

OFFICIAL: Yes. Sometimes this happens, although most of our money goes toward the work that we do. But there are grants. Yes.

INTERVIEWER: Do you think that uh . . . you've created an impact on uh . . . the world educationally and scientifically and culturally?

OFFICIAL: Oh, certainly, certainly! Anything which helps nations to work together and cooperate . . . uh . . . has to contribute to peace.

UNIT 6

INTERVIEWER: So you just returned from a trip?

TRAVELER: Yes, I did!

INTERVIEWER: How was it?

TRAVELER: Oh, I must say that uh . . . I'm happy to be home.

INTERVIEWER: Why's that? What happened?

TRAVELER: Well, . . . I tell you, I took one of these uh . . . special tour package deals and uh . . . I found nothing but frustrations.

INTERVIEWER: Oh, the tour package didn't work out too well?

TRAVELER: Not as the uh . . . material I received claimed it would . . . uh.

INTERVIEWER: What happened?

TRAVELER: Oh, there were all kinds of problems and uh . . . even got started off on the wrong foot uh . . . You get to the airport and then you find out that uh . . . the plane that you're scheduled to go out on . . . uh . . . is going to be delayed about fourteen hours . . . and uh—

INTERVIEWER: Wow!

TRAVELER: . . . you wait around, but uh . . . then you turn around and find out that they've even overbooked the thing . . . and uh . . . so this is frustrating. So there's another two hours uh . . . having them . . . getting that straightened out. . . . And uh . . . So you're exhausted really, by the time you get on the plane.

INTERVIEWER: Well, how was it whe— once you got there?

TRAVELER: Well, I'm afraid to say about the only relaxation I got was on the plane itself because once we got to the uh . . . this big city, why uh . . . we're all anxious to get to our hotel rooms and clean up. And uh . . . come to find out they didn't have enough buses that were scheduled to take all of us that were on this tour package to the hotel, so we had to wait around another half hour for more buses to arrive . . .

INTERVIEWER: Gosh, that sounds terrible!

TRAVELER: Oh, it was!

INTERVIEWER: Did you ever get to see anything that interested you?

TRAVELER: Not really, no . . . uh . . . it uh . . . was just uh . . . a lo—a lot of frustration and uh . . . really, the things that we enjoyed the most were more or less the things that we did outside of the tour package, even though it did involve more pocket money. Why uh . . . pretty soon some of us started to realize if we're going to actually get some money worth . . . uh . . . uh . . . out of our trip here, why we're going to have to go out and do things ourselves.

INTERVIEWER: So you kind of had to go off on your own, huh?

TRAVELER: Right! Yeah, I found this was a true experience.

INTERVIEWER: Well, did you make it home all right?

TRAVELER: Well, we did make it home O.K. and uh . . . uh . . . thank God uh . . . the uh . . . plane was uh . . . uh . . . on time and uh . . . we did have a . . . a fine flight home and uh . . . uh . . . it was also comforting to know that uh . . . the luggage arrived with us this time.

INTERVIEWER: Oh, you lost your luggage the first time, huh?

TRAVELER: Oh, yeah! I thought I'd mentioned that . . . that uh . . . when we got to the hotel, why, come to find out the uh . . . luggage was not there. Waited two whole days for the luggage to arrive.

INTERVIEWER: Oh my gosh! Well, I'm glad you made it home O.K. anyway.

TRAVELER: Well, I'm sure happy to be home. I got some nice pictures.

UNIT 7

INTERVIEWER: I uh . . . suppose that you found much of the initial research . . . uh . . . that you had to do for your new book on the *Titanic* easy to do, but I suppose that as you got into the subject, it . . . it may have become more difficult to track down details.

AUTHOR: Well, in writing a novel you want a good basis in fact, but at some point imagination has to take over. The details—

INTERVIEWER: I see . . .

AUTHOR: . . . that are important are sometimes the imagined ones: sensual, touch, feel, smell. . . . Th . . . the things you have to imagine for a person can come, . . . uh . . . to make a believable character, can come out of your own life as much as it will come out of research, once you have your facts straight.

INTERVIEWER: I see . . . Did you find that to be fertile creative ground?

AUTHOR: Uh . . . it was interesting because it's ground which has been well worked. There's been a movie about the *Titanic*, as you know. A . . . movie made in the '30s or '40s, which is . . . is very sentimental, with a band playing "Nearer My God to Thee," Freddie Bartholomew sinking and there's not a dry eye in the house. Uh . . . to do it . . . Uh . . . in a fresh way was . . . was a challenge and one of the reasons that I was interested in the material. Because you have a situation of . . . a . . . a large and diverse group of people in—caught *in extremis*, really—

INTERVIEWER: Uh-huh.

AUTHOR: . . . and a . . . against a backdrop of an event which was . . . was really one of the major technological achievements of . . . of the day—in 1912 when the *Titanic* was launched. It was said that God himself couldn't sink the *Titanic* and, yet, people uh . . . from vastly different walks of life, caught in different points in their own lives, were uh . . . th . . . thrown into . . . into disaster suddenly, inexorably.

INTERVIEWER: That was uh . . . truly one of the ironies uh . . . attendant to the *Titanic*, was it not?

AUTHOR: Oh, that's one of the things that makes it such a provocative situation and why I think it continues to appeal to the imaginations, not only of the public, but of . . . of writers and film makers.

INTERVIEWER: It's like the Frankenstein monster in that respect.

AUTHOR: In a sense, yes. Technology uh . . . gone awry, technology uh . . . totally violating the expectations of the public . . . and man who wishes to put his faith in machines . . .

UNIT 8

INTERVIEWER: How would you define psychotherapy? Wha—what do you do for people?

PSYCHOTHERAPIST: Uh . . . I help people to change their minds . . . uh . . . about—mostly about . . . ways that they have of dealing with . . . their problems or their lives in general. Uh . . . people that come to me . . . uh . . . tend to . . . uh . . . repeat patterns of behavior that give them problems. And what I do is talk to them and try to show them . . . uh . . . how it is that uh . . . they're repeating things and how that way of repeating things causes a problem for them.

INTERVIEWER: So in other words, it's a self-help program. You're trying to teach them . . . how to help themselves. Would—

PSYCHOTHERAPIST: Well, . . .

INTERVIEWER: . . . that be accurate?

PSYCHOTHERAPIST: . . . some people can help themselves, of course, uh . . . and then others uh . . . have to be taught, through a rather lengthy process called psychotherapy, to help themselves. Some people are more ready to become independent than others. And, of course, uh . . . not everyone is . . . totally independent, you know. You must uh . . . sometimes treat all members of the family.

INTERVIEWER: Why would—say, an average person with . . . with his problems—why would he come to you? Why would you be the best place for him to place his confidence . . . and/or money?

PSYCHOTHERAPIST: Uh . . . well, it depends, of course, on the kind of problem. He may be referred by the hospital or . . . by a doctor or by a—someone that knows me, uh. . . but of course there's different kinds of . . . uh . . . psychotherapists and . . . he would, if he had problems with . . . family, uh . . . since I'm a family therapist, he would come to me.

INTERVIEWER: So, uh . . . what would you say the advantages of . . . going to a psychotherapist were?

PSYCHOTHERAPIST: That you get an outside perspective on a problem that you've probably been keeping to yourself uh . . . is . . . probably the greatest advantage and the second is that the help is really professional. The people are trained . . . to . . . give you that kind of help.

UNIT 9

INTERVIEWER: As an economist, what would you say uh . . . that the effects uh . . . of automation will be in the future?

ECONOMIST: My concern, which is uh . . . uh . . . the antithesis, maybe, of where an economist should be, is regarding —what is it doing to people? What is it doing to society when a man gets up at six o'clock in the morning and goes and plays with a machine all day? What kind of satisfaction is he getting from that? And that's—so I'm sort of a rebel in the . . .

INTERVIEWER: I see. What do you foresee happening?

ECONOMIST: I foresee a need for us to continue to place emphasis on the qualitative life and for man to continue to seek other uh . . . sources of satisfaction. There used to be a great deal of job satisfaction for the farmer, for the butcher, for . . . uh . . . any—It . . . it . . . it was a . . . an occupation that you did because you, intrinsically, got some value from it, but you also got a paycheck. And I personally cannot identify with being a data processor and getting some real uh . . . internal satisfaction from that.

INTERVIEWER: Do you see it leading to more alienation?

ECONOMIST: Yes. I see . . . I sort of envision uh . . . a mass transit uh . . . of people just moving and doing things, with less and less of a dependency upon the mind. However, it takes minds to program the computer, so I am speaking almost schizophrenically about uh . . . my concerns. Because behind the computers are men that are creating this program and feeding it into the computer. The machine is not doing it in absence of human . . . uh . . . skills.

INTERVIEWER: But they are removed from the people who receive—

ECONOMIST: Right.

INTERVIEWER: . . . the skill.

ECONOMIST: So, the economy will prosper and I'm concerned about the well-being of man in this prosperity. Perhaps we're looking at the ability to do things more rapidly with uh . . . a higher . . . a higher production rate . . . uh . . . and, therefore, will be looking, maybe, towards a shorter work week. But . . . uh . . . also, I don't see that really happening because if you can produce things more rapidly uh . . . each day, then why shut down for two days? Just keep producing. Uh . . . but if we could work so that man is having three days on and four days off perhaps there would be some merit to that.

INTERVIEWER: Will this lead to a glut of goods?

ECONOMIST: Well, there's always the supply and demand. Uh . . . if there's a glut, then they're not going to be able to charge as much for those items, so perhaps they will have to store their items in silos and . . . uh . . . and pay farmer—You know how they used to pay the farmers not to plant their fields, . . . and perhaps computers will be paid not to run on certain days.

INTERVIEWER: Kind of a . . . a negative—What positive effects do you see?

ECONOMIST: Oh, possibly, we would have additional leisure time. Uh . . . and with that leisure time would come the ability for man to be able to step back from this interaction with this machine and be . . . and be—again be able to uh . . . focus on the qualitative aspects of human relationships, rather than his relationship uh . . . eight to five with . . . with this machine. Uh . . . I would hope that perhaps there could be uh . . . renewal of the family unit, but I see that as we've increased our ability to produce in . . . in this country, the family unit has become destroyed. Uh . . . I don't see it necessarily as a cause and effect relationship, but these two things have evolved. That . . . the better we've become at business, the worse we've become at raising families.

UNIT 10

JUDGE: One of the more recent cases I had was of a man accused and found guilty of breaking into a house and stealing some money . . .

INTERVIEWER: Well . . . well, was he really guilty, Judge, do you think?

JUDGE: He admitted to the fact that he'd done it. And there were several witnesses saying that he had, indeed, done it. So, I can only assume that he was guilty. He said so, other people said so, he broke into the house, he stole the —

INTERVIEWER: Why . . .

JUDGE: . . . money.

INTERVIEWER: . . . why did he do it?

JUDGE: Well, the reasons were a little muddied. Probably, at least it seemed in the trial, that he did it to get some money to feed his family. You see he'd been out of work for some time. And . . . the . . . uh . . .

INTERVIEWER: Well, did his . . . his—he'd been out of work and he chose to break into a house to get money for his family and, apparently, in front of people that uh . . . could see him do it . . .

JUDGE: Well, his attorney brought testimony that he had indeed uh . . . applied for jobs at several places and was listed with several em . . . employment agencies, including the state employment agency. And so, there weren't any jobs—

INTERVIEWER: . . . and he had no luck.

JUDGE: He'd had no luck and it'd been some time. He had two children. And both of them were uh . . . needing food and needing clothing and all of the things that—

INTERVIEWER: So he was—

JUDGE: . . . children need.

INTERVIEWER: . . . in desperate circumstance. Did . . . did you sentence him?

JUDGE: Yes.

INTERVIEWER: But . . . but what . . . good does it do to put the man into jail when he's obviously in such need?

JUDGE: This particular fellow has been in prison before. That probably had to do with his unemployment—

INTERVIEWER: For—

JUDGE: . . . record.

INTERVIEWER: . . . for the same thing, then?

JUDGE: No, for a different sort of crime.

INTERVIEWER: Huh!

JUDGE: But he ha—did know about crime, so I suppose there are some folks that just have to go back to prison several times.

UNIT 11

INTERVIEWER: Isn't advertising really a kind of lying?

ADVERTISING MAN: I don't think so. Quite often people do try to get away with those types of things, but the Federal Trade Commission is always very quick to jump on them to . . . force them to show evidence to back—

INTERVIEWER: Oh, but—

AD MAN: . . . up any claims.

INTERVIEWER: I mean in your work. I mean, don't . . . don't you actually . . . uh . . . tell lies to get people to buy things? I mean, . . . Let me give you an example, You know, . . . I—a . . . a . . . a movie star says that she uses—a starlet—says that she uses a certain kind of soap every night to make her skin look beautiful and, of course, she doesn't use it at . . . at all, or hardly ever.

AD MAN: I . . . I think if you go back very recently, just within the last year, you'll remember that one of our famous singers and actors and—was uh . . . called down for just that very thing, where he endorsed a product which he didn't use and had to recant what he said in his endorsements.

INTERVIEWER: I see, so what you're saying is that uh . . . you're forced to be honest . . . kind of . . . in the profession?

AD MAN: Well, in some cases that may be true. I won't try to deny that. Uh . . .

INTERVIEWER: Wh . . . What kind of work do you find most interesting in the uh . . . ad business?

AD MAN: I would say, developing new markets, or not so much new markets, but when you have a product which previously people didn't perceive that they needed, but it is an advancement or an improvement over what people previously used . . . and are able to educate people and inform them of a particular thing . . . and they discover it will make their life better and it is something that they could use.

INTERVIEWER: To try to uh . . . kind of advance it to them and . . . uh . . . make them understand what's going on with a new product?

AD MAN: Basically, that's it. This is where a lot of the progress or the amenities in life which we take for granted now, . . . this is how they originally developed. Somebody thought of a new idea and convinced people that it was something they needed and after a period of time, it became what they considered a necessity.

INTERVIEWER: Huh! Would that be true of things, do you suppose, like hula-hoops . . . uh?

AD MAN: Uh . . . no, the same . . . the same process is used as far as trying to promote these things, but I think if something is really a useful product that people can . . . that people can use, that it will find its own place in the marketplace. In other words, the advertising as a promotion will make people aware of a product, but . . . the product's own worth will determine whether or not it's something that people will . . . will bring into their daily lives.

INTERVIEWER: And . . . I suppose that if—if it endures over a long period of time, that that shows that the product really does have uh . . . a stable value and that you're not lying, . . .

AD MAN: Well, I think that's—

INTERVIEWER: . . . if you can—

AD MAN: . . . I think that's a fair assumption. I . . . won't try to tell you that in promoting things, people never lie, but the . . . initial promotion simply gets people to try a product for the first time. And then if the product itself has any merit, then people will continue to use it. So, the quality of a product will determine whether it has any staying power.

UNIT 12

Part 1: An author

INTERVIEWER: What do you like most about being an author?

AUTHOR: I suppose most I like uh . . . the freedom of it, both . . . both physically and imaginatively. I don't have to go to work for somebody else in an office. I make my own hours. I—

INTERVIEWER: Wha—

AUTHOR: —choose my own projects.

INTERVIEWER: —what are your hours?

AUTHOR: My hours, since I have a very young child at home now, are uh . . . are during her nap time. Midday, I get two, maybe three hours to write if I'm lucky, and another two or three hours in the evening.

INTERVIEWER: You write about six hours a day then. Uh . . . how much work can you do in that time?

AUTHOR: Uh . . . it depends on if your muse is with you or not.

INTERVIEWER: I see.

AUTHOR: Uh . . . I used to write much more quickly than I do, but uh . . . I've . . . I've slowed down as I've gotten older. I hope . . . I hope I've gotten better in the process too.

INTERVIEWER: Uh . . . what . . . what kind of writing do you do, mostly?

AUTHOR: Primarily fiction now. I used to write more poetry, but uh . . . I think that's become more and more incorporated into the stories that I write.

INTERVIEWER: Well, that's interesting. How do you do that?

AUTHOR: Uh . . . In the way one chooses one's language, . . . uh . . . by making images very important, in the creation of—of story or character or the evocation of place.

INTERVIEWER: You write uh . . . short stories or novels?

AUTHOR: Both. Time and a place for everything.

Part 2: A supermarket manager

MANAGER: I'm a supermarket manager and . . . and, you know, some people think it's a boring, uh . . . real day-to-day type work. It's . . . it's really not, you know. It doesn't have very much prestige, but uh . . .

INTERVIEWER: Well, do you work with figures a lot and stuff like that?

MANAGER: Oh, there's a certain amount of that, for sure, but it's more working with people.

INTERVIEWER: I . . . that's a . . . I suppose a big part of management . . .

MANAGER: Yeah! . . . yeah . . . eh . . . you know, you work with the customers and you also work with the staff and try to keep people busy and happy and productive and—

INTERVIEWER: It must be one of those kinds of jobs where, you know, if people aren't uh . . . happy at what they're doing, they're certainly not going to do a very good job. Especially, if they're going to meet the public.

MANAGER: Yeah, It's . . . it's . . . you have to figure out little things, like what kind of music to play for what kind of . . . uh . . . which people are on at the certain time of the day—

INTERVIEWER: Oh, so you do, huh? You schedule that uh . . . to . . . like if housewives tend to come in at ten o'clock in the morning and—

MANAGER: Oh, we—

INTERVIEWER: —uh . . . working people at six o'clock at night, huh?

MANAGER: We try to, we try to. And uh . . . it's . . . it's interesting. It's uh . . . a little different each day. Each day is a little different. I find it very fascinating work.

Part 3: A factory worker

INTERVIEWER: What kind of work do you do?

WORKER: I work in a jewelry factory on a kick press.

INTERVIEWER: We—

WORKER: I bend metal for chains.

INTERVIEWER: Oh . . . What's that like? What happens?

WORKER: Well, it's pretty dull. You just take a piece of a . . . unfinished piece out of a bin and you bend it and you put it in the finished piece. And you try not to go to sleep.

INTERVIEWER: Uh-huh.

WORKER: I did fall asleep once. Put a hole right through my finger.

INTERVIEWER: Oh, my gosh! That's—

WORKER: Well, that was nice. I got five days workman's compensation.

INTERVIEWER: Oh, so you didn't have to do anything anymore.

WORKER: Nope! Stayed home and watched TV and had a good time for a week.

INTERVIEWER: Uh . . . uh . . . what do you do for entertainment usually?

WORKER: Go to the fights every weekend. Can't wait for Friday night!

INTERVIEWER: Yeah.

WORKER: Fights Friday night, Saturday night. Save all my money for that. Costs two dollars and fifty cents to get in on Saturday night. Friday night, it's half-price.

UNIT 13

INTERVIEWER: Uh . . . Do you think of yourself as a feminist? Isn't that kind of an extreme position?

WOMAN: Well . . . I'm not an extreme feminist. I feel that women should be able to do what they want. But, I'm not—

INTERVIEWER: Do you mean—

WOMAN: . . . extremist.

INTERVIEWER: . . . do you mean within—that a woman should be able to do anything that she wants? Uh . . . for example, when she's married?

WOMAN: Yes, of course.

INTERVIEWER: Could you tell me more about that? Uh . . . like, she should be able to ge—have whatever kind of job she wants . . .

WOMAN: Well, yes. I think if she wants to feel—or if she feels that she wants to go out and get a job, that's her choice to do what she wants. And, if she has been trained for something specific, that's fantastic. She should be able to go out and use her talents.

INTERVIEWER: Uh . . . You took your husband's name though, didn't you, when . . . when you were married?

WOMAN: Yes, I did. I think that that's conventional and I'm kind of a conventional wife.

INTERVIEWER: I see. You . . . you don't really want to uh . . . be engaged in a protest, so much as . . . as you want to just develop your own potentials.

WOMAN: Right! I want to be equal, but I'm not an extremist.

INTERVIEWER: Uh . . . Do you think—I . . . I think that there are—do you think that there are extreme people in the feminist movement?

WOMAN: Oh, I think in any movement there are extreme people.

INTERVIEWER: Uh . . . how do you see that affecting the . . . the lives of the other people that are involved in the movement?

WOMAN: Well, I think that, to an extent, it's good because it opens more doors for women. Although, if it goes too far it can also close doors.

UNIT 14

Part 1: A young teacher

INTERVIEWER: How do you see inflation affecting your work as a teacher?

TEACHER: Uh . . . I find myself being more involved in union activities to try to get a higher salary.

INTERVIEWER: I see. You need a higher salary now to uh . . . get the same things that you used to get at a previous salary?

TEACHER: Even though I did get a raise this year, I don't seem to be able to buy any—have any more buying power than I had last year.

INTERVIEWER: I see. How does that—how did it affect your uh . . . spending uh . . . patterns?

TEACHER: We—my wife and I spend a lot of time clipping coupons . . .

INTERVIEWER: I see.

TEACHER: . . . watching for sales. We don't buy new cars. Basically, we live somewhat frugally.

INTERVIEWER: Can you still eat the way that you used to?

TEACHER: Pretty much so. Food is inflated, but not quite as much as housing and transportation costs. We've had to move closer to my school, so that we don't have to put as many miles on the car.

INTERVIEWER: How about your personal life? Do you go out as much as you used to?

TEACHER: We really have to budget that kind of activity. Usually, we eat out once a month. And maybe see a show once a month.

Part 2: A supermarket manager

INTERVIEWER: Prices just seem to keep going up and up and up for the things that I buy.

MANAGER: Oh, I know. I know. Last—oh, a few years ago I thought I was doing all right, you know. I was making enough money to get by and now I'm making . . . oh . . . three . . . thousand more dollars a year and I'm not getting by at all well.

INTERVIEWER: So . . . so it's like, although your money has increased—for dollars and—it—it doesn't make any difference because you can't buy any more.

MANAGER: Inflation has just uh . . . skyrocketed.

INTERVIEWER: How does that affect people at your store? Do they buy more or less or—what do they do?

MANAGER: They seem to be buying different . . . ly than . . . than they used to. People are . . . are uh . . . working at being responsible in their—

INTERVIEWER: Oh, so they—

MANAGER: . . . buying

INTERVIEWER: . . . buy different things now? They . . . they don't buy luxuries so much?

MANAGER: . . . more often now.

INTERVIEWER: And they . . . they sp—wha—what do they regard as essentials? I guess that's what they buy now.

MANAGER: Milk and bread!

INTERVIEWER: That's it, huh? And eggs?

MANAGER: Eggs . . . and just the staples.

Part 3: An economist

ECONOMIST: One of the things we need to do is stop our spending. Our—

INTERVIEWER: Do you think spending is really a . . . a ca— a cause, there, of inflation?

ECONOMIST: I definitely think it is and I think the uh—we've been used to charging whatever we needed. We're going to have to look at our money uh—

INTERVIEWER: I see. So you—

ECONOMIST: . . . closer.

INTERVIEWER: . . . you really think—

ECONOMIST: I think we are going to have to analyze what we need to live and maybe live in smaller homes.

INTERVIEWER: Well, are there . . . are there good effects in the economy from this?

ECONOMIST: I think these are good effects. I think we've been spoiled. We have a . . . a lot in America.

INTERVIEWER: Just get too much for nothing, huh? Or, for a little?

ECONOMIST: On credit!

INTERVIEWER: Yeah.

ECONOMIST: And uh . . . do not live within our means. Therefore, we're going to have to just do with less and I don't—

INTERVIEWER: Hm—

ECONOMIST: . . . think it will hurt us a bit.

Part 4: A student

INTERVIEWER: Well, as a student, I suppose you don't have a great deal of earning power, so inflation must affect you.

STUDENT: It affects me in that my parents aren't able to afford to pay for my tuition. So I have been forced into taking part of my study time to devote to earning as much as I can to help pay for that.

INTERVIEWER: So, that kind of cuts into your studies, I suppose . . .

STUDENT: It does to a certain extent, but I've found that with the added pressure of having to earn money, I use my study time more effectively and get more done.

INTERVIEWER: So in that sense, it's kind of a good thing for you.

STUDENT: Yes.

INTERVIEWER: Uh . . . how about your money, though? I mean, for things like entertainment and clothing and such as these?

STUDENT: It doesn't seem as important. Because the time left for entertainment is limited and there are things at the school that we can do without having to spend money.

INTERVIEWER: I see. So you're learning that you have to kind of buckle down and limit yourself?

STUDENT: Yes.

UNIT 15

Part 1: A student

INTERVIEWER: What's it like to . . . to live here . . . right next to the airport, anyway? Must be noisy.

STUDENT: It's like . . . a . . . living in a volcano most of the time, you know. It's . . . it's constant rumbling and uh . . . noise, fear of planes hitting the top of your house, you know. You feel like they're so low.

INTERVIEWER: So tha—that must uh . . . it must be to the point where it's a kind of pollution, huh?

STUDENT: It seems they've gotten worse over the years. I . . . and I've been living here all my life and uh . . . I don't know if the planes are bigger and noisier or—

INTERVIEWER: Have you ever tried to protest that to the city?

STUDENT: Constantly! It doesn't seem to do any good.

INTERVIEWER: They don't respond to you, huh?

STUDENT: No. Uh . . . they say things are being done about it. They're meeting standards, but it's still really bad living right in the path of jumbo jets. And they seem to be coming more frequently all the time.

Part 2: An architect

INTERVIEWER: Well, as an architect, you must have to deal with uh . . . noise pollution quite a bit?

ARCHITECT: Hmm . . . quite a bit. Not only in the business world or the architect designing bui— buildings for offices, in the home use, in the use of school houses, the effect of traffic from the street, the effect of planes overhead, how close the buildings are to each other— Noise comes from all directions and the architect is responsible for cushioning it, providing people with their own quiet space to make as much noise in it as they want to.

INTERVIEWER: Well, that's really good. Uh . . . what are some of the typical sources of noise pollution that you have to deal with?

ARCHITECT: Hmmm . . . the . . . some of the bigger ones are, traffic problems—

INTERVIEWER: Uh-huh.

ARCHITECT: . . . air pollution sounds from planes. One of the ones that's affected people a lot has been the garbage trucks in the morning when they go by and trying to set the house—designing the house far enough off the road so that they don't hear that noise on the streets and waking them up in the morning.

Other pollution . . . uh . . . noise pollution problems are fans. You know, fluorescent lights also create sometimes—

INTERVIEWER: Yes.

ARCHITECT: As an architect—

INTERVIEWER: Yes.

ARCHITECT: We have to take everything into consideration.

INTERVIEWER: So . . . so your design . . . must consider all those things.

ARCHITECT: Whether the face—the . . . the windows face the street where the noise is coming from. Skylights are often a good source of buffering street and horizontal sounds.

INTERVIEWER: I see. Uh . . . do you have to uh . . . design whole environments sometimes?

ARCHITECT: Often. For special playgrounds . . . you would not set a playground right by a main thoroughfare. You would find a geographically quieter place. For condominiums, you would want to develop one that was—gave the impression of seclusion, even if it was right on the main thoroughfare.

INTERVIEWER: I see . . .

ARCHITECT: Peo—People are very touchy about sound in their environment.

INTERVIEWER: Especially if it comes, I suppose, from some alien source.

ARCHITECT: Right. If their peop—if their brothers or their sisters, or their sons or their daughters are making the noise, they can yell at them and say ``Hey, be quiet!'' But if a stranger is making the noise, it's real hard to approach them. And if someone you cannot even talk to, the government, you know, is making the noise, you cannot—you feel helpless.

INTERVIEWER: What do you suppose the effect on the human psyche is?

ARCHITECT: Well, you can probably imagine yourself if you were trying to concentrate, or just think, or read a book, or write a letter, when you had drum playing going on around you and all kinds of sounds, there's an inability to focus, to concentrate, when you're ca—always being bombarded by sound. To have a space of your own that you are in control of, to create an environment, is very important when people are attacked. And they do feel attacked by sounds. They have no way to stop them . . . to offset them. That's where the architect must create a buffer between them and what they are—you know, the sound that is approaching them.

141

INDEX OF GRAMMATICAL ITEMS